W9-BCM-477

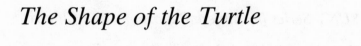

The Shape of the Turtle

SUNY Series in Chinese Philosophy and Culture

David L. Hall and Roger T. Ames, editors

The Shape of the Turtle

Myth, Art, and Cosmos in Early China

SARAH ALLAN

State University of New York Press

Published by
State University of New York Press, Albany

© 1991   State University of New York

All rights reserved

Printed in the United States of America

No part of this book may be used or reproduced
in any manner whatsoever without written permission
except in the case of brief quotations embodied in
critical articles as reviews.

For information, address the State University of New York Press,
State University Plaza, Albany, NY 12246

Production by Christine M. Lynch
Marketing by Dana E. Yanulavich

Library of Congress Cataloguing-in-Publication Data

Allan, Sarah.
    The shape of the turtle : myth, art, and cosmos in early China /
Sarah Allan.
        p.   cm.—(SUNY series in Chinese philosophy and culture)
    Includes bibliographical references.
    ISBN 0-7914-0459-5 (alk. paper).—ISBN 0-7914-0460-9 (pbk. :
alk. paper)
    1. Philosophy, Chinese—To 221 B.C.   2. China—Civilization—To
221 B.C.   3. Mythology, Chinese.   4. China—History—Shang dynasty,
1766–1122 B.C.   5. Cosmology, Chinese.   I. Title.   II. Series.
B126.A44   1991
299'.51'0931—dc20   90-30424
                                                                            CIP

To Nicol Allan

CONTENTS

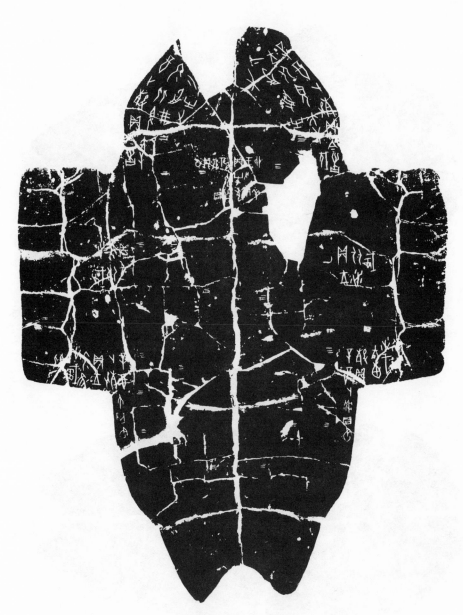

Figure 24 *Heji* 6484

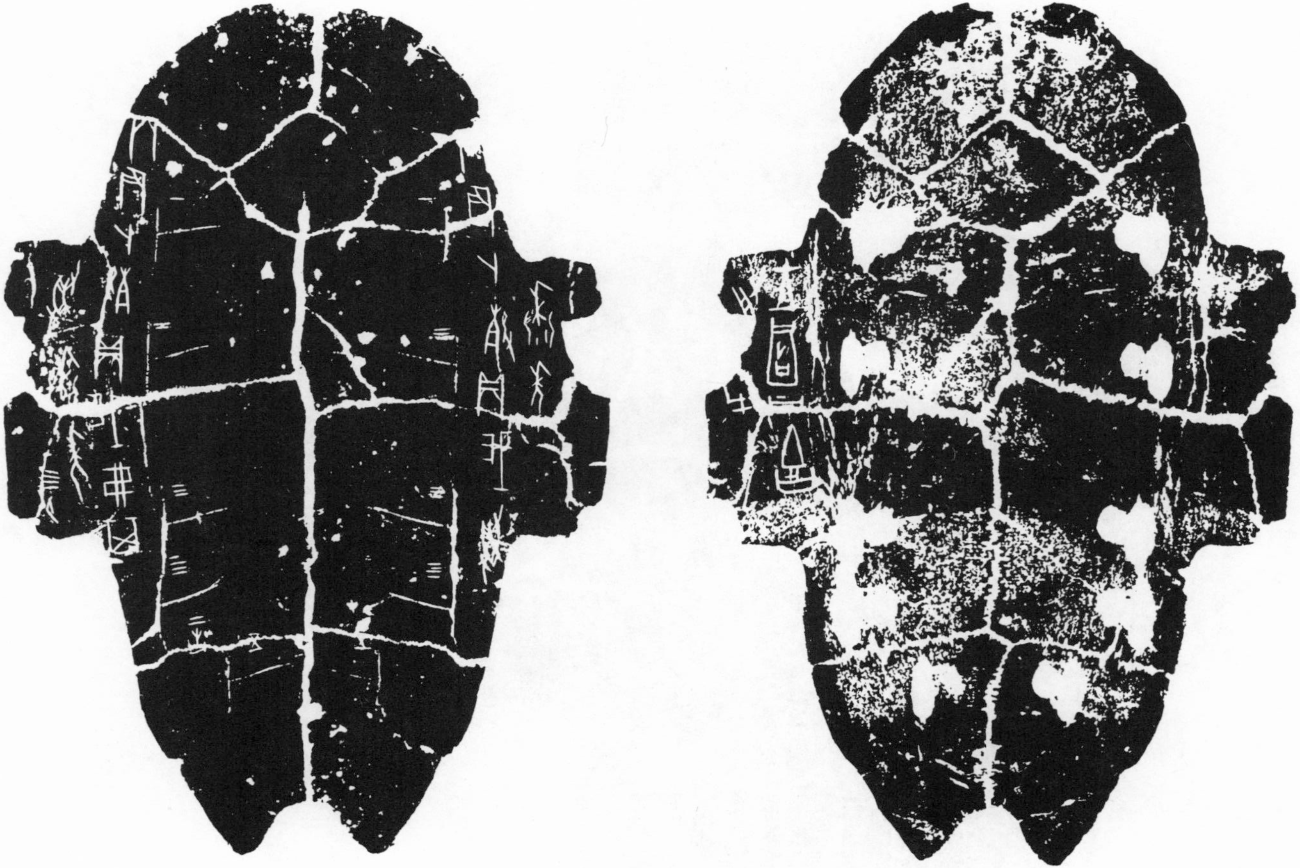

Figure 23 *Heji* 9950

PREFACE

This work has had a long gestation period and, as some readers will recognize, parts of it have been published previously in articles. It is essentially an attempt to answer certain questions which have puzzled me. Some of these questions were first brought to my attention when I was a graduate student at the University of California at Berkeley, studying with Peter Boodberg and Wolfram Eberhard, such as why is there so little myth in early Chinese texts and what was the shape of the cosmos in the minds of the early Chinese? Others I trace back to my undergraduate days at U.C.L.A. where I studied archaeology with Richard Rudolph and took a course in Chinese art history with J. Leroy Davidson, such as what is the meaning of the *taotie* on Shang Dynasty bronzes and what is the relationship between their decor and their ritual purpose? To David Keightley and David Nivison, I owe the problem of how Shang divination worked and to David Keightley, the admonition that I should be able to trace the origin of the structures of Warring States thought which I described in *The Heir and the Sage: Dynastic Legend in Early China*, although if I had taken this admonition seriously at the time, I would still be working to obtain my doctorate.

Some of these questions lead to even more fundamental ones. We cannot understand the problem of myth in early China without understanding the relationship of myth to the structure of religion, nor can we understand the meaning of the *taotie* 饕餮 without considering the problem of meaning in primitive art more generally. No attempt to answer such questions can be definitive. Indeed, any attempt is necessarily both speculative and incomplete and I offer my own solutions herein with a sense of trepidation, and in the belief that such questions must be addressed directly if we are to progress in our understanding of the development of early Chinese thought and if we are to achieve the more complete understanding of the range of possibilities of the human mind which the study of ancient China should allow us. However faulty my own solutions may be, they should at least provoke others to consider these problems.

Although in the Introduction to this work, I have provided a very brief introduction to Shang archaeology in order to make the rest of the work comprehensible to the nonspecialist, I have not made any attempt to provide either a comprehensive account of Shang archaeology or of the contents of the oracle bone inscriptions. I refer the reader to K. C. Chang's *Shang Civilization* for the most comprehensive account of Shang archaeology in English, and to *The Archaeology of Ancient China*, Fourth Edition, for a more recent summary. K. C. Chang, editor, *Studies of Shang Archaeology* also provides useful background and an introduction to current arguments. The best introduction to the contents of Shang oracle bone inscriptions in a Western language is Tsung-tung Chang, *Der Kult der Shang Dynastie im Spiegel der Orakelinschriften*, which includes translations of original inscriptions and an introduction to Shang religion. Léon Vandermeersch, *Wangdao ou la voie royale: Recherches sur l'Esprit des institutions de la Chine archaique* is concerned with the interplay between the social, political and ritual structures and makes extensive use of the oracle bone inscriptions. Those who wish to learn to read the inscriptions for themselves are referred to David Keightley's *Sources of Shang History*, an invaluable reference work, although it is now somewhat dated by the publication of the *Jiaguwen heji* and other recent works. Other general works are included in the bibliography.

ACKNOWLEDGMENTS

Parts of Chapters Two and Three are essentially the same as articles published in the *Bulletin of the School of Oriental and African Studies* and the *Journal of the Royal Asiatic Society*. I would like to thank their editors for permission to reprint them herein.

Another version of this book has been translated into Chinese by my student, Mr. Wang Tao, and will be published by Wenhua Yishu Chubanshe, Beijing. In the course of translation, he made many useful suggestions which I incorporated in both versions. I would like to express my gratitude to him. I also owe thanks to a number of Chinese scholars who have read and commented on draft versions of the text, including Gao Ming, Li Xueqin, Ning Ke, Qi Wenxin, Wang Xu and Yuan Ke; to my colleagues, A. C. Graham and Robert Chard, and students, Gillian Simpson and Colin MacKenzie. Over the years, I have presented almost all of the material in this book to the Early China Seminar, London, and I have greatly benefited from the comments offered by the participants, most importantly, my colleague Paul Thompson. Finally, however, the responsibility for both the opinions and the mistakes in this work must rest with me.

Last, but not least, I would like to thank Nicky Saunter and Lillian Chia for typing the manuscript and helping to prepare it for publication.

I

Introduction to the Shang

In the spring of 1898, the villagers of Xiaotun, near Anyang in northern Henan Province, uncovered fragments of ancient bones with strange markings on them when ploughing their fields and sold them as 'dragon bones', a traditional ingredient of Chinese medicine. In the following year, the palaeographer Wang Yirong 王懿榮 examined the contents of his apothecary's receipt and discovered that his 'dragon bones' were engraved with an ancient form of Chinese writing.[1] These 'dragon bones' or 'oracle bones', as they soon came to be called, were ox scapulae and turtle shells—primarily the undershells or plastrons—which had been used in divination by the kings of the late Shang dynasty.

The oracle bones had been carefully cleaned and trimmed and hollows had been made on one side. Divination was made by applying a hot poker to these hollows, resulting in a crack on the reverse side. This took a conventional shape, represented by the Chinese character *bu* 卜. How the cracks were read remains a mystery, but after they were made, the topic of divination was sometimes engraved beside the crack or, occasionally, across it.[2] Normally, only the topic of divination was recorded, but the scribe sometimes added a note about how the king interpreted the crack and, on rare occasions, recorded what actually happened afterwards.

The site where the bones were found was traditionally called Yinxu 殷墟, the 'Remains of Yin'. Yin is the traditional name for its last capital and an alternative name for the dynasty. According to the *Shiji* 史記, compiled in the second century B.C., the dynasty was founded by Cheng Tang 成湯 and its capital was moved five times. The last capital, south of the Yellow River, that is, in present-day Henan Province, was founded by the nineteenth ruler, Pan Geng 盤庚. He was succeeded by his two brothers and then by his nephew Wu Ding 武丁, who held the rule for fifty-nine years and restored the grandeur of the dynasty, which lasted until its thirtieth king, the evil and incompetent Zhou Xin 紂辛, was overthrown by King Wu 武王, who established the Zhou 周 Dynasty. The Zhou had been a tributary state of the Shang with their homeland in the

1

western Wei River valley, in present-day Shaanxi Province. They established a new capital near modern Xi'an, and Yin fell into ruin.

The period from the fifth to third centuries B.C., known as the Period of the Warring States, was the classical period of Chinese philosophy in which "one hundred schools of thought contended," as the states battled one another for military supremacy. The primary form in which the philosophers expressed their vision of a perfect state and advocated their political philosophy was in terms of ancient sage kings. These included not only rulers of the Shang and Zhou dynasties, but also those of a previous dynasty called the Xia 夏 (traditionally ca. 2200–1760 B.C.) and even earlier sage kings who did not establish hereditary dynasties.[3] However, there are only a few extant texts that predate the Warring States period and none that predate the founding of the Zhou dynasty (ca. 1100–256 B.C.). At the beginning of this century, just as the oracle bone inscriptions were beginning to be deciphered, Chinese scholars had begun to reassess their traditional history and to recognize that it was intermingled with myth and legend. Some, such as the writer and philosopher Hu Shi 胡適, questioned the authenticity of all Chinese history before the Zhou Dynasty.

Mythology has been a focus for academic debate in the West for over twenty-five years. During this same period, our knowledge of ancient China has been dramatically altered by new archaeological discoveries and increasingly sophisticated interpretations of early inscriptions. The major works on Chinese mythology, however, are still those written in the first half of this century—in China, the *Gushibian* 古史辨 volumes edited by Gu Jiegang 顧頡剛; in the West, the works of Henri Maspero, Marcel Granet, Wolfram Eberhard, and Bernhard Karlgren. This work is a reexamination of the problem of myth in ancient China, understood broadly as mythic thinking, including cosmology, divination, art and ritual. It is planned as the first of a series of works on the development of early Chinese thought and will center upon the thought of the late Shang Dynasty (ca. 1700–1100 B.C.),[4] although references will also be made to later periods.

Many writers have made a distinction between the thinking of literate and nonliterate peoples. The oracle bone inscriptions from Yinxu represent a fully developed writing system, but, as I shall argue further on in this chapter, literature rather than literacy transforms mythic thinking and the use of writing was still severely restricted in the Shang Dynasty. Before turning to this argument, however, I will briefly review the historical and archaeological evidence for the Shang as background for the nonspecialist.

The oracle bone inscriptions established the historical authenticity of the Shang but by indirect means. They do not include any records unconnected with divination, nor do they include any extended narrative. Most often they are simply isolated sentences, usually propositions about the future, either proposed sacrifices or other activities of the king or his entourage, or future events in the natural world. Even when an interpretation and record of what happened is recorded, it is stated very briefly and without exposition. Nevertheless, in divinations about ancestral sacrifices, the ancestors are often named and listed in generational order. From these, a genealogy and king list can be compiled. The names can be matched to those of the kings listed in the *Shi ji* and they confirm the historical record, though there is no evidence in the ancestral sacrifices that Cheng Tang had a special role as dynastic founder. He is simply one ancestor, albeit a particularly powerful one, within a genealogy of ancestors which stretches back many generations. Furthermore, the earliest divinations found at Yinxu date from the reign of Wu Ding, rather than from that of his uncle Pan Geng who, according to the traditional accounts, was the king who moved to Yin.

The tradition that Yinxu was the site of the last Shang capital was confirmed when the villagers' discovery of inscribed oracle bones led to the first major archaeological excavation in China. The primary excavations at Yinxu took place between 1928 and 1937 when they were interrupted by the Japanese invasion, but some further excavation has also taken place since 1949. The excavators not only found more oracle bones—the original object of their search; they also uncovered the foundations of large buildings, believed to the temples and palaces, and the vast earthen tombs of the kings, as well as more ordinary dwellings and tombs, bronze, stone, pottery, shell and bone workshops. The excavations revealed that the Shang were a great and powerful dynasty capable of marshaling and maintaining a large labour force over long periods of time, but their rulers were not the benevolent sage kings imagined by later philosophers. The large-scale human as well as animal sacrifice to which the oracle bone divinations referred was confirmed by the discovery of thousands of human sacrifices accompanying the large tombs, buried in building foundations, and in special cemeteries for sacrificial victims.

The primary residential area excavated at Yinxu was in the vicinity of the village of Xiaotun, within the bend of the Huan River. Most important were three groups of large building foundations uncovered north of the village (see figure 1). The largest amongst them was some seventy metres by forty metres and all were constructed of tamped yellow loess, a method used in North China since neolithic times for the building of city walls as well as house foundations. The fine yellow soil was confined in wooden frames, tamped hard and built up layer by layer. Some of the large founda-

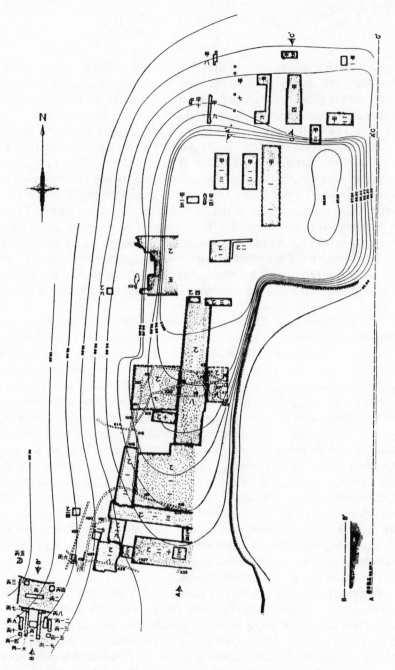

Figure 1 Plan of Shang Dynasty Building Foundations
at Xiaotun, Anyang

From Shi Zhangru, *Xiaotun,* I, part 2, p. 21

tions at Yinxu were as much as three meters in height and made of thirty layers of earth. The walls of the buildings were of wattle and daub; stone or bronze supports held wooden pillars and the roofs were thatched.

Rites in which humans and animals were sacrificed had been performed in association with the buildings in the central and southern sectors, suggesting ritually important palaces and temples, as opposed to the residences in the northern sector which were not associated with such sacrificial rites. In some cases, the sacrifices were performed during the building, presumably to consecrate the structure. Thus, children, adults holding weapons, pigs, oxen, and sheep were found buried within the foundations. In others, the sacrifices were not directly related to the structure and may have been performed after the building was complete, perhaps sacrificial rites performed in association with an established temple. Thus, 185 ceremonial pits were found near the seven large buildings in the central sector which contained 852 human victims, fifteen horses, ten oxen, eighteen sheep, thirty-five dogs and five chariots.[5]

Besides these large house foundations, those of small semisubterranean houses in which the ordinary people continued to live in the same manner as their neolithic ancestors, were excavated, as well as small surface houses found in association with workshops and thought to be those of the artisans. A drainage system was discovered, but no city wall has been found yet and some scholars have questioned whether the extent of the residential areas uncovered thus far is sufficient for the site to merit the designation of the last capital of the Shang Dynasty. The Japanese scholar Miyazaki Ichisada has even argued that Yinxu was a necropolis rather than the capital.[6] However, there is no tradition, either earlier or later, as revealed in either the archaeological or the literary record, of building cities of the dead in China and it is unlikely that the Yinxu site would represent a unique example.

Although the hypothesis that Yinxu was a city of the dead as opposed to a political capital and residential city for the living is unlikely, the primary role of Yin was certainly that of a ritual center for the cult of sacrifice by means of which the Shang kings maintained the health and fertility of their people and their land. In the Zhou Dynasty and later times, the king was defined as the son of Heaven and his palace was the cosmological center from which he maintained the harmony of the empire by performing the appropriate rites as well as benevolent rule. This ritual tradition in which the Chinese king represented his people spiritually before Heaven has its origin in the ritual role of the Shang king whose primary duty was to determine and perform the correct sacrificial rites. As I shall discuss in the course of this work, this role was the reason why the Shang kings continually divined.

The central importance of the ancestral cult is apparent in the vast tombs built for the royal ancestors and the associated sacrificial burials of humans and animals excavated at Xibeigang 西北崗 (near Houjiazhuang 侯家莊), north of the Huan River, as well as by the large number of divination inscriptions about ancestral sacrifices (see figure 2). These excavations included eight large cross-shaped tombs with ramps in the cardinal directions, leading down to a central earthern chamber, and one unfinished tomb, a square pit without ramps. If the unfinished tomb was that of Zhou Xin, who was overthrown by the Zhou, then the number of tombs corresponds to the number of rulers from Wu Ding—the earliest king whose divinations have been uncovered at Yinxu—to the fall of the dynasty.[7] Three other large tombs have been excavated which have only two ramps and some scholars include them among the royal tombs, assuming that Pan Geng rather than Wu Ding moved to Yin, as stated in the historical records. However, although these tombs are impressive, they are significantly smaller than the larger cross-shaped tombs and this cannot be explained by chronology. Thus, they are probably the tombs of other members of the royal family.

In 1975, tomb number five, identifiable by the inscriptions on the bronze vessels as that of Lady (Fu 婦) Hao 好, one of Wu Ding's sixty-four wives, was excavated northwest of Xiaotun.[8] This tomb is small by comparison with the great cross-shaped tombs or even those with only two ramps: it had an earthen pit measuring some 5.6 metres north–south and 4 metres east–west at the opening and 7.5 metres deep, compared, for example, with the pit of Houjiazhuang number 1004, one of the large cross-shaped tombs, which measured 17.9 metres north–south and 15.9 metres east–west at the opening and which was 12 metres deep, and it did not have any ramps. It is nevertheless of critical importance because it is the only large tomb at Yinxu which had not been looted prior to excavation and so it contained a complete complex of ritual artifacts, including over two hundred bronze vessels, more than the number scientifically excavated from all of the other tombs combined. Because bronze vessels inscribed with the owner's name were still in the tomb, it is also the one tomb whose owner can be indisputably identified and matched with the divination inscriptions.

A wooden chamber was placed in the central earthen pits of the large tombs at Yinxu. Though the pits in the vast four-ramp tombs were either rectangular or cross-shaped, all the wooden chambers were cross-shaped. In the other large tombs, both pit and chamber were rectangular. After the chamber was placed in the pit, a ledge was made around it at the level of the roof. Grave goods and sacrifices were placed on this ledge as well as in the chamber and sacrifices might also be placed on the roof of the chamber.

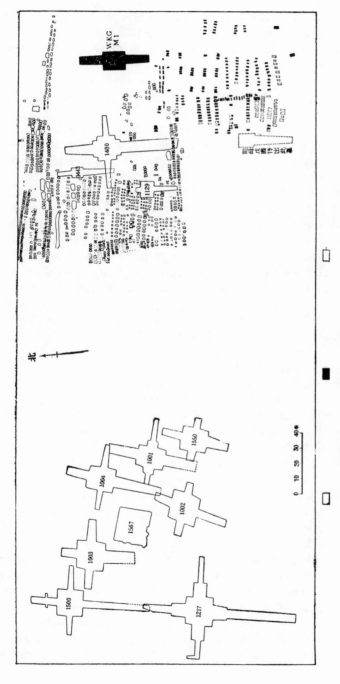

Figure 2 Large tombs, Xibeigang, Houjiazhuang

From Zhongguo Shehui Kexueyuan Kaogu Yanjiusuo, *Xin Zhongguo de kaogu yu faxian*, fig. 61

Human and/or dog sacrifices were also placed in a pit beneath the coffin which was placed in the center of the chamber. This practice was sometimes elaborated, as in the case of Houjiazhuang number 1550 in which there were a further eight pits containing dogs and human victims in the four cardinal directions, northeast, southeast, northwest, and southwest. Sacrifices were also buried along the ramps leading to the central earthen pits.

The scale of human sacrifice at Yinxu is evident from Houjiazhuang number 1001, possibly the tomb of Wu Ding himself, in which some 400 human victims were found, including fifty-nine headless skeletons divided into eleven rows and seventy-three skulls grouped in twenty-seven sets, which were buried along the ramps[9] (See figures 3 & 4). This was the largest number of human sacrifices found in any single tomb and may be compared with the sixteen victims sacrificed for the burial of Fu Hao. Sacrificial burials were also found in pits which were separate from the tombs. For example, in 1950, some seventeen pits with eight to ten headless corpses each were excavated southeast of the large tombs at Houjiazhuang and in 1976, a burial area covering 4,700 square metres, but assumed to be much larger, was excavated which included 191 burial pits and 1,330 human victims, presumably some of the 13,052 human sacrifices which, according to Hu Houxuan's 胡厚宣 calculations, are enumerated in the extant oracle bone inscriptions.[10]

Besides human and animal victims, a great many ritual objects were buried with the ancestors in the large tombs. The most important objects were the bronze vessels which held ritual offerings and which represent the supreme aesthetic achievement of the Shang. Since no other large tomb contained more than a small fraction of its original contents upon excavation, the tomb of Lady Hao may be used to suggest the richness of the original burials. This relatively small tomb contained 1,928 objects and approximately 7,000 cowrie shells. These included 460 bronze objects including both weapons and ritual vessels (but excluding buttons), 750 jade objects, 560 bone objects, five pottery vessels, and a few pieces of stone sculpture and ivory carvings.

When the initial excavations were made at Yinxu, a fully developed bronze culture able to produce bronzes technically unsurpassed even in modern times appeared to rise suddenly without any indigenous origin or development and some scholars assumed that it must have been introduced from the West. Since that time, the indigenous development of China's distinctive bronze culture centered on the North China plain has been gradually revealed. Two sites in Henan Province are particularly important in understanding this development: Zhengzhou 鄭州 including the nearby site

Figure 3 Excavation of tomb 1001 at Houjiazhuang (Xibeigang)

From Liang Siyong and Gao Quxun, *Houjiazhuang 1001-hao da mu*, v. 2, pl. 3, no. 2.

Figure 4 Tomb 1001, Houjiazhuang: headless skeletons on the southern tomb ramp

From Liang Siyong and Gao Quxun, *Houjiazhuang 1001-hao da mu*, v. 2, pl. XXVIII.

of Erligang 二里崗, and Yanshi 偃師, including both Erlitou 二里頭 and Shixianggou 尸鄉溝.

The site at Zhengzhou represented a large settlement, thought by many scholars to be the middle period Shang capital of Ao 隞 (or Xiao 囂). It included a city wall made of tamped earth which measured some 1700 by 1870 meters and had a base approximately thirty meters wide. No large tombs have been discovered yet near Zhengzhou, but bronze workshops and vessels were excavated and the bronze vessels are clearly both technically and aesthetically antecedent to the Yinxu bronzes.[11] Unfortunately, only three inscribed oracle bones of doubtful value have been found at this site and so it is still only at Yinxu that we can begin to read the thoughts of the Shang, as well as observe their material artifacts.[12]

Yanshi Erlitou represents an early stage in the development of Chinese bronze culture.[13] Only seven bronze vessels were found there, all small, undecorated, thinly cast *jue* 爵, a three-legged vessel used for heating and pouring wine which, as I shall discuss in the course of this work, had a particular significance for the Shang. The identities of Erlitou and the nearby site at Shixianggou have excited much debate among Chinese archaeologists in recent years. When Erlitou was excavated in the sixties, it was identified with Bo 亳, the capital of Cheng Tang, the founder of the Shang Dynasty, but some scholars have argued that it is a Xia Dynasty rather than a Shang capital. Shixianggou, a more recently excavated and still incompletely published site, has also been identified with Bo.[14]

The arguments about the location of the Xia Dynasty capitals are based upon an assumption that texts written over a thousand years later are an accurate reflection of prehistory; the oracle bone inscriptions do not refer to a previous dynasty and, in any case, are from the last three hundred years of the Shang Dynasty. In the present work, I will not concern myself with the archaeological argument. I hope, however, to shed light on the meaning of the textual tradition by revealing its origin in Shang mythological dualism.

Shang culture was not limited to Henan Province. Shang bronzes and sites have been discovered throughout most of present-day China. The most important site outside the central plains of the Yellow River region which was the center of Shang culture is Huangpi Panlongcheng 黃陂盤龍城 in the northern part of the southern province of Hubei, where a walled city, palace foundations and bronzes similar to those found at Zhengzhou were excavated. Other important finds include a large cross-shaped tomb in Shandong Province in the far east of China; bronzes from the early Yinxu period near Beijing, pre-dynastic Zhou sites with oracle bones and distinctive bronzes in Shaanxi Province, to the west of Anyang; and scattered sites with bronze vessels in the Yangzi River valley.[15] Late

Figure 5 *Jue* excavated at Yanshixian Erlitou

From *Henansheng Bowuguan*, no. 1

Shang bronzes similar to those from Yinxu have been found in the far western province of Sichuan and, most recently, another bronze culture, inspired by the Shang but stylistically and culturally independent from it, has been discovered at Guanghan 廣漢 in Sichuan Province.[16]

In the present study I will explore various aspects of Shang Dynasty religious thought. In so doing, I will make use of three types of evidence: archaeological artifacts, contemporaneous inscriptions and later texts. Archaeological artifacts are the material manifestations of that thought, reflected, for example, in the shape of tombs and burial practices, ritual vessels and their decoration, etc. Oracle bone inscriptions provide another form of contemporaneous evidence. They are a rich source for the study of religious thought because their primary topic is sacrifice and because they are divination statements. Although they are direct representations of Shang religious thought, because they are exclusively divination records and include no extended discourse or explanatory statements, we must also refer to later texts. These are useful not only because they include later traditions about the Shang, but also because they reflect thought systems which may have developed from the Shang.

In using later texts, I assume that there was a continuity between the Shang and later Chinese civilization. As long as we recognize that later texts are not direct representations of Shang thought, but later transformations of that thought, we may legitimately use them in conjunction with contemporaneous materials. Indeed, all interpretations of oracle bone inscriptions are based upon an assumption of linguistic and epigraphic continuity, without which decipherment could not have begun. But just as characters develop in form and meaning, so too do myths, ideas of cosmos, art motifs, etcetera. Furthermore, these early myths, ideas, etcetera may give rise to a number of different later manifestations depending on place and circumstance (elite or popular culture) and the differences between the later related forms may help us to reconstruct the Shang source, just as modern Chinese dialects help in reconstructing ancient Chinese pronunciation or modern European vocabularies to reconstruct Indo-European.

Although I assume a continuity between the Shang and later Chinese traditions, I believe that there is a fundamental distinction between Shang thought and that represented by surviving Zhou literature. I do not refer here to that change which is inevitable over any passage of time. Nor do I refer to differences in the belief systems of the Shang and Zhou peoples, although I believe that such differences did exist and that they are important in understanding the development of early Chinese thought, as I will discuss in the course of this work, but to an evolutionary change which appears to have taken place some time during the Western Zhou (circa 1100–771 B.C.) as the uses of literacy were extended and a varied body of literature began to develop.

Shang thought was still 'primitive' or, as I prefer to all it, 'mythic'. As Jack Goody has observed, a historic sensibility or awareness of the "pastness of the past" depends upon permanent written records:

. . The Tiv have their genealogies, others their sacred tales about the origin of the world and the way in which man acquired his culture. But all their conceptualizations of the past cannot help being governed by the concerns of the present, merely because there is no body of chronologically ordered statements to which reference can be made . . . Myth and history merge into one: the elements in the cultural heritage which cease to have a contemporary relevance tend to be soon forgotten or transformed; and as the individuals of each generation acquire their vocabulary, their genealogies, and their myths, they are unaware that various words, proper names and stories have dropped out, or that others have changed their names and been replaced. . . .[17]

All interest in the past is because of present concerns, although in societies with a literary tradition, our conception of the past is constrained at least to some degree by written records. The difference between myth and history is not, however, that the history of a literate society is more accurate than the myth of a nonliterate one. Myth is freely conceived. It includes events which not only did not happen, but which *could not have happened,* which are fantastic, breaching the confines of both reality and possibility, for its events are sacred in their nature and not meant to be of this world. In primitive or 'mythic' societies, as I prefer to call them, myth, art, ritual, divination, sacrifice, and cosmology are all manifestations of an integral belief system, generated directly from the religious structure, rather than secondarily from the written records. To use Claude Levi-Strauss's expression, in such societies, people "think in myths". Such thought may make use of real past events as well as present realities, but it is neither concerned with what actually happened nor fettered by real possibility.

Although the manifestations of mythic thought—myths, art, ritual, etc.—are traditional and thus limited by convention in the forms of their expression, they are generated at the time that they are transmitted, performed or created. Once stories or events are recorded, however, the record assumes a life of its own. People begin to think *about* myth rather than in it, to compare different versions, to worry about their inconsistencies, and to wonder about their truth. Where myth and history were once one, they may be distinguished and myth relegated to a special sphere of religion; or they may *not* be distinguished which, as I shall discuss in the following chapter, was the case in China, and then, when the rational literate writer examines the received tradition, he may decide that the myths have been embellished and suppress their supernatural and logically impossible elements.

In a previous book, *The Heir and the Sage: Dynastic Legend in Early China,* I examined the manner in which 'history' was recorded in Chinese texts of the fifth to first centuries B.C. and argued that it was regularly transformed as a means of expressing a philosophic viewpoint. Thus, for example, the relationship between the pre-dynastic rulers Yao 堯 and Shun 舜 , could be expressed as an abdication, usurpation or simply a matter of the changing allegiance of the population, depending upon the writer. Furthermore, I argued that historical legend functioned as myth, to mediate an inherent social conflict, in the case of the legends surrounding passing rule, a conflict between hereditary right and rule by virtue or obligation to one's family and obligation to the larger social group.

Although there are some remnants of an earlier mythology in the legends of the pre-dynastic and Xia rulers, the legends which I have argued functioned as myth, were mostly recounted in a realistic manner. No distinction was made between the pre-dynastic and dynastic period; all of the rulers behaving realistically, if stereotypically, as men of the writers' own time might. Indeed, the same motifs were repeated in the legends of both periods and they were tied together in a single structure, so that it was possible to predict from how a writer related a legend of one period, how he would recount that of another. For example, if he described Shun as usurping the rule from Yao, then he would also say that the first Zhou ruler committed regicide against the Shang king. There is no "sense of the past" in these legends, of a world which has changed, but, as I shall demonstrate herein, the stories of the pre-dynastic past and the Xia Dynasty derive from an earlier mythology.

Many scholars take literacy as the critical factor determining the difference between the thinking of so-called primitive societies and 'advanced' ones. It is not the existence of a writing system and the ability to read, however, which brings about the change, but literature—a corpus of historical records, stories, etc., which may be consulted and compared—which allows us that distance from our own thought and that of our predecessors necessary for critical analysis. Such literature need not develop until some time after the writing system. This, I believe, was the case in early China.

When and where the Chinese writing system originated is not yet clear. The earliest evidence are some symbols engraved on turtle plastrons recently excavated at Wuyang 舞陽 in Henan Province, datable to 8500–7500 B.P.[18] These symbols are not understood but they resemble later Chinese characters and may be a form of protowriting. Although there are a number of examples of isolated symbols later in the neolithic period which may be related to later Chinese writing and some characters on pottery as well as the three oracle bones mentioned above from Zhengzhou, Chinese archaeologists have yet to find the precedents for the oracle bone inscriptions from Yinxu.

Of the oracle bone inscriptions at Yinxu, those of the first period—the reign of Wu Ding—are the greatest in number and the richest and most varied in content. The writing system was also already fully developed. All types of words were represented in the script, though some grammatical particles may sometimes have been omitted. The characters were formed according to all of the same principles as modern Chinese characters and include both semantic and phonetic elements. The pictorial origins of some of these elements are more readily discerned than in the later script, but they are already highly conventionalized and abstracted. Both the writing system and the practice of inscribing divinations on bone must have had a period of development before Yinxu even though the earlier examples have not yet been uncovered.

Although the Shang—or at least the Shang ruler and those priests charged with divining on his behalf—were fully literate, the oracle bone inscriptions are not literature comparable to the extant texts transmitted from Zhou times. They include no extended discourse and they are exclusively records of divination. They are primary evidence of Shang divination as it took place, a direct representation of the ritual. No other narrative is recorded. Possibly, the recording of the divinations led to a consciousness of the system and thus to its standardization, but the oracle bone inscriptions are still thinking in myth—or, in this case, ritual—rather than about it.

We cannot be entirely certain of how writing was used in the Shang since there is always the possibility of undiscovered texts. Early Chinese books were written on bamboo slips tied with string. Such bamboo (or wooden) slips did exist in the Shang Dynasty because the oracle bone inscriptions include the character *ce* 册 (#), a pictograph of the slips, and several related characters which also include this element. They include 嚚 (#)—a picture of bamboo slips placed in a box (later mistaken for a mouth); 洲 (#)—slips sunk in a river; 柵 (#)—slips on an altar; and 典 (#)—slips presented with two hands, to which a box (#) or an altar (#) may also be added. All of these characters are used to describe the offering of ritual promises or oaths recorded on bamboo slips by placing them on the ancestral altars or sinking them in rivers. Divinations were also made about the appointment of military officials in which bamboo slips were used, apparently to sanctify the appointment. These usages indicate that writing held the power of a sacred promise and we know from them that the potential for the development of a literary tradition was present, but they do not indicate that writing was used in the Shang for other than ritual purposes.

Although we cannot be entirely certain that the Shang did not have literature unconnected with ritual, there is no evidence of a lost body of Shang literature in Zhou texts. In an early Western Zhou document included in the *Shang shu* 尚書, the Zhou attempted to persuade the Shang people that their ruler's overthrow was divinely sanctioned, telling them "You know that the earlier men of Yin had documents and records of how Yin superseded the mandate of Xia",[19] but this document does not cite any earlier record and it implies that such records were not extant in the early Western Zhou. Furthermore, Zhou texts do not cite from a lost body of Shang literature, as we would expect if they had such literature.

The earliest extant Chinese texts are the *Shang shu* documents (alternatively called the *Shujing* 書經 '*Book of Documents*'), some of which were written soon after the overthrow of the Shang by the Zhou. These documents appear to derive from inscriptions on bronze ritual vessels. Throughout most of the Yinxu period, these were very simple—names and then simple ancestral dedications. At the end of the Shang, however, the inscriptions began to lengthen and the inscriptions of the early Western Zhou period often commemorate deeds and record speeches in language which is similar to the contemporaneous *Shang shu* documents. This suggests that the document tradition developed from, or at least in tandem with, bronze inscriptions and did not have an origin in earlier Shang documents.

After the *Shang shu,* the next early texts in the Chinese tradition are the hexagram lines of the *Yijing* 易經 or *Book of Changes* and the earliest parts of the *Shijing* 詩經 or *Books of Songs,* both of which were recorded in the early centuries of the Zhou Dynasty. Neither of these texts represents the continuation of a Shang literary tradition. The *Yijing* is associated with the Zhou people and represents another divination tradition. The *Shijing* were originally songs, an oral rather than a literary tradition which was recorded in the Zhou dynasty. These early Zhou texts all suggest that writing gradually expanded in its uses at the beginning of the Zhou Dynasty or, possibly, at the very end of the Shang. With the development of a corpus of documents and different types of texts came changes in patterns of thought. Some of the changes which came about will be indicated herein, but a subsequent volume will also be devoted to tracing and explaining later developments.

In the following chapter, I will argue that the Shang had a myth of ten suns and that their ancestors were classified together with these suns. This totemic classification was the basis of their ritual calendar. In Chapter 3, I will explore the manner in which Shang mythology was transformed into the historical legend of Zhou texts. I will argue that the legend of Yao's abdication to Shun was a transformation of a Shang myth in which the high lord, *di* 帝, appointed the first Shang ruler. I will also argue that the Xia were originally the mythical inverse of the Shang, associated with water, dragons, the moons, darkness and death, as opposed to the fire, birds, suns, light and life, with which the Shang were associated. This myth was transformed into the story of an historical dynasty at the beginning of the Zhou.

Chapters 4 and 5 are concerned with cosmology and divination. In Chapter 4, I ask the question, what was the shape of the cosmos in the minds of the Shang kings and their diviners, and argue that the earth was not a simple square, as in later Chinese cosmology, but a square surrounded by four mythical quadrates in the cardinal directions. This cruciform shape is replicated in the shapes of the royal tombs and is often used to enclose bronze inscriptions. It also provides the origin for numerology based on the number five, as in later five-element theory. Furthermore, the cruciform is the shape of the turtle plastron and the turtle was a model of the cosmos. This recognition provides the key to a new interpretation of Shang divination which I will propose in Chapter 5.

Chapter 6 is concerned with the problem of the meaning of the motifs on bronze ritual vessels. These motifs are readily recognized, but they are continually transformed and they are not representations. I will argue that they are nevertheless iconographically meaningful. In order to understand their meaning, I return to the problem of the nature of myth and its relationship to art in mythological societies. I argue that both the myths and the art of such societies derive directly from the religious structure and that both necessarily breach the bounds of natural reality as a sign of their sacred character. The art alludes to motifs found in other contexts, in this case, eating and sacrifice, the watery underworld, and transformation, but it does not illustrate, and it is characterized by such techniques as distortion, the conjoining of disparate creatures, and double imagery.

II

Sons of Suns

The problem of myth is one that has
concerned Western philosophers from
the time of Plato and the Sophists.

David Bidney,
Myth, Symbolism and Truth [1]

The 'problem of myth' for Western philosophers is a problem of interpret-
ing the meaning of myths and explaining the phenomenon of mythmaking.
The problem of myth for the sinologist is one of finding any myths to interpret and of explaining why there are so few—for mythmaking is generally
assumed to be a universal faculty of mankind. One explanation for this
paucity of myth in the traditional sense of stories of the supernatural in
ancient Chinese texts is the structure of Chinese religion. The focus of
Chinese religion from ancient until modern times has been ancestor
worship; the motive force of which is the belief that people continue to
exist after death, to need food from the living and to exercise power over
them. The belief that people continued to exist and need food after death is
already evident in the neolithic period in which pottery vessels filled with
grain were buried with the dead. In the Shang dynasty, not only were pottery and bronze vessels filled with food offerings buried in tombs, the primary purpose of the elaborate and costly system of oracle bone divination
was to determine the appropriate offerings to be made to the ancestors and
thus prevent their curses or obtain their assistance.

Within this system, the spirits were only important as they related to
the living; they had no life of their own after death. There was no 'other',
supernatural world of gods who were different in kind from human beings
and interacted with one another, like Mount Olympus of the ancient
Greeks where the gods ate ambrosia, drank nectar and enacted the dramas
of their own relationships, occasionally dallying in human affairs and fall-
ing in love with mortals. Nor was there an earlier era, at least in the textual
tradition, before the beginning of time, when gods inhabited the earth.
Gods, when they came to be distinguished from ancestors, were simply

19

other mortals who continued to exercise power after death over people who were not their descendants and to receive offerings from them.[2]

Chinese religion stressed ritual, but the ritual was pragmatic—offerings given in exchange for benevolence or at least for lack of malevolence. Thus although stories of ghosts—the wronged or hungry dead who interfere with the living—and supernatural omens do occur in the early texts, myths in which gods interact with one another in a world of their own do not. Instead, there are stories about the lives of the gods when they were still human beings. These stories may have mythical import. They may function as myth in the sense that they mediate social contradictions,[3] but they appear in the texts as history or historical legend, as human beings interacting with one another at a certain geographical location and within a chronological time scale.

Another explanation for the paucity of myth in ancient Chinese texts is that the myths of an earlier era were historicized by the literati who recorded them in the extant texts, all of which are from the Zhou (ca. 1100–221 B.C.) and Han (206 B.C.–A.D. 220) dynasties. Although the texts do not contain mythical narratives, the accounts of ancient history and the dynastic ancestors do contain events which breach the confines of reality. These take such forms as: (1) cosmogonic events, (2) miraculous conceptions and births, (3) the transformation of people into animals or inanimate objects, (4) impossibly long lives, and (5) confusion of time sequence indicating that events which were once set in an indefinite past have been systematized differently by different writers. This suggests that before the Zhou Dynasty, there were myths which were transformed by later writers into historical accounts and that in some, but not all, texts, their more fantastic elements were excised.

The mythical aura of these accounts of ancient history has been recognized since the beginning of this century and in the last seventy years various attempts have been made to extract the myths from the texts and to demonstrate that accounts which are associated with ancient kings and appear as history in some texts have mythical elements in others. Particularly important as predecessors of the present study are the *Gushibian* 古史辨 ; "Critiques of Ancient History", edited by Gu Jiegang 顧頡剛 and Henri Maspero's "Légendes mythologiques dans le Chou King". The *Gushibian* volumes published in Beijing and Shanghai in the 1920s and 1930s were inspired by Hu Shi's admonition to 'doubt antiquity' and by the realization that the Confucian state and society which its authors wished to challenge were underpinned by the traditional view of ancient history. Written in the form of a continuing debate, they were a bold attempt by a group of scholars led by Gu Jiegang to critically evaluate the received tradition of ancient Chinese history and to scientifically sort fact from fiction.

Gu Jiegang began with the recognition that the actors in Chinese history are like those on the opera stage, exemplars of certain themes about which repeating motifs accrued, the same motifs recurring in association with historical figures of different periods. He then observed that predynastic history can be divided into layers in which as a general rule, the earlier the king, the later he appears in the texts. In the earliest layer, the texts which he dated to the Western Zhou Dynasty (ca. 1100–771 B.C.), history began with Yu 禹, traditionally the founder of the Xia Dynasty (ca. 2200–1700 B.C.); then, in the Spring and Autumn period (722–481 B.C.), the predynastic rulers Yao 堯 and Shun 舜 were placed before Yu in the historical chronology; finally, during the Han dynasty, the Yellow Emperor and his descendant Zhuan Xu 顓頊 were placed prior to Yao and Shun. Gu further argued that not only do many of the ancient rulers have supernatural aspects in some texts, their historical role reflects the governmental organization and social structure of the society of the Zhou and Han Dynasties in which the texts were composed rather than the neolithic age in which the rulers were supposed to have lived.

Maspero's "Légendes mythologiques dans le Chou King" published in 1924 is a much more limited study—of the mythology embedded in the first chapters of the *Shujing* 書經 or *Shang shu* 尚書, the "Book of Documents" or, alternatively "Ancient Documents". Maspero used modern ethnographic data—myths of Chinese minority and other Southeast Asian peoples—and compared differing textual accounts to argue that the historical accounts of the pre-dynastic 'Emperors' Yao 堯, Shun 舜, and Yu 禹 and their ministers were an historicization or 'euhemerization' (Maspero used this term in the reverse of its standard usage) of a more ancient creation mythology.

Before turning to the problem of whether there was a more ancient mythology which has been historicized, the contributions of Marcel Granet and Bernard Karlgren also deserve mention. No one interested in early Chinese thought can fail to be dazzled by Marcel Granet's frequently brilliant insights in recognizing key mythic themes in ancient Chinese history and literature, particularly in *Danses et légendes de la Chine ancienne*. Unfortunately, however, Granet did not accept the authenticity of the oracle bone inscriptions which had not yet been scientifically excavated when he wrote *Danses et légendes* in 1926. Thus, he made no use of this material either in his philological analyses or his historical reconstructions of the development of early Chinese society.

The *Gushibian* authors, Maspero, and Granet all argued that a stratum of myths or mythic themes lay beneath the early Chinese historical tradition. Bernhard Karlgren in "Legends and cults in ancient China", on the other hand, attempted to discover the historical reality which he assumed lay beneath the mythology. Thus he argued that the mythological heroes of the early texts were originally the ancestors of the noble clans who had been mythologized by their descendants. The assumption that myth derives from history is no longer possible. Indeed, it was not tenable at the time as Wolfram Eberhard pointed out in a detailed and effective refutation.[4] More recently, Levi-Strauss's *Mythologiques* has effectively demonstrated, even if one does not accept all of its premises, that myths derive from other myths, and that they are frequently inversions of one another, that they represent a manner of thinking which is above all about the present, not the past.

Although we cannot assume that myth derives from history, the problem which Karlgren confronted is nevertheless a legitimate one: realistic accounts often appear in earlier texts than the apparently mythical versions of the same stories. One explanation for this phenomenon is that the Han texts are much more varied in kind and include a broader range of material than those of the Zhou dynasty, and they are more likely to record folk traditions than the philosophic texts which dominated the preceding period. As Eberhard observed, the date that a story enters the textual tradition is not the date of its origin; it may have a much longer oral history. We cannot assume, however, that within this oral tradition the story will have remained the same.

The problem of dating the material in early Chinese texts is extremely complex, even when we are certain of the date at which the text was compiled which is often not the case. In early times, the texts were not in themselves sacred or canonical; they were living documents, important for the truth which they represented rather than important in themselves. When Sima Qian compiled the *Shiji* 史記 in the second century B.C., he used a variety of ancient sources including the documents in the extant *Shang shu*. In recording the material from these documents, he kept closely to the original, but he also interpreted the archaic language and changed the text to make it understandable to the modern reader. In a study of the 'forged' ancient script (*gu wen* 古文) *Shang shu* text, the *Tang gao* 湯誥, I demonstrated that it was based upon an earlier text, now lost, from which it had excised references to human sacrifice in accordance with Confucian principles. The most complete extant version of the text, quoted in a number of early texts, including the *Mozi* 墨子, is in the *Di-wang shiji*, 帝王世紀 compiled in the third century A.D. and written in the language of that time although the original was probably early Western Zhou (ca. 1100–771 B.C.).[5]

The philosophers of the Greek Enlightenment dealt with the problem of myth either by regarding myths as containing another kind of truth, allegorical, religious or moral, rather than literal or philosophical, or by regarding them sceptically as embroidered history, as did the fourth century B.C. Sicilian philosopher Euhemerus. In ancient China, however, where there was no clearly defined other, supernatural realm, myth and history were always inseparable. Even in Shang times where, as I shall discuss below, the 'high ancestors' (*gao zu* 高祖) were distinguished from immediate ancestors, both types of spirits were, nevertheless, 'ancestors' (*zu* 祖). The enlightened philosophers of the Warring States period who believed in the essential truth of the received accounts could only seek that truth by explaining away or excising those elements of the received tradition which appeared to them to be fantastic or contrary to natural laws.

The historical assessments of the *Gushibian* scholars and, to a lesser extent, Maspero have provided the basis of our historical understanding for the last fifty years. Recently, however, many Chinese and Western scholars have begun to ignore the scholarship of this earlier generation. Not only has the Xia, about which Gu Jiegang and his colleague Yang Kuan 楊寬 remained firmly agnostic, been identified by some scholars with an archaeologically defined neolithic culture centred at Erlitou in Henan Province, but Yu—the flood hero and founder of the Xia Dynasty, Shun and even more ancient rulers such as the Shao Hao 少昊 and the Yellow Emperor are invoked in an attempt to understand the pattern of neolithic China.

There are many reasons for this change of attitude. Most importantly, radiocarbon dating allows us to date neolithic cultures and there is an inevitable tendency to try to relate these to the traditionally accepted historical accounts of the pre-dynastic period. Moreover, relatively advanced neolithic cultures often appear to coincide geographically with the traditionally accepted historical accounts of the homelands of pre-dynastic rulers and this is taken as confirmation of their existence, especially when the ancient textual tradition coincides with later local traditions. However, this phenomenon can also be explained by regarding these accounts as those of the mythical ancestors of the tribes who still inhabit these regions rather than as their former rulers. Since no pre-Yinxu texts have yet been discovered, such problems can only be resolved by a critical evaluation of the origin and meaning of the ancient accounts.

The critiques of ancient history of the *Gushibian* scholars and Maspero were based upon the hypothesis that the myths of an earlier era were made rational and turned into 'history' by the Zhou dynasty literati. But was there a mythology in ancient China, a structure or system of beliefs which has been reinterpreted by later scholars? And if so, what was the nature of this system? Myths are not isolated phenomena. They exist within a social and intellectual structure outside of which they appear incomprehensible or simply irrational. Indeed, as I shall discuss further in Chapter 6 of this work, this apparent irrationality or, to be more precise, the breach of natural reality, is their primary characteristic, the sign that the stories are sacred rather than profane.

If an earlier stratum of mythological thought has been transformed by the Zhou literati, we should expect to find it reflected in the Shang oracle bone inscriptions. These inscriptions are now increasingly accurately interpreted and they provide much information about early Chinese thought which was not available to scholars seeking to interpret ancient Chinese mythology in the early part of this century, but because they are mainly ritual propositions—about offerings to be made to the ancestors and nature spirits who in turn were benevolent or at least lacked malevolence—they do not include mythical narratives or, indeed, narratives of any other kind. Thus, although much information about the nature of Shang religion can be garnered from the inscriptions themselves, the names mentioned have no stories. The pattern of worship can be observed, but it has no explicit rationale. These can only be interpreted in the light of later traditions.

One problem in reconstruction is that there are very few texts from the period immediately following the overthrow of the Shang. Indeed, it is some five centuries before we begin to have a significant corpus of literature. Another problem is that early Chinese texts do not normally recount myth, even euhemerized as history, except in very abbreviated references within the context of other discussion. These references must be pieced together to form an intelligible pattern of interlocking and concordant material, a 'tradition' as I will call it, of stories and beliefs which are consistent in more than one text. I assume that a textual tradition of this type reflected an oral tradition, but the period and region in which it was passed down can usually be defined only in general terms.

Names recorded from an oral tradition frequently differ, reflecting a lack of systemization and differences in the time and place at which they were recorded. In some cases, the names are simply variants, that is the characters are related phonologically or graphically and the figures have the same roles and relationships. Frequently, however, particularly when two traditions which may have a common source are compared, names which are graphically unrelated or only partially related appear to have a common role and have some common kinship relationships. I distinguish these from the above as 'equivalent' or 'structurally equivalent' when their role in two traditions is the same.

An important difference between this work and earlier studies of this same material is that although I assume that the stories continually change with time and place and according to the circumstances in which they were passed down and recorded, I do not assume a single line of development.

An analogy may be made with historical linguistics in which we recognize that there must be a common origin for words in genetically related modern languages and we can reconstruct sound and meaning by studying these later variations. Similarly, a variety of later traditions, both apparently historical and apparently mythical, may derive from an earlier Shang form. Not all later traditions, however, derive from the Shang and we must look for confirmation within the Shang sources themselves.

In this chapter, I will explore the mythology and system of beliefs which surrounded the ten suns in Zhou and Shang texts and inscriptions. First, I will analyse the myth of ten suns rising from the Mulberry Tree as it appears in Zhou and Han texts, including the story of Archer Yi shooting nine of the suns. Secondly, I will analyse the tradition which includes the myth of the origin of the Shang people and the beginning of their dynasty and trace the relationship of this tradition with that of the Mulberry Tree. Thirdly, I will turn to the oracle bone inscriptions for evidence of an antecedent to these two traditions.

My hypothesis is that the Shang had a myth of ten suns and that the Shang ruling group was organized in a totemic relationship to these suns.[6] This myth was specific to the Shang and integrally associated with their rule. When the Zhou, who believed in one sun, conquered the Shang, the myth lost its earlier meaning, and the system its integrity, but the motifs were transformed and continued to occur in other contexts. At the popular level, people continued to believe in ten suns which rose in sequence from the branches of the Mulberry Tree in outlying regions. In the central states, this tradition was known but the ten suns were confined to the mythical past by the story that one day all of them came out at once and nine were shot by Archer Yi. The Shang continued to be associated with many of the motifs of this tradition and the myth of the origin of their tribe from the egg of a black bird is a transformation of the myth of the birth of the ten suns which rose from the Mulberry Tree, but the belief in ten suns had been lost. At the level of official history, as I will discuss in the next chapter, the story of Yao's appointment of Shun includes another transformation of the Shang cosmogonic sun myth.

ONE SUN OR TEN

In the Zhou Dynasty, the tradition that there was only one sun was so widely accepted that Mencius quoted Confucius as saying, "Heaven does not have two suns; the people do not have two kings".[7] This tradition was so dominant from the Zhou Dynasty on that studies of the history of Chinese astronomy, such as those by Maspero, De Saussure and, more recently, Joseph Needham, begin with the assumption that the Chinese believed in one sun.[8] Myth though it was, and although it did not leave any trace upon the history of Chinese astronomy, the belief in ten alternating suns was a strongly competing tradition in ancient China, so much so that in the first century A.D., Wang Chong 王充 launched a spirited denial of the possibility of ten suns perching on the branches of a tree without burning it to cinders.[9]

Wang Chong's account in the *Lun heng* 論衡 of the myth of the ten suns is drawn from two earlier texts, the *Shanhaijing* 山海經, a corpus of mythological geographies drawn together in the Han Dynasty from a variety of sources of different date and origin, and the *Huainanzi* 淮南子, a syncretic philosophical text compiled at the court of Liu An, prince of Huainan (the region south of the Huai River) and presented to the Han emperor Wu Di in 139 B.C. This tradition is also prevalent throughout the *Chuci* 楚辭 corpus, the "Songs of the south" in David Hawkes' translation, including the *Tian wen* 天問 or "Heavenly questions'. Although this section may not be much older in its present form than the purported author of the *Chuci*, Qu Yuan 屈原, who lived in the third century B.C.,[10] it appears to draw upon a more ancient oral tradition.

The prevalence of this myth in the *Chuci* and, to a lesser extent, in the *Huainanzi* indicates an association between the ten-sun tradition and southern China. It might be argued that this was not a Shang tradition retained in the south during the Zhou, but one which originated in the state of Chu. However, an association between Shang and Chu culture has long been conjectured and this hypothesis has recently been confirmed by archaeological excavation.[11] A number of Shang sites in the Chu region have now been excavated, some with bronzes of unusually high quality and size. These include a walled city at Panlongcheng 盤龍城 in the Huangpi 黃陂 District of Hubei Province. This site is earlier than that at Yinxu, and the bronzes excavated at Panlongcheng are similar to those of the middle Shang capital at Zhengzhou Erligang 鄭州二里岡.[12] For the late Shang or Yinxu period, the most extensive finds other than those from Yinxu itself are from Tianhu 天湖 in Luoshan 羅山 County, just south of the Huai River in southern Henan Province. A number of bronzes stylistically indistinguishable from those found at Yinxu have been excavated from this site and the Shang remains lie beneath Chu tombs of the Spring and Autumn and Warring States Period. The artifacts from these tombs are typical of Chu culture.[13] In contrast, very few Western Zhou sites have been excavated in the south.

The large number of Shang sites and paucity of Western Zhou ones from the Chu region suggests that whereas communication between the Shang and the south was easy and regular, Zhou access and influence was much more restricted. The independent status of Chu and the southeastern state of Wu 吳 in the Western Zhou period is also evident in their retention of the title king (*wang* 王) for their rulers. Although Mencius declared that the "people do not have two kings" and the Zhou ruler claimed this title exclusively for the 'son of heaven' (*tianzi* 天子), in the Shang Dynasty, as Qi Wenxin has demonstrated,[14] the rulers of many states used this title and it was recognized by the Shang ruler who was also called king (*wang*).

THE MULBERRY TREE TRADITION

The Mulberry Tree tradition is best known to modern scholars from the myth that one day all ten suns rose at once and Archer Yi 后羿 shot down nine of them. This story may have been used to explain the discrepancy between the conflicting traditions of ten and one suns, but it assumes the motifs of the ten-sun tradition. These include:

1. the Fu Sang 扶桑 Tree in the East at the foot of which is the Valley of the Sun which contains a pool of water;
2. the Ruo Tree 若木 in the West with water at its foot;
3. A watery underworld;
4. Ten as the number of the suns;
5. the suns identified with birds;
6. Xihe 羲和 as the mother of the suns.

According to the *Shuowen* 說文 the Fu Sang is a "spirit tree, that from which the sun(s) go out".[15] The *sang* 桑 or 'mulberry', with its red or white berries, depicted in oracle bone script as a tree with many mouths among its branches 𤔥, provides an apt metaphor for this tree on the branches of which many suns perched. *Fu* (**b'įwo*)[16] 扶 or 榑 is usually interpreted as the name of the mulberry tree and it is sometimes simply called the Fu Tree (*fu mu* 扶木, 榑木). The character 榑 which is used in the *Shuowen* for the sun tree seems not to occur except with reference to this tree,[17] but even in this context the initial syllable *fu* is more commonly written with the homophone 扶 'support'. Scholars have suggested various etymologies based on this character: among them, that the name refers to the support of the tree for the suns[18] and that two trees supported one another.[19] However, **b'įwo* was an initial syllable before many plant names in the *Shijing* 詩經.[20] This, together with the variation between the two characters in this instance, suggests that *fu* was originally an initial syllable which designated plants rather than the name of the tree. Thus, the Fu Sang Tree was originally simply *the* Mulberry Tree and the Fu Mu, *the* Tree.

The references to the Mulberry Tree tradition in the *Shanhaijing*, *Huainanzi* and *Chuci* are generally in accordance, with only minor discrepancies. The most explicit descriptions of the tree are those in *Shanhaijing*:

Above the Tang Valley 湯谷 is the Fu Sang. [The Valley] is where-
in the ten suns bathe. It is north of the Black Tooth Tribe. In
the swirling water is a great tree. Nine suns dwell on its lower
branches; one sun, on its uppermost branch.

> *Shanhaijing* (*Haiwaidongjing* 海外東經) 9/97a–b.

and:

On the top of a mountain named Nieyaojundi is the Fu Tree 扶木.
Although its trunk is three hundred li, its leaves are like those of
mustard. The valley there is called the Warm Springs Valley
溫源谷 (i.e. Tang Valley-Guo Pu). Above the Tang Valley 湯谷 is
the Fu Tree. When one sun reaches it, another sun goes out; all of
them carried by birds.

> *Shanhaijing* (*Dahuangdongjing* 大荒東經) 14/65a–b.

The name of the valley from which the suns rise is written in these
passages as Tang (**t'âng*) 湯 with a water radical—the same character
which is used in Zhou texts for the name of the founder of the Shang
dynasty. It may also be written with one of three homophones pronounced
Yang (*dịang)— 暘,[21] 陽,[22] 崵,[23] Tang has a meaning of 'hot water' and
the commentator Guo Pu 郭璞 (A.D. 276–324) interprets the name of the
valley as a reference to the heat of the water in which the suns bathe (9/
97b). This interpretation is supported by the reference to the valley as the
'Warm Springs Valley' in the *Dahuangdongjing* passage, an apparently
inadvertent error based on *tang* meaning hot water which does not occur in
other texts.[24]
    When the valley from which the suns rise is called the Tang 湯
Valley—with the water radical—the name of the valley includes the pool
of water in which the ten suns bathe. However, with a sun or slope radical,
the 'Hot Water Valley' becomes the 'Sun Valley'. In this case, the pool of
water sometimes has another name. For example, in the *Huainanzi* (3/9a–
b): "The sun comes out of the Yang Valley (暘谷) and bathes in the Xian
Pool (咸池)." The variation of the radical indicates that it was not originally present and the phonetic 昜 itself carries the meaning of sun.[25] Mythically, there is always a valley which contains a pool of water for the suns
to bathe in.
    Corresponding to the Fu Sang in the far east—the precise location
varies—is a Ruo Tree 若木 in the far west. The ten suns perch on its branches after their long journey across the sky. The following passage from the
Huainanzi (4/3a) also includes a third tree, an *axis mundi* to use Mircea
Eliade's term,[26] which connects heaven above with the earth below:

The Fu Tree is in Yang Zhou 陽州 and is that which the suns touch upon.[27] The Jian Tree is in Du Guang and is that which the many spirits 眾帝 descend from above. . . . The Ruo Tree is West of the Jian Tree 健木. When the ten suns are on the tips of its branches, it illuminates the earth below.

The reference to a third tree besides the Fu Tree and the Ruo Tree in this passage is unusual as is the usage of *di* 帝 in a collective sense for spirits which inhabit the heavens.[28]

At the foot of the Ruo Tree, there is a gorge, called the Yu Yuan 虞淵 which has been identified by Chen Bingliang with the Feather Abyss 羽淵 where, as I shall discuss below, the sun-ravens shed their feathers when they were shot by the Archer Yi.[29] In it there is water, as at the foot of the Fu Sang. According to the *Tian wen,* the sun(s) "go out from *Tang gu* 湯谷 (the Hot Water Valley) and stop at *Meng si* 蒙汜 " (the 'Hidden Stream').[30] More specifically, *si* is a stream which returns to its source and the water at the foot of the Ruo Tree is also called the Ruo River 若水. The location of the Ruo River has caused some confusion. Although, according to the *Shanhaijing,* the Ruo River has its source at the Ruo Tree,[31] it also appears in association with the Kong Sang 空桑, the Hollow Mulberry, which some scholars have identified with the Fu Sang.[32]

Mizukami Shizuo has argued on the basis of the similarity between the character *ruo* and some forms of *sang* in the oracle bone script and the confusion in the myth tradition that the Fu Sang and Ruo Tree are identical.[33] However, both the *Chuci* and the *Huainanzi* regularly mention both trees and a tree in the west on which the sun-birds perch in the evening is a logical counterpart of the Mulberry Tree in the east from which they set out in the morning. The Ruo River's appearance in both east and west can be explained by regarding it not as an ordinary river, but as another name for the watery underworld also known as the 'Yellow Spring' (*Huang Quan* 黃泉), which ran everywhere beneath the earth and which came to the surface at the feet of the Fu Sang and Ruo Tree.

In Han Dynasty tomb art, the region beneath the earth is depicted with turtles, dragons, and large fishlike creatures.[34] The earliest reference to the Yellow Springs which I have found is in a passage from the *Zuozhuan* 左傳 in which Duke Zhuang of Qing who had been wronged by his mother swore to her that "we shall not meet one another until we reach the Yellow Springs".[35] These, then, were the land of the dead, but later on, when the duke regretted his harshness towards his mother, he accepted advice that "if you scoop out the earth until you reach the springs (*quan* 泉) and then, having dug a tunnel, meet with one another, who could say that it is contrary [to your oath]." This device suggests that all underground springs were branches of the Yellow Springs. The *Mencius, Xunzi* and *Huainanzi* also record the belief that worms "eat soil and drink from the Yellow Springs".[36] Similarly, Wang Chong observed in the *Lun heng* that people do not like to work in mines because they are "next to the Yellow Springs".[37]

Thus water ran beneath the earth, just as the sky surmounted it. This dualism is sometimes made explicit, as for example, in the *Zhuangzi* 莊子 which speaks of "treading the Yellow Springs and climbing to the great sky (*da huang* 大皇)".[38] The great flood was a problem of controlling these waters when they threatened to rise up to the sky and the Xia ancestors are regularly associated with the Ruo River, the color yellow, and the netherworld. The oracle bone inscriptions name a number of different springs and even today there are many natural springs bubbling up from the yellow loess in the Anyang region. Thus a belief that water ran everywhere beneath the earth would have been a natural assumption in this region. The Ruo Tree in the West was the place where the suns set and entered this watery underworld, that is the Ruo River, or, alternatively, the Yellow Springs, for yellow was the color of earth. Yellow or bright (*huang* 黃) and black or dark (*xuan* 玄) are a natural primitive color system and they are the colors used for the animals sacrificed in the oracle bone inscriptions.

These suns, which bathed in a pool of water and dwelt on the branches of the Mulberry Tree, were thought to be birds, as these motifs suggest. In a passage from the *Shanhaijing* (14/65a–b) translated above, the suns were described as being "carried by birds" but the *Huainanzi* (7/2a) describes the birds as being inside the suns: "Inside the suns(s), there are *jun* 踆 raven(s); in the moon(s), toad(s)." Similarly, in Han dynasty tomb art, the sun is frequently depicted with a bird inside it and the moon with a toad or a hare and cassia tree.[39]

Han tomb murals most frequently include one sun and one moon, but there are some examples in which the Mulberry Tree and its many suns are depicted. One example is the funerary pendant excavated in 1972 from Han tomb number one at Mawangdui 馬王堆, near Changsha in Hunan Province—formerly within the boundaries of the state of Chu. The tomb dates to the early Western Han Dynasty. Here, nine suns are depicted on the branches of a tree, the twisting trunk of which is consistent with the form of a mulberry. Eight of the suns are simple orange discs but that at the top of the tree in the left-hand corner of the pendant contains a black bird, possibly a raven, standing on two legs. A moon in the opposite corner contains a toad.[40] The absence of the tenth sun has caused puzzlement, but since this is a depiction of the deceased journeying to the world of the

Figure 6 Yangshao pottery fragment from Miaodigou,
Henan Province, with 3-legged bird motif

From Wu Shan, *Zhongguo Yinshiqi shidai taoqi yi shu*, p. 51

dead, I suspect the tenth sun is travelling across the sky of the human world above.[41]

In Han mural art, the Mulberry Tree is most often depicted as part of a scene which includes Archer Yi about to shoot at the sun-birds. The suns are depicted simply as birds, but the archer's drawn bow identifies the scene.[42] Whether the bird carries the sun, is in the sun, or is the sun is thus ill-defined because the relationship is a mythical one. Mythically, the suns and birds are the same and this presents a problem for the Han illustrator.

In the *Huainanzi* passage quoted above (7/2a), the bird in the sun was called a *jun*-raven. According to the Eastern Han commentator, Gao You, the *jun*-raven was three-legged and Wang Chong, writing in the first century A.D., substitutes 'three-legged' (三足) for *jun* 踆. Gao You's annotation is based on an identification of the name of the bird with the character 蹲, meaning 'to crouch'. I suspect, however, that the name of the bird is related to that of Di Jun 帝俊, the husband of Xihe in this same tradition and so, presumably, the father of the sun-birds. The characters are the same except for the addition of a ' 亻 ' human radical to Di Jun and of a '足' foot radical to his descendants, the sun-birds. Thus, we may suppose the origin of both was 夋.

The earliest depiction of a three-legged bird is on neolithic pottery of the Miaodigou (Yangshao) culture in Henan Province (see figure 6).[43] In Han tomb art, however, sun-birds are depicted with either two legs, as in the Mawangdui pendant, or three (see figure 7). Izushi and M. Loewe have related the number of legs of the sun-bird to the development of *yin-yang* and five element theory in the early Han dynasty in which three was the

Figure 7 Painting from Mawangdui tomb no. 1
(Han Dynasty)

From *Hunansheng bowuguan*, pl. 79

yang number and so that of the sun.[44] Although the three legs of the sun-bird may have been understood in this manner in the Han dynasty, there is another reason for linking the suns with the number three—the ten suns appear three times a month. The ten-day week and thirty-day month were the basic calendric units from Shang times on.

Every morning when the sun-bird which was to fly that day across the sky arose in Sun Valley, it was bathed by its mother Xihe in the pool of water there:

"Beyond the South-eastern Sea amidst the Sweet Waters is the Tribe of Xihe. There is a woman named Xihe who regularly bathes the suns in the Sweet Springs. Xihe is the wife of Di Jun. It is she who gave birth to the ten suns (生十日)."

Shanhaijing (*Dahuangnanjing* 大荒南經) 15/7b.

The *Shanhaijing* commentator Guo Pu quotes a similar passage from the *Gui zang* 歸藏:

"Behold their ascent to the sky! A time of brightness, then a time of darkness, as the sons of Xihe go out from Sun 陽 Valley.[45]"

The *Gui zang* was already lost by the Han Dynasty and Maspero considered that in its present form it could not pre-date the fourth century. Nevertheless, the text was traditionally thought to be the Shang equivalent of the *Yijing* 易經 and it may be significant that this text, which was associated with the Shang, records this myth complex and in language which is not derivative from other extant texts.[46]

Besides Xihe, the *Shanhaijing* names two other women as wives of Di Jun. One is Chang Xi 常羲, the western counterpart of Xihe. She gave birth to the twelve moons whom she bathes in a pool of water in the West, just as Xihe bathes her sun-children in the East.[47] The cult of Chang Xi is much less developed than that of Xihe, just as that of the Ruo Tree is less developed than that of the Mulberry Tree. However, she has also been identified with Chang E 常娥 (or Heng E 姮娥), the goddess who fled to the moon after having stolen the elixir of immortality from Archer Yi[48] and Chang Yi 常義, the second wife of Di Ku 帝嚳.[49] Since Xi (*χia*), E (*$ng\hat{a}$*) and Yi (*$ngia$*) are closely related phonetically (the same word family in Karlgren's reconstruction) and their roles are similar, these figures are probably variants of the same original moon goddess.

The other wife, E Huang 娥皇, is more directly connected with the human world for she gave birth to the 'Tribe of Three-bodied People' (the number recalls the three legs of the ravens).[50] They in turn bore Yi Jun

義均 .[51] Here there is a connection with the Shang for, as Chen Mengjia 陳夢家 has observed, Yi Jun may be related to Shang Jun 商均, the son but not the successor of Shun who was enfeoffed in Shang.[52] E Huang is also named as a wife of Shun[53] and in the *Shanhaijing* (15/68b), E Huang and the Three-bodied Tribe carry the surname Tao 姚 which is that of Yao. This suggests that the two Jun 均 are not only structurally equivalent but variants of the same person, the Shang in the one referring to the association with the Shang people.

Di Jun has been identified with both Di Ku and Shun whose wives, Chang Yi (Di Ku) and E Huang (Shun), he shared. Jun 夋 was the personal name of Di Ku, the progenitor of the Shang who mysteriously impregnated his wife by means of the egg of a black bird.[54] Guo Pu also identified the two figures in his commentary to the *Shanhaijing* (16/73b) and this identification has been generally accepted by modern scholars since the studies of Wang Guowei 王國維, both because of the given name Jun, and because of the overlap of roles and relationships including the wife Chang Xi (or Yi).[55] Clearly, the two figures are structurally equivalent and although the names are alternatives rather than variants, they were associated very early and could refer to the same original myth figure.

Shun and Jun have also been identified.[56] This is based on the phonetic similarity of *jun* 俊 (**tsiwən*) and *shun* 舜 (**śiwən*) and on an overlap of roles and relationships including their common wife E Huang. Guo Pu considers Jun a phonetic borrowing for Shun in *Shanhaijing* (16/73b). This suggests that the names are variants. The roles of Shun and Di Ku are also sometimes interchangeable. For example, the Shang performed the *di* 禘 rite to Shun in the *Guoyu* 國語[57] but to Di Ku in the *Liji* 禮記.[58] Thus all three names may have a common source. The importance of these identifications will become clear in the following discussion. For clarification, I also refer the reader to the chart, in figure 8.

The preceding description of the Mulberry Tree tradition is based on the *Huainanzi* and *Shanhaijing* accounts because, although these texts are relatively late, they contain explicit narratives. However, the motifs of this tradition—the Fu Sang (and the Ruo Tree in the west), Sun Valley and the pool of water in which the suns bathe, the suns as birds, and ten as the number of the suns—also appear consistently throughout the works in the *Chuci* corpus. In the works of the *Chuci* in which the poet-shaman ascends into the other world, he frequently refers to these motifs as a sign of his ascent and supernatural power. This begins with the *Li sao* 離騷: "I ordered Xihe to stop the passage of time. . . . I watered my horses at the Xian Pool and tethered my horse to the Fu Sang. I broke a branch of the Ruo Tree with which to brush off the sun. . .".[59]

The author of the *Jiu zhang* 九章 (*Bei hui feng* 悲回風) writes in a

Figure 8 Transformations of Shang myth figures

I. The Mulberry Tree Tradition

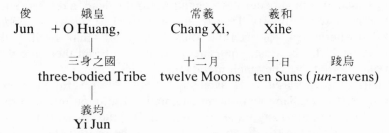

俊　　　娥皇　　　　　　常義　　　　羲和
Jun　+ O Huang,　　　　Chang Xi,　　Xihe
　　　　　｜
　　　　三身之國　　　　十二月　　　十日　　　　踆鳥
　　three-bodied Tribe　twelve Moons　ten Suns (*jun*-ravens)
　　　　　｜
　　　　義均
　　　　Yi Jun

II. The Shang Origin Myth

　　　玄鳥
　　　Black Bird
　譽　　　　簡狄　　　　常義
　Ku　+　Jian Di,　Chang Yi
　　　　　｜
　　　　商契
　　　　Shang Xie

III. The Oracle Bone Inscriptions

（俊；　夒？　夔？）
Jun　Nao　Kui　　　（西母）Western Mother　　（東母）Eastern Mother
　　　（娥）
　　　　O

（王亥）
Wang Hai
　｜
（上甲）
Shang Jia (ancestors henceforth named according to ten suns)

IV. The Historical Tradition

　　　帝　　堯
　　　Di (Yao) + No recorded wife

舜　　　　娥皇　　　女英　　　丹朱　　十子
Shun　+　O Huang,　Nü Ying　Dan Zhu (ten sons)
　　　　　｜
　　　　商均
　　　　Shang Jun

similar vein: "I broke a branch from the Ruo Tree with which to screen the light".[60] And the poet-shaman in *Ai shi ming* 哀時命: "I caught my left sleeve on the Fu Sang. . .".[61] In the "Summoning of the soul" song *Zhao hun* 招魂 which presumably derives from a rite for the dead, a reference to the ten suns of the Mulberry Tree tradition is used to signify a region beyond that where men—or even the souls of the dead—may dwell: "Oh Soul, come back! In the East, you cannot dwell. . . . From there the ten suns go out alternately. They melt metal and dissolve stone. . . ."[62]

Similarly, the *Tian wen* or 'Heavenly questions' asks several questions which refer to the Fu Sang myth in an enigmatic form. One refers to the suns travelling from the Tang Valley to Meng Si 蒙汜 the 'Stream of Darkness' (also mentioned in the *Huainanzi* 淮南子 as the resting place of the setting sun) and asks, "from brightness until darkness, how many miles is (the sun's) journey?"[63] Another, "When Xihe has not yet risen, how do the Ruo Flowers glow?"[64] And also, in reference to the myth of Archer Yi shooting the suns, "Why did Yi shoot the suns? Why did the ravens shed their feathers?"[65]

THE MYTH OF ARCHER YI

The tradition of ten suns rising from the Mulberry Tree has been best known since Han times through the myth that once in the time of Yao the ten suns came out together, their great heat threatening to destroy the world until Yao ordered Archer Yi to shoot nine of them. However, this myth presupposes the Mulberry Tree tradition and assumes the same motifs although Xihe plays no role in the story. There were ten suns. The suns were birds—as in the *Tian wen* question quoted above: "Why did Yi shoot the suns? Why did the ravens shed their feathers?" And the sunbirds dwelt on the Mulberry Tree—Han tomb murals of Yi shooting the suns show them as birds in a tree. Because it assumes the same motifs, it can only have arisen after the Mulberry Tree tradition *per se,* but it relegated the ten alternating suns to a distant era, thus explaining away the tradition (which I am hypothesizing was a Shang tradition replaced in Zhou times by the belief in a single sun) without directly opposing it: once there were ten suns, but now there is only one.

The most explicit early reference to this myth is in the *Huainanzi* (8/5a–b). Here, the myth of Yi shooting the ten suns is placed in the context of a larger cosmogony myth which has certain structural parallels to the *Yao dian* 堯典, as will be discussed below. The passage begins with a description of a time of perfect peace in which "people entrusted their infants to the safety of nests and placed their excess grain at the head of the fields. Tigers and leopards could be pulled by the tail; vipers and snakes could be trod upon. . . ." But the peace was broken: "When it came to the time of Yao, the ten suns came out together, withering the crops of grain and killing the grasses, so that the people had nothing to eat. . ." Various monsters also appeared, but Yao sent Yi to punish them and "shoot the ten suns". Because of Yao's success, he became the first ruler.

The time of Yao in which the ten suns appeared was followed by the time of Shun in which the waters were fanned by the evil Gong Gong 共工 until they "reached the Hollow Mulberry" (*kong sang* 空桑) but Shun appointed Yu to dig the river channels and open up passages so that the water could run into the sea. In this passage, then, the time of Yao was the era in which perfect harmony was lost to the world and heaven and earth separated (because of a ritual breach implied by the disobedience of the ten suns?). The appearance of the ten suns in the sky also contrasts with the following era in which water flooded the earth: a time of fire, then a time of water. The story of Yi shooting the ten suns has a further mythical dimension for an Yi is associated with the west and the moon in other myths. He was given the elixir of immortality by Xi Wang Mu 西王母, the Queen Mother of the West, but it was stolen by his wife Chang E (that is Chang Yi, see p. 33) who fled with it to the moon.[66] Yi in shooting the suns may have represented the forces of the west and the moon in battle with those of the east and the sun.[67]

This myth is usually interpreted to mean that Yi shot down nine of the ten suns, destroying them so that afterwards there was only one sun left which came out every day. Wang Yi so interprets the *Tian wen* question quoted above: "The nine birds inside [the suns] all died, dropping their feathers and wings, so that one sun from among them was left."[68] This interpretation accepts the tradition of ten suns rising from the Mulberry Tree, but assigns it to an era in the mythological past. Thus, where the belief in ten suns was heterodox in Zhou times, the myth of Archer Yi could still be accepted.

The coexistence of the two beliefs is evident in three related passages, two from the *Zhuangzi* (fifth century B.C.) and one from the *Lüshi chunqiu* 呂氏春秋 (third century B.C.), all of which refer to the light of the sun or suns as a metaphor for virtue and refer to the time of Yao. These passages appear to have a common source, but the *Zhuangzi,* at least in its present form, rejects the ten sun tradition. In the *Lüshi chunqiu* (22/9b), Yao, who wishes to cede the throne to Xu You, explains, "If the ten suns rise, and the beacon fires are not [let to] expire, is this not too troublesome!" But in the equivalent passage in the *Zhuangzi,* Yao says to Xu You 許由, "If the sun and moon rise. . . ."[69] This can be correlated to another passage in the *Zhuangzi* which the commentators relate to the *Huainanzi* passage discussed above (8/5a). Here, Shun in reply to a question from Yao about whether to force the submission of certain tribes says, "Formerly, the ten suns came out together and the ten thousand things were all illuminated. . . ."[70]

However, the myth of Archer Yi was not always interpreted to mean that the nine were destroyed. They may merely have been frightened into better behaviour. Wang Chong who discusses this myth in the *Lunheng* 論衡 says that Yi shot the ten suns and "therefore they were not seen together again on the same day".[71] Other texts also refer to the ten suns coming out together in later times. For example, according to the *Huainanzi* (15/6b), the ten suns appeared as an ill omen at the end of the Shang dynasty. Similarly, in the authentic *Bamboo Annals*, the ten suns appeared together as an ill omen near the end of the Xia dynasty.[72]

Because of the ambiguity about whether the suns were destroyed when Archer Yi shot them, this myth allowed some people to continue to believe in ten suns which rose from the branches of the Mulberry Tree while others accepted that there was only one sun. Since the myth of Archer Yi assumes the motifs of the Mulberry Tree tradition, it could only have arisen after that tradition, although the two traditions coexisted in late Zhou and Han texts. The prevalence of the Mulberry Tree tradition in the *Chuci* and to a lesser extent in the *Huainanzi,* as well as the portrayal of the nine suns on the Mulberry Tree in the Mawangdui painting, indicate an association in Zhou and Han times with Southern China, but as discussed above, Shang influence had extended into what became the semi-independent state of Chu in Zhou times.

I have suggested that the Mulberry Tree tradition derived from a Shang tradition which lost its integrity when the Shang were conquered by the Zhou and a belief in a single sun replaced that in ten suns as the orthodox belief. The Mulberry Tree tradition as I have described it is a late Zhou and Han tradition of Southern China and has no particular association with the Shang. However, the same motifs—with the exception of ten as the number of the suns—are intimately associated with the Shang in another tradition about the origin of the Shang people and their dynasty which is recorded in the broad range of Zhou texts. As I will discuss later, the Shang origin myth is a transformation deriving from the same source as the myth of Xihe giving birth to the ten suns. The Shang are also associated with the motifs of the Mulberry Tree tradition in: the name of their altar, the story of the great drought at the beginning of the dynasty, the myth of the birth of Yi Yin, and the name of the founder of the dynasty.

THE SHANG ORIGIN MYTH

In the Mulberry Tree tradition, the suns were birds which were bathed by their mother Xihe in the pool of water in the Valley of the Sun at the foot of the Mulberry Tree. Xihe was married to Di Jun who was also married to

Chang Yi, the mother of the moons and to E Huang, the mother of the Three-bodied Tribe, who in turn gave birth to Yi Jun. In their origin myth, the Shang were born of a black bird which, I will argue, can be identified with the sun-bird.

The earliest references to the origin of the Shang are in the *Shang song* 商頌 section of the *Shijing*. The *Xuan niao* 玄鳥 (*Mao* 毛 303) states:

"Heaven commanded that black bird (*xuan niao* 玄鳥).
It descended and gave birth to Shang.
The land of Yin in which they dwelt was vast.
Therefore Di 帝 ordered martial Tang. . ."

The *Chang fa* 長發 (*Mao* 304) also states:

Wise and brilliant was Shang
And long-lived its fortune.
The flooding water spread forth,
And Yu brought order to the lands below.
Both small and large states were delineated.
And the border was long.
When the lady of You Rong 有娀 was nubile,
Di appointed (*li* 立) his son and gave birth
    to the Shang.

The *Shang song* are the hymns of the Shang rulers as they were passed down among their descendants who were enfeoffed in the state of Song 宋 during the Zhou dynasty. The reference to Tian 天 'Heaven' in the first line of *Xuan niao* may indicate Zhou influence. Later in the verse, however, and in the *Chang fa,* the high god is referred to as 'Di' Lord (that is the Lord on high) which accords with Shang usage. We may assume that these verses have suffered some changes before being recorded. Nevertheless, they are as close to authentic Shang tradition as is possible within the extant Zhou texts.

In terms of our discussion in the following chapter of the Xia myth, it is significant that Yu appears here in a hymn to the Shang ancestors. There are no Xia hymns within the *Shijing,* as we would have expected if they were a dynasty with living descendants. The only reference to Yu is this one, in which he appears after the beginning reference to Shang, as though he were a part of their own tradition. Yao and Shun also go unmentioned, but this is to be expected if, as I will argue, Yao was a transformation of the High Lord, Di and Shun of Di Ku 帝嚳.

Questions about this myth also occur in the *Tian wen* section of the

Chuci which, as discussed above, contains questions relating to the Fu Sang tradition: 'When Jian Di 簡狄 was in the tower, how did Ku favor her? When the black bird brought its gift, how did the woman become blessed?" (*Chuci* 3/22a) Here, the Lady of You Rong is named as Jian Di and Di Ku rather than the black bird is the progenitor.

For the answers to these questions, we must turn to a later text, the *Shiji*:

> Xie 契 of Yin's mother was called Jian Di. A woman of the You Rong clan, she was the second concubine of Di Ku. Three persons (including Jian Di) were going to bathe. They saw a black bird drop an egg. Jian Di took it and swallowed it. Thus, she became pregnant and gave birth to Xie.[73]

The tower is missing from this version, but the Shang ancestor was born of the egg which Jian Di swallowed. Clearly, there is a relationship between this myth and that of Di Jun. Di Jun was the father of the *jun*-ravens, the black birds in the sun, and of the 'Three-bodied Tribe' who bore Yi Jun, that is, Shang Jun 商均, that is, the Shang.[75] Di Ku bore the Shang by means of a black bird. Di Jun and Di Ku have been identified, as discussed above. Thus, the bird which gave birth to the Shang was the same as the bird in the suns. (The *Shiji* passage also mentions the motifs of bathing and the number three. These may be weakened transformations of earlier myth motifs.)

A raven is black and *wu* 烏 also means dark or black. The earliest forms of the Shang origin myth only identify the bird as a *xuan niao*, but in the *Lüshi chunqiu* the bird is identified as a swallow (*yan* 燕) and this identification is often followed by later texts. According to the *Lüshi chunqiu* (6/6b), Di ordered a swallow to go and look at two beautiful women of the You Rong clan for whom a nine-storied tower had been built where they ate and drank to the accompaniment of drums. Attracted to the bird, the two women competed to catch it and put it in a jade box. When the younger one (Jian Di) opened it, it flew out leaving behind two eggs. The reference to two eggs is unusual—could the second have been swallowed by Di Ku's other wife Chang Yi and given birth to the moons?—but the colorful detail in the passage suggests a relatively late version of the story, even though the *Lüshi chunqiu* was compiled earlier than the *Shiji*. The two women eating and drinking in a tower to the accompaniment of drums is also reminiscent of the motif of the bad wives of Zhou Xin 紂辛, the last Shang king.[76]

The black bird which gave birth to the Shang thus seems originally to have been undifferentiated with regard to species, but in color matches the sun-bird.[77] The identification of Di Ku and Di Jun suggests that the bird in the suns was also that which gave birth to the Shang. Further evidence to support this interpretation is found in the significance given to the mulberry in myth and ritual associated with the beginning of the Shang dynasty.

THE SHANG AND THE MULBERRY TREE

The altar of the state of Song in which the descendants of the Shang kings were enfeoffed by the Zhou was at Sang Lin 桑林 the 'Mulberry Grove'. The *Lüshi chunqiu* (15/2b) explains, "When Wu Wang conquered the Shang . . . he enfeoffed the descendants of Cheng Tang at Song 宋 so that they could give offerings at Sang Lin." The *Mozi* and the *Zuozhuan* also name Sang Lin as the altar of the state of Song.[78] Yang Kuan and others have further argued that there is an etymological connection between Song (*song)—a tree under a roof, Sang (*sâng)—the mulberry and sun tree, and Shang (*śiang)—the name of the city after which the Shang are called.[79]

Edouard Chavannes and Marcel Granet called Sang Lin an earth altar,[80] but its role as a sun altar and importance in the mythology associated with the Shang are apparent in the story of a great drought which occurred at the beginning of the dynasty. This drought occurred when the Shang defeated the Xia and lasted for five or seven years. The crops failed, the rivers dried up and the heat was so great it 'braised sand and melted stone',[81] but Tang offered himself as a sacrifice for his people to Shang Di at the altar of Sang Lin and the rain fell.

This event is recorded in a number of texts, of which the *Mozi* (ca. fifth century B.C.) is the earliest. As I have argued elsewhere, all of the extant accounts derive from a single original text, the original *Tang gao* 湯誥 or 'Announcement of Tang' of the *Ancient documents* or *Shang shu*.[82] The most complete version of the text although it is in modernized form is from the *Diwang shiji* 帝王世紀, compiled by Huangfu Mi 皇甫謐 in the third century A.D. from unnamed earlier sources:

> After Tang smote Jie, there was a great drought for seven years and the Luo River dried up. He ordered someone to take a three-legged *ding* 鼎 vessel and make an invocation to the mountains and rivers. It said, "Is it that the government is not frugal? That we are causing the people to be harried? That food bribes are common? That slanderers flourish? That palaces are being built? That women's advice is followed? Why has the lack of rain reached such an extreme?" The Yin scribe divined by crack-making and said," Prayer should be made with human (offering)." Tang said, "Those

for whom I am asking for rain are the people. If it is necessary to make a prayer using human offering, I ask that I should be it myself." Thereupon, he fasted and abstained, cut his hair and pared his nails, and regarding himself as a sacrificial victim, prayed at the altar of the Mulberry Grove. He said, "I, your little son Lu, dare to use a dark (玄) sacrificial victim and announce to the Lord of Heaven above: If there be wrongdoing in the ten thousand regions, the wrong is upon my person. If I myself have wronged, do not extend it to the ten thousand regions. Do not let one man's dullness cause the High Lord, spectres and spirits to harm the people's life." Before he had finished speaking, a great rain came, covering an area of many thousand li.

All versions of the text including the *Mozi* name the Mulberry Grove, Sang Lin, as the place of offering. This suggests that Sang Lin was not only a place in the state of Song, but the name of the Shang altar wherever it was located. Besides the naming of the altar as the Mulberry Grove, the mention of a three-legged *ding* for the offering and a black (*xuan*) offering recall the three-legged black bird of the Mulberry tree tradition.

Although this cannot be taken as a Shang text, many of its references do recall actual Shang practice and the role which the king assumes at the completion of the story is an accurate encapsulation of the role of the Shang king. Rain is a major subject of divination in the oracle bone inscriptions and drought was sent down upon the king by Di, the Lord on High. In this text, the king responded by a rite of invocation (*zhu* 祝) which was a Shang rite and made his offering in a *ding*-tripod, the archetypical Shang offering vessel. Having made his invocation, Tang had a divination made in the traditional Shang manner, by cracking an oracle bone. The 'scribe'— *shi* 史 —made the crack; *shi* is a Shang title of an official possibly involved in bone-cracking. Human offerings were a normal part of Shang ritual and divinations about whether animals or humans should be offered and in what combination are frequent. Indeed, there is a particular Shang ritual to which this may be a reference—the *chi* 赤 (or *jiao* 烄) in which a human was burnt or exposed to the sun in prayer for rain. This rite is particularly apt because the offerings were not slaves or prisoners of war, as in most offerings, but shamans or sacred cripples.[83] In some versions of the text, the king refers to himself as 'I, one man' (*yu yi ren* 余一人), a standard form of self-reference in oracle bone inscriptions as well as in Zhou texts.

There is no record in the oracle bone inscriptions of a king offering himself in sacrifice and it is difficult to imagine such an inscription. Yet, in a sense, the Shang kings were already offerings: they served as physical as well as spiritual mediums between the spirits and their people. The king's toothache and other illnesses were as much omens of displeasure as the curses which might be visited on his land in the form of drought or bad harvest and he divined in the same manner about both. The Shang king did not give offerings directly to the Lord on high, who stood at the apex of the hierarchy of ancestral and nature spirits and exercised the most awesome powers, controlling both weather phenomena such as rainfall and the major affairs of state such as warfare and city building, but his ancestors could intercede on his behalf, as I will discuss below, and he divined to determine the consent of the Lord for his major activities.

In the textual tradition, Tang was founding king of the Shang dynasty and this story is about his assumption of the sacred role of king. In offering himself as a sacrifice, he both becomes a conduit to the spirits—the primary priest, who may determine the will of the Lord by divination—and, as he does so on behalf of his people, he assumes the sacred role of king. The theme of a royal offering to appease the Lord on high after a previous dynasty had been defeated also occurs in the *Shang shu, Jin teng* 金縢 in a story set at the beginning of the Zhou dynasty when Wu Wang fell ill and the Duke of Zhou prayed in his stead, asking that the sins of the dynasty be visited upon himself, but the site is not the Mulberry Grove, nor was there a drought. These motifs are specifically associated with the Shang.

The heat of the drought recalls the heat of the ten suns which appeared together in Yao's time and it may be a weakened version of the same theme, symbolizing the connection of the Shang with the sun or suns. This symbolism is reinforced by the myth in *Huainanzi* (16/6a) (a text in which the ten sun myth is prevalent), that the ten suns appeared together as an omen when Wu Wang fought Zhou Xin at the end of the Shang dynasty. The drought myth is also an inversion of the flood myth associated with the beginning of the Xia dynasty. At the beginning of the Xia, the rivers flooded; at the beginning of the Shang, they dried up.

The Shang are also associated with the mulberry tree in the myth of the birth of Yi Yin 伊尹 and this myth similarly includes an opposition between the motifs associated with the sun and those of the flood. In Zhou legend and the *Shiji,* Yi Yin is the minister of Cheng Tang, the dynastic founder of the Shang, and the regent of his grandson Tai Jia 太甲. Tang raised him up from his work as a cook in the entourage of his bride, a lady of the You Xin 有莘 clan. The theme is that of the 'founding minister' and as such he parallels Taigong Wang at the beginning of the Zhou dynasty.[84] In Shang oracle bone inscriptions, however, Yi Yin is worshipped as though he were an important ancestor of the Shang. K. C. Chang has theorized that the Shang kingship alternated between two politically prominent lineages which were related by a system of cross-cousin marriage and that Yi Yin was the head of the alternative group at the time that Tang was ruler.[85] Qi Wenxin 齊文心, however, has argued that Yin 尹 was an official title in Shang times and Yi 伊, the name of a state along the Yi River basin. Thus Yi Yin would have been an *yin*-officer of the Yi state who assisted the Shang founder.[86]

Although Yi Yin is Tang's minister in the historical tradition, the story of his birth suggests the cosmogonic myth which included the great flood. The first reference to his birth is in the *Chuci, Tian wen:* "In the tree by the water's edge, they got that little child. Why did they so despise him that they sent him in the entourage of the woman of You Xin 有辛?"[87] The question posed seems to be why he was not recognized for what he was, but in early Chinese mythology, children born of spirits, such as Hou Ji 后稷 whose mother was impregnated when she stepped on the High Lord or Di Ku's footprint in the Mulberry Grove, are frequently abandoned.

The *Lüshi chunqiu* is the earliest text to give a full account of the myth. The text explains that the woman of You Xin found Yi Yin in the Hollow Mulberry (*kong sang*) when she was picking mulberries. His birth is explained thus:

> His mother lived by the Yi River. When she was pregnant, she dreamed that a spirit said to her, 'When the mortar emits water go east and do not look back.' The next day she saw water coming from inside the mortar and told her neighbours. She went east for ten li and looked back. The city was completely flooded. Consequently, her body was changed into a hollow mulberry tree.
>
> *Lüshi chunqiu* (14/4a)

In the *Huainanzi* passage (8/5a) discussed above with reference to the myth of the ten suns coming out together, the flood drained by Yu was fanned by Gong Gong" until it pressed the Hollow Mulberry." This suggests that the flood which Yi Yin's mother saw was the same as the great flood at the time of Yao.

The Hollow Mulberry (sometimes called the *qiong sang* 窮桑) is often mentioned in early texts as a dwelling place of the gods or cosmic tree which served as an *axis mundi* between heaven and earth.[88] Its relationship with the Yellow Emperor and the high ancestors of the Xia will be discussed in the following chapter. The *Gui zang* describes it thus: "The Hollow Mulberry, luxuriant and vast, extends to the eight extremes (of the world). There is Xihe who controls the comings and goings of the sun and moon to make light and darkness."[89] The *Gui zang* also records that "Chi You 蚩尤 attacked the Hollow Mulberry in which Di lived."[90] Di in this case must be understood as Huang Di 黃帝, the Yellow Emperor, since another fragment of the *Gui zang* tells of Huang Di killing Chi You. Di Shao Hao and Di Zhuan Xu also lived at Hollow Mulberry, according to other texts.[91] And in the legend of later times, Confucius—a native of the state of Lu and reputedly a descendant of the Shang—was born at Hollow Mulberry after his mother dreamed of Xuan Di 玄帝, the 'Black Emperor'. Xuan Di's identity is uncertain, but the term *xuan* suggests a connection with the black bird myth.[92]

Marcel Granet identified the Hollow Mulberry with the Fu Sang and Xihe was mentioned in connection with the Hollow Mulberry in the *Gui zang*.[93] In this transformation of the mulberry motif, however, the tree in the west is called the Kong Tong 空桐 'Hollow Paulownia'.[94] Kong Tong was a dark place of death and disgrace as opposed to the Kong Sang, the seat of the gods, for it was to Kong Tong that Yi Yin banished Tai Jia 太甲 when he found him unfit to rule and it was there that Cheng Tang died.[95] The Hollow Mulberry and its counterpart are thus an important part of the mythology surrounding the founding of the dynasty.

A myth in which Cheng Tang is associated with the springs in which the suns bathed corresponds to that in which Yi Yin was born from the Hollow Mulberry, although the record is less explicit than with Yi Yin. According to the *Chuci Tian wen,* "Tang emerged from the Deep Springs (Chong Quan 重泉)."[96] Mori Yasutaro has related these to those of Sun Valley.[97] Tang is also connected to these springs by his name—the valley and its pool of water are often called Tang Gu 湯谷, as discussed above. In oracle bone inscriptions Tang is written with a character antecedent of the homonym 唐 (the clan name of Yao). However, he is also called 𠦏 which some scholars transliterate as *xian* 咸, the name of the pool of water when the valley is called Yang Gu 陽谷.[98] The name Xian also occurs in the *Book of documents*.[99]

The Shang, then, are consistently associated with the motifs of the Mulberry Tree tradition in Zhou texts. Their first ancestor was born from the egg of a bird sent by Di Ku who as Di Jun was husband of Xihe and father of the sun-birds. When a drought occurred at the beginning of the dynasty, their founder Tang prayed at the Mulberry Grove. Yi Yin, his minister, was born from the Hollow Mulberry, a transformation of the Fu Sang, and he himself is associated with the pool of water in the Valley of the Sun.

Between the earliest texts which record this tradition about the origin of the Shang and their dynasty and the end of the Shang are some five or six centuries in which Zhou creeds had replaced those of the Shang as the orthodoxy of the central plains of Northern China, but since few texts remain to us from this intervening period, if we are to reconstruct Shang belief we must turn directly to the Shang oracle bone inscriptions. These texts are of limited usefulness because they are mainly ritual propositions in which the Shang king attempted to determine the appropriate offerings to be made to the ancestors in order to ensure the welfare of himself and his people. Since they do not record mythical narratives or include any expository writing, they do not provide direct evidence about the myth and logic underlying the rites. Nevertheless, the pattern of names and ritual suggests an earlier myth from which the Mulberry Tree and Shang origin traditions derived and these traditions provide a key to their interpretation.

TOTEMISM IN THE SHANG DYNASTY

In the following I will argue that the Shang rulers had a totemic relationship with the ten suns which were also thought to be birds. I regard 'totemism' as a system of classification rather than a social institution, by means of which primitive man gives order to and perceives the world in which he lives and which includes an analogy between man and animals or other natural objects. Magic, in such a system, is the manipulation of categories within the system to achieve practical results. It is logical but assumes absolute determinism, its limitations being those of the classification system.[100] A system of this type in which the Shang ancestors were classified with the ten suns was the basis for the Shang ritual calendar and an earlier form of the myth traditions described above provides its rationale.

There is no direct record in the oracle bone inscriptions of a ceremony such as that described above in which Cheng Tang offered himself as a human sacrifice in order to save his people from drought.[101] Nevertheless, as discussed above, the king was the one man who, by giving offerings to the nature deities and to his ancestors who could in turn intercede on his behalf with Shang Di, was able to ensure the welfare of his people. The offerings involved the manipulation of a number of categories and he was responsible for determining the correct ceremony and ensuring that it was properly carried out. Otherwise curses befell his people in the form of bad weather and disastrous harvest or other natural calamity, and his person in the form of illness or accident.

This magical system is the primary subject of the oracle bone propositions. Not only did the ancestor have to be worshipped on the proper day, but the ceremony, animal or combination of animals (including humans), their preparation, number, sex and color were all suitable subjects of divination. In the first period, the king ascertained that the categories were correct by offering substitutions; by the fifth, the ritual had become so codified that the king had merely to announce and verify the ritual form of divinations which had become predictably auspicious.[102] Other inscriptions were mostly concerned with determining whether there would be misfortune over a given time span or in a particular circumstance, or whether the High Lord or ancestors would give blessings of harvest, hunt and good weather or other assistance. All of these, even such propositions as 'It will rain; it will not rain' may be interpreted as an attempt to determine whether the king had obtained the favor of, or would be cursed by the spirits. This system will be discussed in greater detail in Chapter Four.

Claude Levi-Strauss has argued that totemic systems are lived rather than conceived and tend to have few myths. Whether this was true of the Shang cannot be determined because there are no narratives, but the vast energy devoted to the divination process in preparing and cracking the bones and recording divinations[103] implies that sacrifice was the focus of Shang religion. Nevertheless, indirect evidence can be found for an earlier form of the Mulberry Tree and Shang origin traditions—in the characters for east and west, the names of the ancestors of the remote era, and the pattern of offerings to the immediate ancestors.

The Fu Sang tree itself is never mentioned in the oracle bone inscriptions. Mulberry (*Sang* 桑) is a place name in the east in the oracle bone inscriptions,[104] but it has no unusual significance—nor should we expect it to have unless, like the suns themselves, which do receive offerings in the oracle bone inscriptions, it was an object of worship.[105] However, a belief in the Fu Sang tree is implied by the characters for east and west.

As mentioned at the beginning of this chapter, east (**tung*) was understood in the *Shuowen* and by its commentators to be a tree and a sun, that is the *fu sang* tree.[106] This understanding of the character has been challenged by many scholars and two alternative readings of the structure of the character have been proposed—that it is either a bundle of faggots tied together or a bag tied at both ends.[107] The evidence from the oracle bone inscriptions, however, supports the *Shuowen,* as I will explain below.

Oracle bone characters, like those in later Chinese writing, are made up of combinations of meaning elements and/or sound elements. The meaning elements are more pictographic than in later Chinese characters, but they are nevertheless highly abstracted, so that a few strokes conventionally suggest a complex picture. The conventions, however, are not rigid, like they become in later writing, particularly after the unification of the script under the Qin Dynasty (221–206 B.C.). Not only did the calligraphy change over the three centuries of the late Shang dynasty, more than one style of writing coexisted and the engraver himself often took shortcuts which changed the structure of the character.[108] Sound elements, as in later Chinese script, are usually characters, originally made up of meaning elements, which are borrowed to become the whole or part of another character. Thus, it has been suggested that the character now written as 束 (*śiuk), to bind, tie together, and that now written as 橐 (*t'âk), a bag made by tying up two open ends, were borrowed for phonetic reasons for the character 東 (*tung) and that originally it was not a picture of a sun and tree.

This problem can best be resolved if we begin with the oracle bone characters rather than their modern descendants and analyse the alternative meaning families before turning to the character which means 'east'. I have listed the various forms of the character east in figure 9, line 1. The three characters in line 2 all include a bundle of faggots. 2a has two dots at the side which represent fire and this character means to offer a sacrifice by burning it. This is the sacrifice most frequently offered to the spirit of the east. 2b is a picture of the faggots tied together. This character is often read as 束 (*śi̯uk). 2c is an offering in which the faggots tied together are placed upon an altar. The meaning element of faggots in a bundle common to these three characters resembles a tree (line 5), but it can be distinguished from it because the lines cross in the middle. In the character for east, however, although there is one variation (1b) in which the circle has a cross inside, the tree element has no such cross.

Line 3 has characters with the meaning element of silk threads intertwined. 3a means thread and is a modern radical (糸). 3b may be equivalent to 3a or to 3c which includes a hand element, 索 (*sâk), to 'twist a rope'; 4a has only two examples in Shima Kunio's oracle bone index. It may be a variation of 3a. Many scholars have suggested that it is 束, to bind or tie, but the context of one of Shima's example suggests that it is a place name and a variation of 4b, thought to be the origin of the character 橐, a bag tied at both ends'. These characters are similar to east in line 1, but they can be distinguished by not having a vertical line representing the trunk of the tree through the center except for 3a which has two circles and so could not be 束. Only 1d lacks this line and since there are only two examples of this variation out of many hundred, it may justifiably be regarded as an oddity.

Let us now turn to east. If the characters in line 1 are compared with line 5, 'tree' and line 6, variations on the character for 'sun' the resemblance to these elements rather than to those discussed above will, I believe, be apparent. We do not know what the cross in 1b means, but such a variation does occur in the character for sun (6b).[109] The two lines in 1c are a mystery as well, but they are not very common and may be another form of the two crossed lines. In any case, they have no relationship to the alternatives which have been proposed. Finally, east has

Figure 9 East and related oracle bone characters

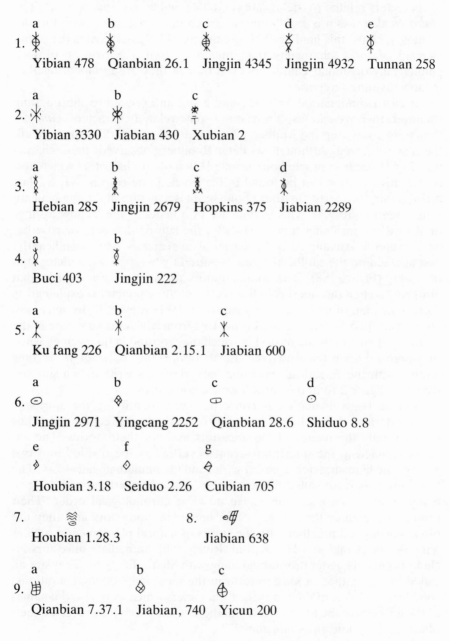

	a	b	c	d	e
1.					
	Yibian 478	Qianbian 26.1	Jingjin 4345	Jingjin 4932	Tunnan 258

	a	b	c
2.			
	Yibian 3330	Jiabian 430	Xubian 2

	a	b	c	d
3.				
	Hebian 285	Jingjin 2679	Hopkins 375	Jiabian 2289

	a	b
4.		
	Buci 403	Jingjin 222

	a	b	c
5.			
	Ku fang 226	Qianbian 2.15.1	Jiabian 600

	a	b	c	d
6.				
	Jingjin 2971	Yingcang 2252	Qianbian 28.6	Shiduo 8.8

	e	f	g
	Houbian 3.18	Seiduo 2.26	Cuibian 705

7. Houbian 1.28.3   8. Jiabian 638

	a	b	c
9.			
	Qianbian 7.37.1	Jiabian, 740	Yicun 200

a final 'ng' in Karlgren's reconstruction as opposed to the 'k' in the group of characters related to 'tie' (*śiuk) and 'bag tied at two ends' (*t'âk). The *Shuowen* also says it is 動 (*d'ung) and a group of characters with the element 重 all have this final ng.[110] It seems more likely that east is the sound element of those characters than that it is itself a borrowing of such phonetically dissimilar characters even though they are grouped together in later rhyming categories.

If east is understood as a tree and a sun and related to the Fu Sang tradition, then we can also understood some related characters. *Gao* 杲, 'bright' is a sun atop the Mulberry Tree and *yao* 杳, 'dark' a sun beneath the roots of a tree. Although, as Peter Boodberg observed, these characters do not occur in oracle bone script,[111] two other characters which also reflect this tradition can be found in the oracle bone corpus. *Xi* 昔, 'last night' (later, 'formerly', in oracle bone script is a picture of the sun beneath water (see Figure 9.7). This is evidence of a belief in the Yellow Springs or Ruo River in Shang times—visually, the sun neither set nor rose beneath water at Anyang or at the earlier Shang capitals. Most significantly, east as a sun on the Mulberry Tree, is paired by 'west' *xi* 西, a pictograph of a nest (Figure 9.8). The commentators to the *Shuowen* explain that birds roost when the sun sets in the West and this character is explained as a phonetic loan of *qi* 栖, meaning 'to roost'.[112] However, if the suns *were* birds, then, just as *dong* 東, east is the tree from which the suns rose in the morning, then west is the nest(s) in which they roosted in the evening when they perched upon the Ruo Tree. Furthermore, the character *yi* 翌, now written with the 立 radical, meaning 'next day' was written as a sun and wing (see figure 5.8) in the earliest oracle bone form.

Oracle bone divination is concerned with identifying the spirits to whom offerings should be made and discovering their precise needs; thus we have only the names of the ancestors and not their stories. The ancestors named in the inscriptions can, nevertheless, be divided into two groups: the high ancestors (*gao zu* 高祖) and the immediate ancestors. The high ancestors were called by personal names, often written with suggestively graphic characters, and have no clear chronological order. Their powers are greater than those of the immediate ancestors and they are often worshipped together with the spirits of natural phenomenon such as Yue 岳, the 'Peak' and He 河, the 'River'. The immediate ancestors include twenty-six generations, beginning with Shang Jia 上甲. They are all called by an epithet (a kinship term in the most immediate generations) combined with one of the ten cyclical characters which were also the names of the ten days of the Shang week and those upon which they received their offerings, later known as *tian gan* 天干.

The distinction in naming style between the immediate and high ancestors and lack of a clear order for the high ancestors suggests that a group of mythical ancestors originally set simply in the remote past have been combined with a real genealogy. Since both groups were 'ancestors' (*zu* 祖), there is no ideological differentiation—the high ancestors were not designated gods as opposed to men—and in combining the two groups, the seeds for later historicization of the figures of the remote past were sown. Although there are no narratives in the inscriptions about these figures, their names suggest an antecedent to the Mulberry Tree Tradition and the Shang Origin Myth.

The highest ancestor whose name is recorded in Shang oracle bone inscriptions is called 夋 (variously 夋, 夋 in period I). This character was first transcribed by Wang Guowei as Jun 俊 and although other transcriptions, the most popular of which are Nao 夒 and Kui 夔, have been suggested since, I believe Jun has the greatest justification for the following reasons.[113] Jun 俊 was the husband of Xihe, the mother of the ten suns, and father of the *jun* 踆 sun-birds in the Mulberry Tree tradition, as discussed above. 夋 was also the name of Di Ku who sent the black bird which gave birth to the Shang. Thus, if the character is *jun* 俊 (= 夋), the high ancestor named in the oracle bone inscriptions would correspond precisely to the father of the ten suns in the Mulberry Tree tradition and the progenitor of the Shang in their origin myth. The identification with Di Ku (that is Jun) is further supported by the tendency recorded in oracle bone inscriptions to worship this figure on the *xin* 辛 day of the ten-day week, for Di Ku was also called Gao Xin Shi 高辛氏 in Zhou texts.[114] It was Shang practice for the immediate ancestors whose names included one of the ten cyclical characters to be worshipped on the corresponding day.

There is also graphic justification. The character *jun* 夋 (presumably the original form) consists of a human figure with a head which may be turned (允) 允 and a leg and a foot (夊) 夊.[115] The name of the Shang ancestor includes a head which Wu Qichang 吳其昌 believed to the beaked[116] and a human figure with a large foot (sometimes omitted when the figure assumes a sitting or squatting position). Thus there is a general correspondence, except that in *jun* the head is not that of a bird although the myth figure has many bird associations. The foot in both cases may reflect the peculiar, possibly bird-like gait or stance suggested by the *Shuowen* definition— 夋行夋夋也一曰倨也 and the squatting figure suggests a source for the definition of 踆 as 蹲 crouching discussed above.[117]

Because of the lack of prominence of the head element in Jun and the resemblance of an oracle bone character which many scholars identify with this one (夒) (*Jiabian* 甲編 2236) to a monkey, Wang later transcribed it as

Nao which one source cited in the *Shuowen* defines as a mother ape. Although many oracle bone scholars prefer this transcription, I do not think that it is justified. Nao is an extremely rare character and I have been unable to find any examples in early texts other than the definition in the *Shuowen*. Since the king list recorded in the *Shiji* corresponds well to the names of immediate ancestors, it is unlikely that the name of the highest ancestor would be totally forgotten to later generations. Nor are the Shang mythically or otherwise ever identified with a monkey. Indeed, the animalistic form of the character can be better explained by the evolution of the character *jun*. In the oracle bone inscriptions, the character 夋 is also used for an animal which is caught or netted by hunters, the name of which is presumably a homonym of that of the ancestor. The *Shuowen* and *Erya* 爾雅 both refer to a wild animal, the identity of which is unclear, called *suan* 狻.[118] This probably derives from the same Shang character and provides an explanation for its evolution which Nao cannot adequately provide.

   Kui 夔 is another common transcription for this character. Scholars who use this transcription, including, most recently, Akatsuka Kiyoshi, regard it as an alternative form of Nao which derives from a period III variant of the Shang character which has lines on the head. The *Shuowen* defines *kui* as a one-legged dragon. The single leg agrees with the Shang character and the lines on the head are interpreted as a horn or horns. However, even in the examples given by Akatsuka, the lines on the top of the head do not resemble horns, as in this bone form with four straight lines— 夋 (*Yibian* 乙編 4718), or this bronze form in which what looks like plumage is matched by a feather-like tail— 夔 (*Sandai* 三代 11.34).[119] Furthermore, although Song scholars identified the *kui* dragon with a dragon motif which is common on Shang bronze vessels, there is no early textual association between this character and the Shang and although *kui* is more common than *nao* 夒, with a few occurrences in early texts, it is nevertheless a rare character. Some scholars identify *kui* with *nao* and *nao* with *jun*.[120] Regardless of the transcription, most continue to equate the figure with Di Ku. If he is Di Ku, however, Jun seems a more likely transcription of the oracle bone character.[121]

   According to the *Shanhaijing*, Di Jun's wives included Xihe, the mother of the ten suns and Chang Xi, the mother of the twelve moons. Among the remote ancestors of the Shang (or nature deities as these are not clearly distinguishable) are two female ancestors called Dong Mu 東母 'Eastern Mother' and Xi Mu 西母 'Western Mother'. Their worship is related to that of the rising and setting suns[122] or the suns and moons [123] which suggests that they are the antecedents of Xihe and Chang Xi although there can be no conclusive proof.[124] Dong Mu is the more frequently worshipped, as would be expected in light of the Shang identification with the suns.

As discussed above, Di Jun's wives also included E Huang, the mother of the three-bodied people in the *Shanhaijing*, but the wife of Shun and mother of Shang Jun in the historical tradition. Her structural equivalent in the Shang origin myth was Jian Di who swallowed the egg of the Black Bird (*xuan niao*) sent by Ku. The female ancestor E 娥 () in the oracle bone inscriptions is identified by most scholars as E Huang.[125] Like Wang Hai, 王亥 her name is mentioned together with the nature deities Yue 岳 'Mountain' and He 河 'River' and she is invoked in prayers for good harvest and capable of sending curses.[126]

There is no name corresponding to Jian Di in the oracle bone inscriptions, but dedications on a bronze vessel to a Black Bird Lady confirm that this was authentic Shang myth. The name consists of *fu* 婦 'Lady' + *xuan niao* 玄鳥 'black bird' over *nü* 女 'woman':

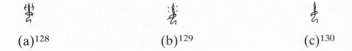

As Yu Xingwu has argued, these inscriptions probably refer to women of the You Rong clan who continued to marry Shang kings rather than to the original woman who gave birth to the egg of the black bird, but they nevertheless prove the antiquity of the myth.[127]

This character is not listed by Shima Kunio in his index of oracle bone inscriptions, but he does list three characters which may refer to the same name. The first of these three characters consists of two hands, the element which Yu Xingwu transcribes as *xuan* black and a bird head identical to that of the high ancestor Jun over *nü* woman:

(a)[128]   (b)[129]   (c)[130]

The hands and bird head thus replace the bird of the bronze inscription form. This character has been transcribed as *ku* 嚳, but the female element is more likely to imply the woman whom he impregnated with the black bird egg. The character is also preceded by (or may include) the element *wo* 我 and this may tie it to E 娥 (*wo* + *nü*). The evidence is far too sparse to be conclusive, but it is worth noting that there are connections here with the black bird lady, Ku (as a female), Jun (also female), and E.

The second and third characters may be abbreviated forms of the same name. The third one is called *fu* 婦 'Lady' in some inscriptions, as is the bronze inscription figure, and she is the only Fu X in Shima Kunio's index who could possibly be identified with the bronze inscriptions. One inscription refers to illness and another is apparently a divination to determine whether she should be offered as a burning sacrifice so she was apparently a living consort rather than an ancestor, but this would support Yu Xingwu's supposition that the name continued to be used.

The myth that the Shang were born from the egg of a black bird is further implied in the oracle bone inscriptions by the figure of Wang Hai 王亥. Wang Hai was the father of Shang Jia 上甲, the first of the Shang ancestors to be called by one of the ten cyclical characters. Thus his position is pivotal between the remote ancestors and the immediate ones placed in a clear genealogical order. His importance to the Shang is evident from his title Gao Zu 高祖 which he shares exclusively with the highest ancestor Jun and the dynastic founder Tang (Gao Zu Yi 高祖乙). His name is also the only one among those of the Shang ancestors to include a character from the cycle of twelve rather than the cycle of ten. Most striking in light of his pivotal position is that a bird is often drawn over the cyclical character *hai:* 𦏧 [131]

According to the *Shijing* which included the earliest record of the Shang origin myth, Heaven sent down a black bird (玄鳥) and it gave birth to the Shang. This progeny, called simply 'Shang' and 'Xuan Wang' (the 'Black King') in the *Shijing,* was called Xie 契 in later texts as discussed above. Zhou texts consistently refer to Xie as the first ancestor of the Shang in contrast to Qi 啓, the ancestor of the Xia, and Hou Ji 后稷, the ancestor of Zhou.[132] Wang Hai's position as the father of the first immediate ancestor and the bird drawn over his name identify him as Xie, the 'Black King'.[133]

In the light of evidence for the Mulberry Tree tradition originating with the Shang, ten suns must have risen on the ten days of the Shang week. I argued above that the bird which gave birth to the Shang in their origin myth was originally the same bird as that in the ten suns. Wang Hai, as the bird over his name indicates, was the Shang king actually born of the bird egg. From the time of his son Shang Jia 上甲 on, the ancestors of the Shang kings were called by names which included one of ten cyclical characters also used to designate the days of the week on which they were worshipped. These characters, now called *tian gan* 'heavenly stems' were called the *shi ri* 十日, 'ten suns' or simply *jia yi* 甲乙, after the first two characters in the cycle, *jia* and *yi,* in Zhou and early Han texts. *Ri* is an ambiguous term meaning both day and sun as well as referring to the cyclical character which classified these. The ten-day week, however, was not called *shi ri* but a *xun* 旬. In Zhou texts the primary meaning of *ri* as sun is occasionally evident in its use with reference to the cyclical characters, as in the *Zuo zhuan*: "Heaven has ten suns (*shi ri* 十日); men have ten ranks."[134] This is not common, for the Zhou did not have a myth of ten suns, but in the *Lun heng,* Wang Chong (who is also the first writer I have found to use *gan* and *zhi* 支 for the cycles of ten and twelve) explicitly associates the *shi ri,* used in his time for a type of geomancy, with the ten-sun tradition.[135]

The oracle bone inscriptions do not discuss the ten suns directly and we cannot be certain what the Shang called these cyclical characters, but there is some contemporaneous evidence that it was also *ri.* In the oracle inscriptions, *ri* and a cyclical character are interchangeable in many contexts. For example, *jin ri* 今日 'today' could also be described as *jin jia* 今甲 'now *jia*' if it were a *jia*-day; *yi ri* 翌日, 'the next day' as *yi yi* 翌乙, 'the next *yi*'. In bronze inscriptions, a sun may be drawn over a cyclical character (e.g. 𝌆, 𝌆) or omitted (𝌆) in identical contexts. There is also an unusual set of inscriptions on three excavated ritual weapons in which the ancestral names were recorded as *Fu ri gui* 父日癸, *Xiong ri gui* 兄日癸, and so on,[136] rather than the more usual *Fu gui* 'Father gui', *Xiong gui* 'Elder brother gui. . .'. *Fu gui* is not a name but a category made up of two elements: *fu,* a kinship term for father and father's brothers, and *gui* a ritual classification for ancestors worshipped on the *gui* day or when the *gui* sun was present. *Fu ri gui* is also a category—there are more than one such in a single inscription—and the meaning is probably the same in both cases: "father belonging to the cyclical category (that is sun) *gui*'.

The traditional explanation for the posthumous naming system of the Shang is that they were called according to the cyclical date of their birth (*sheng ri* 生日). The first reference to this system is not until the first century A.D. (*Baihu tong de lun* 白虎通德論 8/9b) and it has been disputed by some modern scholars. Most convincingly, K. C. Chang has argued that statistically the categories could not have been assigned according to the accident of birth and they were hereditary exogamous social groups.[137] If the traditional explanation is correct, it implies that after Wang Hai or Xie's miraculous conception from the egg of the sun-bird, his descendants were metaphorically born of the sun which appeared on their day of birth. If Chang is correct—the dispute is too complex to be dealt with here—it is nevertheless possible that the names were assigned according to the date of a birth ritual rather than actual birth date and that they were still considered to be born of the sun with which they were classified.

However the ancestors received their names, an identification with one of the ten suns appears to be the basis of the ritual calendar in which they were worshipped on the day with the corresponding classification. In the oracle bone inscriptions, rites are also sometimes directed at the sun (*ri*) itself, presumably the one which was present on the day of the rite. As Chen Mengjia has observed, the rites for worshipping the sun were also those used for the ancestors.[138] One such is *bin* 賓, to 'play host to' or 'receive as guest'. For example:

> Cracked on the *yizi* day, the king will play host to the sun (*bin ri*). He will not play host to the sun.[139]"

Frequently, an ancestor and the sun were worshipped together:

> "Cracked on the *guiwei* day, Ge divining, on the next *jiashen* day, the king will play host to Shang Jia and sun (*bin Shang Jia ri*). The king read the divination and said: 'auspicious'. . . .[140]"

It is possible in this case that *ri* refers not simply to the sun, but to the cyclical category generally—the sun and the *jia* ancestors present on that day.

I have cited examples of the *bin* rite because it is frequently used with reference to the sun and because it will recur in this context in the *Book of Documents*, but it also provides another key to the rationale of the ritual week. The *bin*-ritual is unique because the king not only played host to his ancestors on the day corresponding to the cyclical character of their name, his ancestors could also *bin* higher ancestors of the same category on that day or even the High Lord.[141] From this we can infer that the names of the ancestors were present and capable of receiving offerings and able to communicate with one another and Shang Di on the day the sun with which they were classified was also present. Other factors came into consideration, probably including the moon, as offerings were not made to each ancestor every week. Nevertheless, the evidence indicates that the Shang ancestors were totemically identified with one of the ten suns and that this was a primary assumption of their ritual calendar. In the following chapter I will discuss the transformation of the Shang origin myth into the legend of Yao's abdication to Shun. I will also discuss how the dualism of fire and water implicit in this Shang myth system underlies the story of the Xia dynasty which preceded the Shang.

III

From Myth to History

In the previous chapter, I discussed the relationship between the Mulberry Tree tradition and the Shang origin myth and traced the origin of both traditions to a Shang antecedent which provided the rationale for Shang totemism. I suggested that this system which was specific to the Shang lost its integrity when the Shang were conquered by the Zhou, but its motifs were transformed in outlying regions into a belief in ten suns who were the sons of Xihe and dwelt on the Mulberry Tree in the east and in the central plains into the Shang origin myth.

In the following, I will analyse the relationship between the myth tradition already described and the historical schemes which developed in the Zhou and Han dynasties. In the previous discussion, the great cosmic events—the flooding waters which rose up and pressed the Hollow Mulberry and Gong Gong's butting of Bu Zhou Mountain in the northwest of the world, causing the earth and sky to tilt towards one another—took place 'in the time of Yao'. Although the *Shijing* 詩經 which records the myth of the birth of the first Shang ancestor from the egg of a black bird does not mention any ruler earlier than Yu, other Zhou texts conventionally begin their references to ancient history with the reign of Yao. In the following, I will first examine the story of Yao's abdication to Shun as it appears in the *Shang shu Yao dian* 尚書 · 堯典. I will argue that the 'Yao' of the historical tradition was a transformation of the Lord on high, Shang Di 上帝, and that the story of Yao's abdication to Shun was originally a story of Di's appointment of the first Shang ancestor, 夋, in the oracle bone inscriptions.

Although, as I will discuss below, Yao's appointment of Shun is a transformation of the Shang origin myth, in the historical tradition Shun was succeeded by Yu, the founder of the Xia dynasty who preceded the Shang. Furthermore in the early Han dynasty, the Yellow Emperor Huang Di and his descendant Zhuan Xu were placed before Yao in the historical sequence. I noted above that in the Zhou traditions which originated with the Shang, there was an opposition between the Mulberry Tree in the east and the Ruo Tree in the west, the suns and moons, fire and water, birds and dragons, black and yellow, the sky and the Yellow Springs in which the Shang were regularly associated with the Mulberry Tree, the east, the ten suns, fire, birds, black, and the sky. This dualism provides the key to our understanding of the Xia and their ancestor, the Yellow Emperor, for the Xia were the mythical inverse of the Shang and, as I will argue below, the Yellow Emperor, originally the Lord of the underworld.

FROM YAO TO SHUN

The date of the *Yaodian* is uncertain. Most scholars place it some time in the Zhou Dynasty, estimates ranging from the beginning of the dynasty to the fourth or third centuries B.C. Joseph Needham, who has accepted a date of eighth to fifth centuries B.C. as most likely on philological grounds, has observed that it nevertheless presents a riddle because calculations based on star positions point to a date in the third millennium B.C.[1] The problem of the date is largely insoluble because it was probably, as Karlgren observed, compiled by a Zhou writer from more than one source.[2] The language is often archaic and is not entirely understood. I will argue in the following that it has some philological and philosophical origins in the Shang; however, the text in its present form is undoubtedly Zhou and it includes another transformation of the myth traditions described above.

The *Yaodian* or 'Annals of Yao' is the first chapter of the *Shang shu*. This reflects the early Zhou tradition that history began with the time of Yao. Not only is Yao the first ruler mentioned in many texts, but the great cosmological events are associated with his reign. In the *Huainanzi* 淮南子 passage (8/5a–b) discussed above, the ten suns came out in the time of Yao followed by the great deluge. Other scourges included Gong Gong 共工 who knocked down Bu Zhou Mountain and made heaven tilt towards the earth in the north-west. In the *Yaodian* itself, Yao first orders the four brothers Xi and He (a transformation of Xihe, mother of the ten suns, as I will discuss below) to go to the four directions where they are responsible for the astronomical bodies and the seasons—and then turns earthward to the problem of the flood.

Yao's origin is mysterious. He has no family other than his son Dan Zhu 丹朱 (or tens sons, depending on the text) and his two daughters whom he gave in marriage to Shun. The *Shiji* 史記 gives his father as Di Ku.[3] This implies a relationship between Yao and Di Ku, but Yao has no clear genealogy in other early texts. The early texts never mention a mother. There is no story of his birth, miraculous or natural. Nor are there any early references to his wife.

In the *Shuowen* 說文, *Yao* 堯 is glossed as *gao* 高, 'high'. There is a Yao Mountain in the *Shanhaijing* 山海經, but *yao* is not a word used in any other context.[4] In Zhou texts, Yao is sometimes called Tang Yao 唐堯, i.e. Yao of the Tang clan. Since the founder of the Shang dynasty's name was written with this character in the oracle bone inscriptions, this may imply a connection with the Shang—that he was the high one of Tang.[5] In the *Yaodian*, however, the name Yao only occurs in the first line: "Di Yao was called Fang Xun." From then on, the protagonist is called simply *di* 帝.

In Zhou texts, *di* has four usages: (1) As a title for pre-dynastic rulers up to Di Yu 帝禹 whose son Qi was the ancestor of the Xia. This usage extends to Yao's son Dan Zhu although, according to the historical tradition, Shun replaced him as Yao's successor.[6] (2) As a title for Shang ancestors in the main line of descent. This originally Shang usage is sometimes followed in Zhou texts for Shang rulers such as Di Yi 帝乙 and Di Xin 帝辛, but it was not used by the Zhou for their own ancestors. (3) Occasionally as a collective term for 'spirits' (of the ancestors?), as in the *Huainanzi* (4/3a) discussed above. (4) Di may stand for Shang Di 上帝, the high god of the Shang who was equated by the Zhou with their own deity Tian 天 'Heaven'.[7] This is the only Shang or Zhou usage of *di* in which the character stands alone without name or modifier. Nor did *di* refer to living rulers before the late Warring States Period. Thus, the *di* of the *Yaodian* did not originally mean emperor as it has been interpreted following later usage, but Shang Di, the high lord.

An examination of the *Yaodian* reveals that although its protagonist may in some part be Di Yao, a former ruler who was called Fang Xun 放勳, he is also the High Lord. There are also traces of a cosmogonic myth similar in structure to that in the *Huainanzi* (8/5a–b) already discussed. Di first arranges for the movement of the suns, now transformed into the singular, and the other heavenly bodies and then turns to the flooded earth. In a transformation of the myth traditions described above, he appoints Shun (equivalent to Ku- the progenitor of the Shang- and Jun) to have charge over the earth. Shun in turn appoints Yu 禹 and Yu's descendants are followed by the Shang. Once again there is an implied dualism of Xia and Shang, water and fire or suns—but I will restrict myself here to a discussion of the sun mythology.

The first section of the *Yaodian* is a preface in praise of Di who "covered the four extremes (of the earth) horizontally and reached to (the worlds) above and below."[8] This line which I take as a direct reference to Di rather than as a description of his influence is followed by a passage in verse describing his transforming virtue. The terms in which he is described suggest a human ruler, but both the verse form and the language indicate a distinct origin from the text which follows.[9]

The second section concerns the heavens and the calendar. Di first charges Xihe to "calculate and delineate (*li xiang* 曆象) the sun, the moon and (the other) heavenly bodies and respectfully give the people the seasons."[10] Thus Xihe is a transformation of the mother of the ten suns in what I have called the Fu Sang tradition as Maspero and others have observed. She retains her connection with the sun but she "calculates and delineates" (if *li xiang* is interpreted correctly) the sun rather than ordering her sun children. "Giving the people seasons" (*shou ren shi* 授人時) may be either a godly or an astronomical act, depending upon the interpretation.

As the passage continues, Di separately orders four brothers Xi Zhong 羲仲 , Xi Shu 羲叔, He Zhong 和仲, and He Shu 和叔 to the east, south, west and north, respectively. These four have traditionally been interpreted as the sons of Xihe and because their names imply younger brothers, the Xihe of the first line is often interpreted as meaning the elder brothers Xi and He. As Karlgren has observed, however, this would have to be written as Xi Bo 羲伯 and He Bo 和伯, not Xihe.[11] These four younger brothers Xi and He are not named in any other early text. By their names they are linked with Xihe, the mother of the ten suns, but their charge also suggests an origin in the spirits of the four directions or quadrates. These will be discussed in detail in chapter 4.

The language of this section links the *Yaodian*, the oracle bone inscriptions, and the Mulberry Tree tradition. Di first ordered Xi Zhong to the east to dwell with the Yu Yi 嵎夷 at a place called Yang Gu 陽谷 — the Valley of the Sun in the Fu Sang tradition. There he was to "respectfully play host to the rising sun"—*bin chu ri* 賓出日. *Bin*, as discussed above, was a rite performed both by the king and his ancestors in Shang times and was commonly performed to the sun. "And arrange and regulate the works of the east. When the day is of medium length and the asterism is Niao 鳥 'Bird' thus determine mid-spring." The Niao is a star named as an object of worship in the oracle bone inscriptions.[12] Its worship may be an aspect of the Shang identification with birds and the East.

The passage continues by naming the people in the east as the Xi (*qi min xi* 其民析). Traditionally, this character was interpreted as a verb meaning 'to disperse' but as Chen Mengjia has demonstrated, there is a correspondence between the people of the four directions in the *Yaodian* and the names given the four directions in the *Dahuangjing* 大荒經 section of the *Shanhaijing*. (This is the section which also describes Xihe as the mother of the ten suns and Chang Yi as the mother of the moons.) They also correspond to the names of the four directions given in oracle bone inscriptions which list the four directions and names them and their winds: a chart is given in Chapter 4, p. 82.[13]

The *Dahuangjing* also names the winds of each direction, calling the

East Wind, Jun 俊, a further tie to the sun birth myth.[14] The winds may also be birds as the oracle bone character for *feng* 風, 'wind' is a pictograph of a bird which has been identified with the phoenix (*feng* 鳳).[15]

The passage concludes as Di, having ordered the four brothers separately, charges them collectively (here: Xi ji He 羲暨和) to fix the intercalary month with a reference to the year as having 366 days—*san bai you liu xun you liu ri* 三百有六旬有六日. As Joseph Needham has observed, the insertion of the particle *you* between the powers of ten is a feature of Shang oracle bone inscriptions in the early periods which does not occur in other Zhou texts.[16]

The links which this passage provides between the Shang inscriptions and the *Shanhaijing* are a confirmation of my hypothesis that the Mulberry Tree tradition had its origin in the Shang. There is some evidence of euhemerization in the description of Xihe as "calculating and delineating" but Xi Zhong also travels to Yang Gu, the mythical Valley of the Sun. Generally, the text is ambiguous about whether these are astronomical officials of an earthly court or divine ones determining the heavenly movements and providing a sacred calendar. In light of what we now know about the hierarchical ordering in Shang religion from the oracle bone inscriptions, we can no longer assume, as Maspero did, that the bureaucratic air of a text such as this one indicates a tampering with an earlier mythical tradition. A transformation has occurred, however, and in the person of Xihe. She is no longer the mother of the ten suns but, it seems, of the four quadrates or directions. The ten suns, however, are not lost but reappear in another guise.

Having ordered Xihe, Di looks for a successor or an assistant (the language is ambiguous): "who will carefully attend to this? I will raise and use him."[17] His descendant, the prince Zhu (*yin zi Zhu* 胤子朱) is recommended to him but he rejects him. Zhu is called Dan Zhu 丹朱 in the *Shiji* and other texts. Dan means 'cinnabar' or 'red'. Zhu, according to the *Shuowen*, is a tree with a red heart (*chi xin mu* 赤心木),[18] and it may mean either 'red' or as 珠, 'pearl' or 'bead'. In the *Lüshi chunqiu* 呂氏春秋 (1/11b), however, Yao has ten sons whom he rejects in favor of Shun. Thus Dan Zhu, the 'Red Pearl' appears to be another transformation of the ten sun motif, here rejected in favor of Shun, another transformation of Di Ku and Di Jun.

Having also rejected Gong Gong, in other texts the destroyer of Bu Zhou Mountain, the pillar of the sky in the northeast, Di turns from the heavens to the problem of the flooded earth: "O, you Si Yue 四岳, voluminously the waters everywhere are injurious, extensively they embrace the mountains and rise above the hills . . . ."[19] Structurally this section balances that in which Di concerned himself with the sun and the heavens, just as the flood was juxtaposed to the coming out of the ten suns in the cosmogonic myth of *Huainanzi*. With regard to the Shang origin of the motifs of this text, it is noteworthy that although Yue 岳 'Peak' is a powerful nature deity in the oracle bone inscriptions, the Si Yue 四岳 (嶽) 'Four Peaks', to my knowledge, only appear in Zhou texts which refer directly to the *Shang shu*.

Finally, Di, now taking a more human form, observes that he has been on the throne for seventy years, and asks to yield to the Si Yue. When they refuse he asks whom he might promote. All reply: "There is an unmarried man below called Shun of Yu."[20] With Shun we clearly enter the realm of human beings. He is not only 'below' but described in human terms: "the son of a blind man; his father was stupid, his mother was deceitful, (his brother) Xiang was arrogant. . . .."[21] Di decides to try him and sends down (*jiang* 降) his two daughters to wive him. These are identified elsewhere as E Huang 娥皇 and Nü Ying 女英. E Huang bore Shang Jun 商鈞 (that is, the Shang, see p. 34). Shun, as previously discussed, can be identified with Ku and Jun. Thus, this is another transformation of the myth of the birth of the Shang.

Di tests Shun before yielding his power to him three years after his appointment. In part, the test is one of obedience to ritual; in part a mythical challenge by what I take to be nature spirits: "He was sent into the great foothill forest but violent wind, thunder and rain did not lead him astray."[22] The underlying theme of this text is thus the ordering of the cosmos and the appointment of Shun—a transformation of the Shang progenitor—to the position of human ruler by the high lord. The ordering of the heavens includes a transformation of the myth of the birth of ten suns in the Fu Mulberry tradition, both in the ordering of Xihe by Di and in Di's heir or ten heirs Dan Zhu. Shun, that is Di Ku and Di Jun, receives the High Lord's command and his own daughters and they bear the line which became the Shang.

In *The Heir and the Sage*, I have discussed this story as one in which the Emperor Yao abdicated to Shun and traced its relationship to the subsequent legends of dynastic change and continuation in which themes of heredity and virtue were repeatedly transformed and contrasted. The texts which I used were primarily those of the Warring States period. In the *Yaodian*, however, there remain traces of what was originally a cosmogonic myth of the Shang people. The act which came to symbolize a breach of the hereditary principle in later times was here the giving of the heavenly charge by the high lord to the progenitor of the Shang. This, then, was the Shang myth underlying the Zhou textual traditions of Shun's succession to Yao.

THE MYTH OF THE XIA DYNASTY

As I have already discussed, by the mid-nineteen thirties, the works of
Henri Maspero and other scholars in the West and of Gu Jiegang 顧頡剛
and his compatriots in China had clearly established the originally mythological character of Yu 禹, the founder of the Xia dynasty (traditionally
ca. 2200–1760 B.C.) and of the rulers who preceded him in traditional
Chinese historiography.[23] The excavations near Anyang of late Shang
palaces, tombs and inscribed oracle bones had also established the authenticity of the Shang dynasty which followed the Xia, or at least of the
latter part of it. In 1936, Chen Mengjia 陳夢家 published an article in
which he related the Xia king list to the Shang and argued that the two
periods were the same.[24] For the next forty years, the question of the authenticity of the Xia was left largely in abeyance although most scholars did
continue to assume that the Xia dynasty, which was hereditarily like the
Shang, would some day be authenticated by archaeological excavation.

Recently, however, Chinese scholars have begun to classify archaeological finds, as 'Xia'. What has brought about this change? The most important excavations of the major Xia site, Erlitou in Henan Province, were
done before 1964 but at that time they were classified as 'early Shang'.[25]
No new inscriptions which could confirm the existence of an earlier dynasty
have been found. Indeed, although Tang 湯, traditionally the founder of
the Shang dynasty, is revered in the oracle bone inscriptions as a high
ancestor, the genealogy goes back to Wang Hai 王亥, the first mythical
ancestor of the Shang, without any indication that this was the critical juncture at which the dynasty was founded or that other rulers were defeated.
The primary cause of this change appears to be the introduction of
radiocarbon dating: we now know that finds at Erlitou and other sites date
to within the traditional Xia period.[26]

In the following, I shall reconstruct the role of the Xia in early Chinese
mythology and argue that the Shang had a myth of the Xia as a previous
people who were their inverse, a dark and watery people who had been
overcome by the Shang sun-kings. This myth was transformed into a previous dynasty when the Zhou conquerors of the Shang proposed the theory
of a changing mandate of Heaven. To demonstrate that there was a Shang
myth about the Xia is not to prove that the Xia were a myth. Nevertheless,
an historical reconstruction should not be based on materials which are
part of a mythological system.

Within the Zhou textual tradition the Xia is a critical juncture. Yao
passed the rule to Shun and Shun to Yu 禹. Both successions were non-
hereditary, but Yu passed the rule to his son Qi and thus established the
first hereditary dynasty. Yet, according to Zhou legend, Shun did not con-

tinue to rule but abdicated in favor of Yu who founded the Xia. Only when the last Xia ruler Jie 桀 was defeated by Tang was the Shang Dynasty established. Why was the Shang rule not continued if their progenitor was appointed by the High Lord?

The Xia are ubiquitous in Zhou texts, including those chapters from the *Shang shu* which may de dated to the early Western Zhou.[27] In these the new Zhou kings sought to legitimize their overthrow of the Shang by citing the precedent of a Xia dynasty overthrown by the Shang and arguing that the mandate of Heaven is not constant. For this propaganda which was addressed to the Yin (that is Shang) people to have been effective, the Shang must have believed that a Xia people had preceded them and lost the favor of the High Lord. The problem is to determine the nature and meaning of this belief.

In the following, I shall demonstrate that the mythical themes associated with the Xia are an inversion of those associated with the Shang in Shang mythology. The relationship is similar to that of later *yin-yang* dualism of which it was the harbinger. The Shang were identified with the ten suns, birds, the Mulberry Tree, the east, the sky and life. The Xia, on the other hand, were identified with water creatures such as dragons and turtles, the Ruo Tree, the west, the Yellow Springs and death. This dualism was part of a single mythological system which preceded and laid the foundation for the Zhou theory of a dynastic cycle and the changing mandate of Heaven.[28]

The genealogy of the Xia rulers can be divided into three eras: The earliest, a clearly mythological period, is from the 'Yellow Lord' Huang Di to Yu the flood hero's son Qi. Next there is the period from Tai Kang to Shao Kang in which rule was usurped by the descendants of Yi. Finally, there is the period from Yu to the last king Jie when the Xia are supposed to have reigned over 'all-under-heaven'. I will be primarily concerned with the first, mythological period, but I will conclude with some remarks about the two following periods and the historicity of the Xia.

THE 'YELLOW LORD' HUANG DI AND THE YELLOW SPRINGS

In the *Xia annals* of the *Shiji*, the Xia ancestry is traced from Yu 禹 back to Huang Di, the Yellow Lord.[29] *The Annals of the Five Emperors*, the first chapter of the *Shiji*, also begins with Huang Di. Thus, by the end of the second century B.C., Huang Di was regarded as the first ruler of China. This tradition, as Yang Kuan observed in the *Gushibian*, did not begin until the late Warring States period.[30] But even in the texts of the late Warring States and early Han, history conventionally begins with the time of Yao.[31] Yao, as I noted above, was a transformation of Shang Di, the

High Lord of Shang religion, and he is called simply Di in the *Shang shu Yaodian*.

Huang Di was credited with the ancestry of many ancient tribes, but he is particularly associated with the Xia, so much so that Chen Mengjia attempted to identify him with Yu 禹.[32] His surname, for example, was You Nai (or Xiong) Shi 有熊氏 or, alternatively, Xuan Yuan Shi 軒轅氏. As I shall discuss below, both Yu and his father Gun turned into a yellow 熊, three-legged turtle or dragon. Xuan Yuan is also the Heavenly or Black Turtle (*tian* 天 or *xuan* 玄黿) and in some versions of the myth this is the name of the mountain through which Yu passed when he turned into a 熊.[33]

Yang Kuan, on the other hand, argued that Huang Di was Shang Di.[34] This is based on a series: Shang Di 上帝, Huang Shang Di 皇上帝, Huang Di 皇帝, Huang Di 黃帝—in which Huang Di 黃帝, the Yellow Lord is supposed to have originated with a taboo for the character *huang* 皇, 'august' referring to the High Lord. *Huang* 黃, 'yellow' and *huang* 皇, 'august' were homophones in classical Chinese (**g'wâng*), but their meaning is quite distinct and it is unlikely that the cult of the Yellow Emperor, which was very popular in the late Warring States and Han times, could have derived from a taboo character. *Huang*, august (originally a shining sun over earth) refers to the sky (as in *da huang* 大皇) and it was used as an adjective to describe Shang Di as early as the *Shijing*.[35] (Only after the 'First Emperor' of Qin styled himself *Shi Huangdi*, did *huangdi* come to refer to an earthly ruler rather than the August Lord.) *Huang* 黃, yellow on the other hand, is the color of the springs which ran under the earth and in oracle bone inscriptions it is one of two colors, yellow-bright, as opposed to *xuan* 玄 dark, the color of the sky and sun-birds, in a primitive color dualism. This suggests that the Yellow Lord may have originally been the Lord of the underworld, the counterpart of Shang Di, the Lord on High.

In five element theory, Huang Di was associated with the earth, yellow, dragons, and the center. According to the *Lüshi chunqiu* (13/4a) which was written in the late third century B.C. and includes one of the earliest formulations of five-element theory, "In the time of the Yellow Lord, Heaven first caused large earthworms and mole-crickets to appear. The Lord said, 'The spirit of earth is in ascendancy'. The spirit of earth was in ascendancy, therefore he esteemed yellow as his color and took soil as his concern." Earthworms, as mentioned above, both eat soil and drink from the Yellow Springs. Mole-crickets, bore in the earth and sing sadly in the evening.[36] The *Huainanzi* (3/3a), about a century later, stated, "As for the central land, its lord is the Yellow Lord, . . . his animal, the yellow dragon.' Elsewhere in the *Huainanzi* (4/11a), we are told that the Yellow Dragon born of the ether of the central earth (after a number of transformations) hides in the Yellow Springs. The yellow earth and the yellow springs which run beneath it are thus connected.

However, Huang Di is not only the Lord of the central region. He is frequently identified with a cult of immortality associated with the Kunlun 崑崙 Mountains in the far west of China. At the foot of the Kunlun Mountains, there was a Ruo (*ńi̯ok) 弱 River identifiable with the 若 (*ńi̯ak) River which had its source at the Ruo Tree.[37] This was the birthplace of Huang Di's descendants, as I shall discuss below. It may also have been an entry to the land of the dead. (Ultimately all waters must have derived from the Yellow Springs). The Kunlun Mountains were also the home of Xi Wang Mu 西王母, the Queen Mother of the west who gave the Archer Yi the elixir of immortality.

In ancient China there were two souls, the *hun* 魂 and the *po* 魄, the ethereal and the corporeal, the heavenly and the earthly.[38] The *hun* ascended whereas the *po* settled. Thus, the Yellow Springs may not have been simply the land of the dead, but more precisely, the land of the *po* souls. The origin of this belief in two souls is difficult to determine because only the *hun* soul was the object of the ancestral cult. There was also a reluctance to discuss what happened to a person after death before the late Warring States Period when the two souls began to be discussed in connection with the developing *yin-yang* theory. The earliest reference which I have found is a discussion of ghosts without tombs in the *Zuozhuan* 左傳 (*Zhao Gong* 昭公 7): "When men are born and begin to move, it is called *po*. When the *po* is already born, the *yang* (element) is called *hun*. As the form and spirit become greater, the *hun* and *po* become stronger. . . . When ordinary men and women are killed by violence, the *hun* and *po* are still able to attach themselves to people. . . ."[39]

In Shang times, the Lord on high, Shang Di—usually called simply Di—was the lord of the spirit world, issuing commands to the natural phenomenon and standing at the apex of the hierarchy of ancestral spirits. However, the Shang not only divined to determine the approval of Di and their ancestors before performing certain acts, they also divined about the approval of 'below and above' (*xia shang* 下上).[40] Only in Zhou times, was Shang Di identified with *Tian* 天, heaven. If a Lord of the Yellow Springs, that is a Lord Below, existed, he, like the *po* soul, had no cult. In the late Warring States Period, however, men began to attempt to preserve themselves not simply as ancestors, that is *hun* souls receiving offerings, but corporeally, by prolonging life and by preservation of the corpse, as at Mawangdui. This may explain the sudden prominence of the Yellow Lord.

With the rise of the Warring States cults of immortality, the Lord of the netherworld was transformed into the Lord of the western paradise. In five-element theory, however, he became the Lord of the center. In this guise, he fought the Red Lord Yan Di 炎帝 (that is Chi You 蚩尤), whose emblem was fire, for possession of the Hollow Mulberry—perhaps a new transformation of the earlier fire and water dualism.[41] In the historiography, there also became five emperors: Huang Di, Zhuan Xu (his descendant, as discussed below), Yao, Shun and Yu.

CHANG YI TO ZHUAN XU

According to the *Shiji*, Huang Di had a son by the "Woman of the Western Mound" Lei Zu 縲祖, called Chang Yi 昌意.[42] In the *Shanhaijing*, Lei Zu is written as 雷祖, 'thunder ancestress'.[43] Chang Yi and his descendants are identified with the west, water and death or immortality. In the *Xia Annals*, Chang Yi was the father of Zhuan Xu 顓頊, but in the *Shanhaijing*, Han Liu 韓流 intervenes between the two generations:

> Huang Di's wife Lei Zu gave birth to Chang Yi. Chang Yi descended and made his home in the Ruo River. He begot Han Liu. Han Liu had a long throat and small ears, a human face with a pig's snout, a scaly body, thighs like wheel rims and pettitoed feet. He took Zhuozi 淖子 who was called A Nü 阿女 as his wife; she bore Di Zhuan Xu.[44]

The *Guben zhushu jinian* 古本竹書紀年 also records that Chang Yi descended and made his home in the Ruo River although in that confusion of sequence which is characteristic of this mythological era, Chang Yi and his son—called Han Huang 韓荒 in this text—are placed before Huang Di.[45] The Ruo River, as I noted above, had its source at the Ruo Tree, the western counterpart of the Fu Sang.

These texts might have been interpreted as 'made his home *at* the Ruo River', but since Han Liu's appearance is that of a dragon, I assume he lived in the river. Di Zhuan Xu is also described as a water creature in the *Shanhaijing*: "There is a fish which is withered on one side. Its name is Yu Fu 魚婦 ('Fish Lady'). When Zhuan Xu had died, he thus came to life again. The wind blew from the North, and then the sky became a great spring of water. A snake was transformed into a fish. This is what is called Yu Fu: Zhuan Xu who had died come to life again."[46] The term 'withered on one side' (*pian ku* 偏枯) is also used for Zhuan Xu's descendant, the flood hero Yu.[47]

Earlier in the same section of the *Shanhaijing*, it also states that ". . . there is a mountain called the Great Wasteland Mountain which is where the sun and moon set. There are people there who have three faces.

These are the sons of Zhuan Xu. They have three faces and one arm. Three-faced people don't die."[48] These three-faced descendants of Zhuan Xu appear to be an inversion of the three-bodied sons of Xihe, the mother of the ten suns. The Xia are further identified with the far west—where the sun and moon set—and with life beyond death.

The *Lüshi chunqiu* (5/9a) also states that Di Zhuan Xu was "born from the Ruo River" and adds, "he actually made his home in the Hollow Mulberry. Thereupon, he rose up and became Lord (*di*). When heaven was harmonized, the principal wind blew. . . . Di Zhuan Xu liked its sound and so he ordered the Flying Dragons to make sounds which imitated the eight winds and bestowed the name 'Containing Clouds' on (the music) for making sacrifice to the High Lord." The Hollow Mulberry in this passage is an *axis mundi*, allowing access to the heavens. Zhuan Xu's retinue were dragons, those which fly on clouds—clouds rose from springs as water mist and fell again as rain, thus although dragons were water creatures, they sometime ascended to the skies.[49]

As the second of the five lords, however, Zhuan Xu was opposed by Gong Gong. According to the *Huainanzi* (3/1a–b), "Long ago, Gong Gong contested with Zhuan Xu to become Di. He became angry and butted Bu Zhou Mountain (in the northwest corner of the earth), breaking the pillar of heaven and severing earth's cord. Heaven inclined in the northwest, so the sun and moon, stars and constellations move in that direction; earth did not fill up the southeast, so the water and dust turn towards there." Elsewhere in the *Huainanzi* (15/1b), we are told that when Zhuan Xu contested with Gong Gong, Gong Gong caused a 'water catastrophe'.[50]

The earliest reference to Gong Gong's rampage is in the *Chuci Tian wen* 楚辭 · 天問 (ca. fifty century B.C.), "When Kang Hui 康回 was greatly angered, why did the earth incline in the southeast? How were the nine states divided and why were the river valleys made deep?"[51] The first of these two questions refers to Gong Gong's butting of Bu Zhou Mountain; the second to Yu's division of the central kingdom into nine states and dredging of the riverbeds to drain the flooding waters. Thus the tilting of the earth and the flooding are once again linked. The *Tian wen* do not, however, tell us when these events occurred except by reference to Yu's solution.

As I mentioned above, the historical sequence of five lords which is related to five-element theory is later than that of Yao, Shun and Yu. Most frequently, the great flood is placed during this period and this tradition is also recorded in the *Huainanzi* (8/5b): "During the time of Shun, Gong Gong stirred up and made swell the flooding waters (*zhen tao hong shui* 振滔洪水) until they pressed the Hollow Mulberry." According to the *Lüshi chunqiu* (14/3b–4a), the mother of Yi Yin, traditionally the minister of the Shang dynasty founder Tang, turned into a hollow mulberry when she turned around to look back upon the flood which was emerging from her kitchen mortar. This flood was undoubtedly the great flood—other records indicated a drought rather than a flood at the beginning of the dynasty[52]—and the tree from which Yi Yin was supernaturally born was the *axis mundi*, but because these stories were originally myths, placed in that time 'long ago' there is confusion when they are placed in historical order.

These events are also transformations of the cosmogonic myth in the *Shang shu Yaodian*. Therein, Di (that is Shang Di)[53] having first arranged the heavens and the calendar, then turned to the lower world where "voluminously the great waters everywhere are injurious, extensively they embrace the mountains and rise above the hills, vastly they swell up to heaven (*tao tian* 滔天)"[54] Having first rejected his son Dan Zhu and then Gong Gong who also 'swelled up to heaven 滔天' (*tao tian*), he then turned to Zhuan Xu's son Gun to allay the flooding, as I shall discuss below. In all of these stories, there is a symmetry of sky and water, a battle between the rising waters and the heaven represented by the High Lord or by the Hollow Mulberry which allows access to the skies.

In the *Tian wen*, the flooding waters are called *hong quan* 洪泉, 'flooding springs' and it seems that those waters which surged to heaven and pressed the Hollow Mulberry in cosmic battle of sky and water were those which were later confined to the netherworld from which they watered the riverbeds.[55] In the *Mencius* (5/11b, 3A.4), we are told, "In the time of Yao, the world was not yet level, and the flooding waters flowed laterally (that is not in riverbeds), inundating the world." Although this passage does not mention the tilting of the earth caused by the attack on Bu Zhou Mountain, the sense is similar. In no text is the flood ever attributed to rainfall, nor is there any suggestion of divine punishment. William Boltz has identified the etymonic root of Gong Gong as bellicose or wanton[56] and there is a battle between order and disorder, and between the high and the low in the story of the flood, but the biblical concepts of sin, guilt and retribution are completely absent.

GUN

Gun 鯀 whose name may be divided into *xuan yu* 玄魚 'dark fish' tried, according to the *Chuci Tian wen*, to allay the flood by following a pattern made by owls and turtles, symbols of night and water: "the owls and turtles linked together, tail in mouth; why did Gun follow them?"[57] According to the Shanhaijing, "Gun stole Di's swelling mould (*xi rang* 息壤) and thus dammed up the flooding waters"[58] but his attempts failed and he was executed by Di.[59]

Although Gun was executed, he did not die but was transformed into a yellow *nai* 熊, a three-legged turtle or possibly a dragon,[60] and thus he gave birth to Yu. The earliest reference to this story is once again that in the *Tian wen*, "Long he lay cast off on Yu Shan. Why did he not rot for three years? Lord Gun brought forth Yu from his belly. How was he transformed?" and again, "When Gun came to the end of his westward journey, how did he cross the heights? He turned into a yellow turtle, how did the shamans bring him back to life?"[61] The answer to the questions may be found in the *Gui zang* 歸藏, "When Gun had been dead for three years and did not putrefy, they cut him open with a knife of Wu. He was transformed into a yellow turtle (熊). They tore him open with a knife of Wu 吳 and thus he gave birth to Yu. '[62] And in two almost identical passages in the *Zuozhuan* (*Zhao Gong* 昭公 7) and the *Guoyu* 國語 (*Jin yu* 晉語 8, 14/4b): "Long ago, when Yao executed Gun on Yu 羽 ('Feather') Mountain, his spirit was transformed into a yellow turtle (熊) and thus he entered the Yu Yuan ('Feather Abyss').

This story has many of the motifs discussed above in association with the Xia ancestors. The Yellow Lord Huang Di had the surname 熊. According to the *Shanhaijing*, Zhuan Xu's descendants were three-bodied, matching the three-faced descendants of Shun. Gun was a three-legged turtle rather than three-bodied, but as such he is a counterpart for the three-legged sun-bird of the Shang. The Feather 羽 (*giwo) Abyss is the 虞 (*ngiwo) Abyss, the gorge where the sun set at the foot of the Ruo Tree[63]—the land of death and entry to the Yellow Springs.

YU AND QI

Yu 禹 (*giwo) was born when Gun was transformed and his name is phonetically identical with that of the Feather Abyss. It means *chong* 蟲, a class of animals usually translated as insects but which includes both dragons and tortoises. The story of how Yu dredged the riverbed and built up the high land so that the water flowed peacefully in channels to the sea is the best known of early Chinese myths and need not be recounted in detail here. Just as Gun followed a pattern made by owls and turtles, Yu followed yellow dragons.[64] Yu's wife was the Lady of Tu Mountain 塗山. She is sometimes identified as Nü Gua 女媧 who, in still another version of the cosmogonic myth recorded in the *Huainanzi* (3/6b), cut off the four legs of a turtle to prop up the sky when all four poles were broken causing fire and flood.[65] This story may give a clue to the origin of the three-legged tortoise for if only Bu Zhou Mountain were broken, as in other versions of the myth, only one leg would have been needed to prop up the sky.

Yu also had a miraculous transformation resulting in the supernatural birth of his son Qi 啓. The earliest reference to this story is probably a line from the *Tian wen* which refers to a diligent son who slew his mother.[66] A late account explains that when controlling the flood, Yu passed through Han Yuan Mountain (Han Xuan was one of Huang Di's surnames) and was transformed into a 熊. The Lady of Tu Mountain saw him and fled in fright. When she reached Song Gao Mountain 嵩高山, she turned into a stone, Yu said, "Return my son to me" and the stone broke open, giving birth to Qi.[67]

Thus far we have been within a mythical era, a time long ago when the world was first taking shape before there was a separation between the supernatural and human worlds. Yu gave the world its physical order when he controlled the flooding. He also gave it its political order for he harmonized the nine states and had cast the nine sacrificial *ding* 鼎 vessels. Qi whose name means 'Beginning' was the last of the Xia ancestors to be born miraculously. He was also the first hereditary ruler in the historiography of ancient China. His reign was that in which heaven and earth were separated and his role was transitional.

Qi still had access to heaven from which he took music, the *Jiu ge* 九歌, the *Jiu bian* 九辯, and, according to some texts, the *Jiu shao* 九韶. This tradition goes back to the *Tian wen* and *Li sao* 離騷 of the *Chuci*[68] and is made explicit in the *Shanhaijing*: West of the Floating Sands (that is in the extreme west), there is someone with green snakes in his ears who rides a mount of two dragons. His name is Xia Hou Qi 夏后啓. Qi ascended and played host to (*bin* 嬪) heaven three times. He obtained the *Jiu ge* and *Jiu bian* and descended . . ."[69] Yu had cast the *ding*; now, with the sacred music, sacrifice could be made by those below.

The stories of the era from Huang Di to Qi are clearly myths in the traditional sense of stories of the supernatural set in a time long ago. From the time of Qi, heaven and earth were separated and the Xia dynasty begins officially. But it begins strangely—with the loss of the state.

TAI KANG TO SHAO KANG: AN INTERREGNUM

According to the *Shiji*, "When the Xia ruler Di Qi died, his son Tai Kang 太康 was established (on the throne). Di Tai Kang lost his state and the five brothers all fled to Luo Nei 洛汭; they made the *Song of Five Brothers*. When Tai Kang died, his younger brother Zhong Kang 中康 was established (on the throne); this was Di Zhong Kang. In the time of Di Zhong Kang, the Xi 羲 and He 和 behaved lasciviously, disrupting the seasons and throwing the days into confusion. Yin 胤 went to correct them and made the *Yin Zheng* 胤徵. When Zhong Kang died, his son Di Xiang 帝相 was established. When Di Xiang died, his son Shao Kang was established.[70]

The Xia dynasty thus began with the loss of the state. Although the *Shiji* does not record to whom Tai Kang lost rule, other texts record that it was usurped by Yi 羿, possibly the same Yi 羿 as the archer who shot down the ten suns, and there is an echo of this in the *Shiji* reference to Xi and He (mythologically Xihe, the mother of the suns) creating confusion. Yi was cuckolded and then murdered by Han Zhuo who fed him to his sons who refused to eat him and died. Han Zhuo continued Yi's rule and passed it on to his son Jiao 浇 (or 奡), but Shao Kang whose pregnant mother had escaped, returned and killed Jiao, restoring the dynasty.[71]

This interregnum from Tai Kang to Shao Kang, as Lü Simian 呂思勉 observed in the *Gushibian*, appears to be an insertion.[72] The story forms an integral whole which can be separated from the following king list. It is distinguished by the naming style of the kings. This style is that of the Shang rulers: Kang is probably a substitution for the cyclical character Geng 庚 based upon a taboo.[73] This naming style is used only by Kong Jia 孔甲 and, in alternative genealogies, Yin Jia 胤甲 who, as I shall discuss below, are also distinguished from the rest of the king list. Logically, a dynasty cannot begin with usurpation. Indeed, if there were a dynasty in this period, it is that of Yi.

THE KING LIST: YÚ TO JIE

According to the Xia Annals of the *Shiji*, Di Shao Kang was succeeded by his son Di Yú 予. The *Guoyu* also refers to Yú's ability to follow the lead of Yu 禹, a further indication that this is in some sense a new beginning.[74] The *Shiji* lists nine kings between Yú 予 and the last Xia king Jie, but the only ruler about whom other than genealogical information is included is Kong Jia. Kong Jia is also the only ruler in the *Shiji* king list identified in the Shang naming style, that is with one of the ten cyclical characters which also represented the ten suns and the ten days of the week. Significantly, the story of Kong Jia is mythological and involves dragons, the water creatures with whom, as I have shown above, the Xia were consistently associated.

The *Shiji* Annals tell us that Kong Jia was attracted to magic and the supernatural and was lascivious and disorderly. The virtue of the Xia declined and many lords rebelled. Heaven sent down two dragons, a male and female, but Kong Jia could not feed them as he had no descendant of the Dragon-feeding clan in his service. He appointed a descendant of Yao who had studied training dragons from the Dragon-feeding clan, but the female died and he fed it to the Xia ruler. When Kong Jia requested the dragon, he fled in fright.

The *Guben zhushu jinian* genealogy is slightly different from that in the *Shiji* and it does not include Kong Jia. It does, however, include a Yin Jia who is not in the Shiji genealogy but may be identifiable with Di Jin 廑.

Yin Jia "dwelt at the Western River. Heaven had an ominous disaster: the ten suns came out together. In that year, Yin Jia died."[75]

Both of these stories are about the decline of the Xia. The supernatural motifs which signify this decline are consistent with the mythological pattern established above. In the first story, the Xia declined after the Xia ruler ate a dragon—a creature of his own kind for his ancestors were such creatures. In the second, the ruler who lived on the Western River (once again the Xia are associated with the west and water) is cursed with an omen of ten suns, the symbol of the Shang kings.

CONCLUSION

The historical legends of Yao and Shun and of a Xia dynasty founded by Yu derive from Shang myth. Within the Shang myth system, their ancestors were identified with the ten suns which were also birds which was the basis of their ritual calendar and they had a myth of descent from a sun-bird. This Shang origin myth occurs in Zhou texts in several forms: as the myth of Di Ku 帝嚳 and the black bird (*xuan niao* 玄鳥) who impregnated Jian Di 簡狄 to give birth to Shang Xie 商契; as the story of Xihe 羲和 who gave birth to the ten suns (the *jun*-ravens 踆鳥) and whose husband was called Jun 俊; and, in the historical tradition, as Yao's appointment of Shun who, with Yao's daughter E Huang 娥皇, was the progenitor of Shang Jun 商均 (see figure 8).

Within the Shang myth system, there was also a dualism, the antecedent of later *yin-yang* theory, in which the suns, sky, birds, east, life, the Lord on High were opposed to the moons, watery underworld, dragons, west, death, the Lord below . . ., and a myth in which the Shang ancestors who were identified with the suns, east, . . ., had vanquished a previous people, the Xia, identified with the underworld, dragons, west, ... When the Zhou conquered the Shang, this myth was reinterpreted in the light of their own historical context as a similar historical event at an earlier period and the Xia came to be regarded as a political dynasty. Later, Huang Di 黃帝, originally the lord of the underworld or Yellow Springs and thus closely associated with the Xia, was also transformed into an historical ruler and, with his descendant Zhuan Xu 顓頊, placed before Yao, who was a transformation of the Lord on High, Shang Di 上帝, in the historical sequence. Thus, the historical accounts from Huang Di to the Xia may all be understood as deriving from a Shang myth system.

IV

The Shape of the Cosmos

Who can tell the story of the beginning of
    utmost antiquity?
By what means can we examine the time
    when the above and the below had not
    yet taken form?
Who can fathom the twilight before day
    and night?
How can we know the form of
    insubstantial matter?

Chuci Tian wen 楚辭. 天問

In the far east of the world, there was the Fusang tree from which the ten suns rose; in the far west, the Ruo tree on which they set. Beneath the earth was water; above sky. But what was the shape of the cosmos in the minds of the Shang kings and their diviners? This question, like so many others concerning Shang thought, cannot be answered directly by consulting the oracle bone inscriptions. Indeed, the first references to the shape of the cosmos are the questions posed in the *Chuci Tian wen* 楚辭. 天問, as much as eight centuries after the fall of the Shang dynasty, and direct speculation about the shape of the cosmos is associated in the textual tradition with the rise and development of five-element (*wu xing* 五行) theory in the third century B.C., most importantly with the philosopher of the *yin-yang* 陰陽 school Zou Yan 鄒衍, though it undoubtedly had a longer history.

Although cosmological theories were a relatively late development in the Chinese philosophical tradition, cosmology was, nevertheless, of critical importance to the Shang kings in their attempts to ensure the well-being of their dead ancestors and the harmony and prosperity of their state by means of divination and ritual sacrifice. We have already seen that the Shang kings identified themselves totemically with the ten suns who rose from the Mulberry Tree on the ten days of the week and that this tree had a counterpart in the west. Furthermore, the sky above had a counterpart in the Yellow Springs which ran everywhere beneath the earth.

74

In the following, I will first examine the problem of the shape of the earth as it was understood by the Shang. I will first argue that the *si fang* 四方 , conventionally translated as the 'four directions' were four mythical lands which surrounded a central square. Thus, the shape of the Shang earth was that of a cruciform or the Chinese character *ya* 亞. I will then review the occurrences of the *ya* shape in various archaeological contexts and discuss its significance with reference to Mircea Eliade's theory of the symbolism of the center. I will further argue that a *ya*-shaped earth and lands above and below were the origin of later numerological theories based on five and six. Finally, I will argue that the plastron of the turtle which was used in Shang divination was also, roughly speaking, *ya*-shaped and that it functioned as a model of the Shang cosmos. This understanding provides the basis for a new interpretation of Shang divination in which the divination cracks are interpreted as artificially produced omens.

THE FOUR QUADRATES (*SI FANG* 四方)

According to the *Zhou bisuanjing* 周髀算經 (1/17b) and the *Huainanzi* 淮南子 (3/9a), "Heaven is round and the earth, square" 天圓地方. This tradition was prevalent throughout later Chinese history and it undoubtedly has an earlier origin than the *Zhou bisuanjing* which was compiled in the third century B.C. where it appears in the context of mathematics, although this is the first explicit statement about the shape of the earth and the sky which I have discovered. But did it originate with the Zhou whose high god was Tian 天, 'Heaven'? Or can it be traced back to the Shang? The key to the solution of this problem lies in understanding the nature of the four *fang* 方, squares or quadrates as I shall translate them for reasons which will become clear in the following discussion.

In Shang oracle bone inscriptions, the four quadrates are mentioned collectively, as the *si fang* 四方, and individually, as the eastern quadrate 東方 , western quadrate 西方, southern quadrate 南方, and northern quadrate 北方. They are the objects of the *di*-sacrifice and the homes of the winds. northeast, southeast, northwest and southwest also occur in the oracle bone inscriptions, so the Shang recognized eight directions altogether, but they are never called *fang* and their sacrifice is characteristically the *ji* 戠 ; it is never the *di* 禘.

The term *si fang* 四方 occurs frequently in Zhou dynasty texts. In the oldest sections of the *Shijing* 詩經, the *Song* 頌, and *Da Ya* 大雅 sections which may date to the Western Zhou dynasty, the term refers to the outlying regions of the world and their rulers or people and by extension comes to mean simply the entire world. For example:

"The city of Shang was well-ordered, the pole (*ji* 極) of the four quadrates."

(305, *Shang song Yin wu* 商頌.殷武)

"The four quadrates came to congratulate him."

(243, *Da ya Xia wu* 大雅.下武)

"The four quadrates were at peace."

(262, *Da ya Jiang han* 大雅.江漢)

Si fang in Zhou texts and, indeed, in oracle bone inscriptions has conventionally been interpreted and translated as the 'four directions', but, the standard meaning of the *fang* is 'square' or 'rectangle' (hence my translation quadrate which includes both). By extension it may also mean 'cube' as in *Mozi* 墨子, "One side of a cube (方) is not a cube, but one side of a wooden cube (方木) is the wooden cube."[1] This meaning is also evident in the frequent contrast of *fang* with *yuan* 圓, as in the expression "Heaven is round and the earth, square" or the *Zhuangzi*, "The carpenter's square (*ju* 矩) is not square (*fang* 方); the compasses (*gui* 規) cannot make a circle (*yuan* 圓)."[2]

With the advent of five-element theory, there were five *fang*, those of the north, south, east, west and center, and these are also conventionally translated, albeit somewhat nonsensically, as the five 'directions'. The center is not a direction. The meaning of *fang* is spatial, not linear, but it has not been understood as direction because there is a contradiction between the idea of four square spaces located in the cardinal directions and that of a square world. If the *fang* were squares, then they would have to lie outside a central square and the earth would have to be cruciform or *ya* 亞 -shaped. This, I shall argue below, was the shape of the earth as it was understood by the Shang and traces of this early belief are still evident in later texts.

What, then, did *fang* mean in the Shang dynasty? The meaning square or rectangle is first attested unequivocally by the expression *fang ding* 方鼎, 'square *ding*-vessel' which first occurs in early Western Zhou bronze inscriptions.[3] However, this meaning is also attested by an analysis of the character, itself. In oracle bone inscriptions of the reign of Wu Ding—the first period of Dong Zuobin's five periods—*fang* is written as 方. A variety of explanations have been given for this character, but most scholars agree that the *Shuowen* 說文 explanation, "boats side by side" (並船也) is incorrect. One often cited explanation, that of Xu Zhongshu 徐中舒, is that "*fang* represents a plough. The short horizontal line above is the horizontal piece of wood at the top of the handle. The long horizontal below is the place where the foot treads."[4] However, Xu cannot explain the two short lines at the sides, regarding them simply as ornament, nor is there a clear relationship between this interpretation of the character and its usage.

Rather than regarding the character as a whole, I believe that it can best be understood by dividing it into two elements: 冖 and 刂. 刂 has been interpreted as *ren* 人, 'man' and as *dao* 刀, 'knife' but in my opinion, the hook at the bottom of this element more closely resembles the oracle bone form of *dao*: 刂 than the straight or slightly jagged leg of *ren* 𠆢, 𠂊. The horizontal element of this character is often interpreted as a rack from which weapons were hung or, if the other element is a man rather than a prisoner, a rack worn as a cangue by a prisoner.[5] I suspect, however, that it is a type of carpenter's square. This is supported by the evolution of the character *ju* 矩, 'carpenter's square'. This character does not occur in the extant oracle bone inscriptions, but in early Western Zhou bronze inscriptions it is written as a man (rather than the arrow: 矢 of the later character) holding a tool: 𢀜.[6] In light of the meaning of the word, this must be a carpenter's tool used for making squares. As the *Zhou bisuanjing* 周髀算經 (1/2b) states, "Circles come from squares (*fang* 方) and squares come from carpenter's squares (*ju* 矩)." The character *gong* 工 is also a representation of this tool according to Li Xiaoding.[7] The function of the knife may thus have been to mark the squares. The line at the top of the character in some alternative forms of *fang* (𠀟) could then be explained as a mark on the third side of the square.

The character *wu* 巫 (written in the *Shuowen* as (𢂾) is also closely related. In the oracle bone form: 𠀆, the tool rather than the knife or man element (the *Shuowen* form is still unclear) is reduplicated, but whichever element is reduplicated, both forms of the character derive from *fang* and indicate repetition or reduplication. This repetition may be a reference to the four *fang*. In oracle bone inscriptions of the *Shi* 𠂤 and *Li* 歷 diviner-groups, the character *wu* is used instead of *fang* with reference to the four quadrates.[8] Shima Kunio's oracle bone index, the *Inkyo bokuji sorui*, lists eight inscriptions which include the expression *wu di* 𠀆�, all of which belong to the *Shi* or *Li* diviner-groups, as do the two inscriptions which include the formula *di yu wu* � 于 𠀆.[9] This pattern parallels that of *fang di* 𠀟 � and *di yu fang* � 于 𠀟 in which *di* is the name of a sacrifice and *fang* refers to the four quadrates to which the sacrifice is made. Where *fang* (or *wu*) precedes the verb *di*, it modifies it: "perform the four-quadrate-*di*-sacrifice"; where it comes after the verb and preposition *yu* 于, it is an object: "perform the *di*-sacrifice to the quadrates." The *di*-sacrifice is also offered to the northern and eastern quadrates (*Heji* 34140; *Cui* 1311) and one inscription (*Xu* 1.2.4; *Yizun* 81) refers to the four 𠀆. In these instances, *wu* is equivalent to *fang* and refers to the quadrates of the cardinal directions.[10]

The character *di* 帝, written in oracle bone script as 粟 may also be related. As a noun, this character refers to Shang Di, the Lord on High, the high god of the Shang inscriptions. It is also used as a title for Shang ancestors in the main line of descent. As a verb (禘), it refers to the *di*-sacrifice. This was the highest of the Shang sacrificial rites and it was offered to Yue 岳, the 'Peak' and He 河, the 'River' as well as to the four quadrates. When the character functions as a verb, a square □ is some-times substituted for the element 予: 粟. Many scholars take this character as a phonetic loan deriving from the homophone 蒂 and believe it to be a pictograph of the calyx of a flower, but I have never been able to see the resemblance.[11] The substitution of a square for the horizontal element 𝖸 in the verbal form suggests that this element is also a square. In a few examples, a circle is substituted for the square (粟). This is probably simply an engraver's shortcut, but it could also refer to the sky—the home of Shang Di who ruled the *fang* below. In the inscriptions *Cui* 1311 to which I have referred above, *di* is written as 粟. Some scholars have taken this as a significant variation, but since there is also a small circle in the character 予 , both are probably the result of a small piece of dirt or sand under the rubbing paper or some problem with the bone rather than a part of the original character.

That 'square' was the primary meaning of *fang* can also be seen from the substitution of a square for this element in the character *wei* 衛 (衛): 衛 = 韋 (衛).[12].

The meaning of square may also be seen in the identity of 方 with ㄷ. Both characters, now pronounced *fang*, are reconstructed by Bernhard Karlgren as *pi̯wang*. 'ㄷ' is a pictograph of a square container. Thus it means a cube and by extension is also used to mean square just as '方' is a square and, as I have already noted, by extension, a cube. The sound and meaning of the two characters were the same and so we must assume that they are different ways of representing the same spoken word. This identity is also apparent in the substitution of ㄷ for the element 工 in the later form of the character *ju* 矩. Conversely, *yang* 央 which means 'center' is written in oracle bone script as 央, but as 央 in Western Zhou bronze inscriptions. The center is thus *tian* 天, 'sky' or *da* 大, 'large' (depending on the inter-pretation of this element) and a square. If the center is a square, then the *fang*, which are also squares, must be at its sides, forming a cross or *ya* 亞 -shape.

In the oracle bone inscriptions, *fang* not only refers to the four *fang* of the north, south, east and west, it also refers to tribes with which the Shang were frequently at war, such as the *Hu fang* 胡方. Shima Kunio lists some forty-two such tribes in his *Inkyo bokuji sorui*. This usage has been explained as meaning *bang* (*pǔng*) 邦 or *guo* 國. However, both terms refer to a state of some type and there are so many of these that any form of political organization, especially a state with a walled city implied by the term *guo*, is unlikely. A more likely explanation is that the primary meaning of *fang*, square has been extended to mean a land, the space of which is only vaguely defined, just as the later Classical Chinese expression '地方百里', 'a territory of a hundred li square' does not imply that the territory was actually square, but is simply a rough indication of size. Thus, the *Hu fang* were the people of the Hu land.

Another explanation which has been offered for *fang* when it is used with reference to these tribes is that it stands for *pang* 旁, side.[13] The *fang* tribes would thus be the people from regions on the sides of the Shang state. This interpretation is supported by the interchangeability of the characters *fang* and *pang* in, for example, the new text and old text versions of the *Shang shu* 尚書. A character which has been identified as *pang*, the name of one of the *fang* tribes, does occur in the oracle bone inscriptions. Significantly, it is written as 𠂤, which may be interpreted as a square (or land) beside another square (or land). the four *fang* might also be so interpreted, but the meaning is nevertheless the same—they were squares (or, more roughly speaking, quadrates) on the four sides of a central square.

The four *fang* or quadrates were the homes of the four winds. This is evident from divinations about a rite to pacify the wind (*ning feng* 寧風) which was performed to the *fang*. It is also made explicit in two unusual inscriptions, both of which are from the reign of Wu Ding, the first period according to Dong Zuobin's periodization. One of them, an ox scapula, is not a divination inscription, but simply records the name of each of the four quadrates and the name of its wind: "The eastern quadrate is called Xi; its wind is called Xie. The southern quadrate is called. . ." (*Heji* 合集 14294; see figure 10). The names are listed in figure 12. The other is a nearly complete turtle plastron, the upper part of which is engraved with a series of six divinations (see figure 11). The first, third and fifth inscriptions are on the left side of the plastron and are written vertically from right to left. The second, fourth and sixth inscriptions are written on the right side of plastron, also vertically, but with the columns going from left to right. The numbers 1, 2, 3 and 4 are written beside the accompanying divination cracks which indicates that each divination was made four times.

The inscription reads:

Xinhai day, Nei divining, this first month, the Lord will command rain. On the evening of the fourth day, *jiayin*, [it really rained]. 1, 2, 3, 4.

Figure 10 *Heji* 14294

Figure 11 *Heji* 14925

Figure 12 The names of the four quadates

		Heji 14294	Heji 14295	Hopkins 472	Jingjin 4316	Qianbian 4.42.6	Shangshu Yaodian	Shijing (32)	Huainauzi 13/3a	Lushi 4/2	Erya, Zhong/6a
E	Quadrate	析(析)	析(析)	析(析)			析				
	Wind	劦(劦)	劦(巛)								
	People										
S	Quadrate	(桼)	兂(兂)								
	Wind	兂(兂)	(兮)					凱	巨 (Gao You: 愷)	巨 (凱)	凱
	People						因				
W	Quadrate	彝	彝(彝)								
	Wind	彝(彝)					夷				
	People										
N	Quadrate	勹(勹)	勹(勹)								
	Wind	殴(殴)	殴(殴)				隩				
	People										

Cracked on the *xinhai* day, Nei divining, this first month, [the lord] shall not command rain. 1, 2, 3, 4.

Cracked on the *xinhai* day, Nei divining, offer the *di*-sacrifice to the Northern quadrate which is called 勹; [its wind] is called 阪. Prayer for harvest. [First month]. 1, 2, 3, 4.

Cracked on the *xinhai* day, Nei divining, offer the *di*-sacrifice to the Southern quadrate which is called 屴; its wind is called 丬. Prayer for harvest. First month. 1, 2, 3, 4.

Cracked on the *xinhai* day, Nei divining, offer the *di*-sacrifice to the Eastern quadrate which is called 析; its wind is called 劦. Prayer for harvest. 1, 2, 3, 4.

Cracked on the *xinhai* day, Nei divining, offer the *di*-sacrifice to the Western quadrate which is called 彝; its wind is called 未. Prayer for harvest. 1, 2, 3, 4.

(*Heji* 14295)

Although the names of the quadrates and winds of the south and west have been reversed on the scapula and plastron and there is also some graphic variation in the writing of the names, the names on the two bones are nevertheless identifiable. The names of the quadrates and their winds are not often recorded in other inscriptions—offerings are simply made to the *fang*, winds, east, west, but there are a few isolated references in other divinations.

Some scholars have identified the four *fang*, 'quadrates' with the four *tu* 土, 'lands'.[14] The four *tu* (named individually as the eastern *tu*, western *tu*, but never collectively as the 'four lands', were lands, which lay to the north, south, east and west of the Shang. The central position of the Shang is evident in the expression 'Central Shang' (Zhong Shang 中商) and also in the following fifth period divination:

The *yisi* day, the king made the crack, divining, this year, Shang shall receive harvest. The king read the crack and said 'fortunate'.

The Eastern land shall receive harvest.
The Southern land shall receive harvest.

The Western land shall receive harvest.
The Northern land shall receive harvest.

Heji 36975

I believe, however, that a distinction can be made between the *tu* and the *fang*. Although the character 土 is also used in the oracle bone inscriptions for *she* 社, 'earth altar' these four *tu* were clearly real lands. Most divinations about them are concerned with whether they will receive harvest or suffer drought. However, I have not found any divinations about whether the *fang* will suffer drought and the only inscriptions which refer to the *fang* receiving harvest are from the Li diviner group in which the character *wu* is substituted with reference to the four quadrates (*Heji* 33244, *Tunnan* 屯南 443). The four *fang* are also the objects of the *di*-sacrifice, whereas the *tu* are not.

The different in usage between *tu* and *fang* suggests that whereas *tu* were real lands to the north, south, east and west of the Shang from whom they received harvest grain, the *fang* were primarily important as spiritual entities. The *fang* or quadrates may have overlapped with real lands, but the term referred primarily to spirit lands, the homes of the winds with power over rain and harvest.

This impression that the four quadrates were spirit lands is confirmed by later textual tradition. In the *Chuci Zhao hun* 楚辭. 招魂, the 'Summons of the Soul' the dead or dying man is called back from each of the four quadrates by Wu Yang 巫陽, the 'sorcerer' Yang:

> Oh soul, come back! Why leave your old home and go to the four quadrates (*si fang* 四方)? Leaving your happy abode, you shall meet with misfortune.

> Oh soul, come back! You cannot lodge in the Eastern quadrate. There are giants there, tall as a thousand men, who seek souls. The ten suns rise from there one by one; they melt metal and liquify stone. There, everyone is accustomed to it, but you, soul, would surely dissipate. Come back! You cannot dwell there!

> Oh soul, come back! In the Southern quadrate you cannot bide. They tattoo their foreheads and blacken their teeth. They use human meat for sacrifice and make a broth of the bones. There are masses of vipers and a great fox who can leap a thousand miles. And an enormous python with nine heads who darts back and

forth, swallowing men to satisfy his appetite. Come back! You cannot wander long there.

Oh soul, come back! The horror of the Western quadrate is drifting sands for a thousand miles. They swirl around and enter the Thunder Abyss; they grind everything down and cannot be stopped. And if, by chance, you should escape, a world of desolation is beyond. The red ants are like elephants and the dark wasps like jugs. . . .

Oh soul, come back, you cannot bide in the Northern quadrate. The layered ice soars into the sky. There is flying snow for a thousand miles. . . .

Having called the soul back from the four quadrates, Wu Yang then turns to the land above, Heaven, and to the underworld, here called You Du 幽都 , the 'Dark City'.

Oh soul, come back! Do not climb up to the sky. There are tigers and leopards at the nine gates which snap at men from the world below and cause them harm. There is a man with nine heads who can pluck up nine thousand trees. He looks about like a ravenous wolf, pacing to and fro. He hangs men for amusement and tosses them into the deep abyss. . . .

Oh soul, come back! Do not descend into the Dark City. The body of the Lord of the earth is twisted nine times and his horns are very sharp . . . He has three eyes, a tiger head and the body of an ox. . . .[15]

The other 'summons' poem in the *Chuci*, the *Da zhao* 大招, 'Great Summons' is very similar to the *Zhao hun*, but it only includes the four quadrates.

In the 'Summons of the Soul' the four quadrates partake of the characteristics of the directions in which they lie—the north is cold, the south is hot and has tattooed men, . . . —but they are clearly lands in which human beings cannot survive, inhuman and full of monsters. Like the sky above and the underworld below with which they are combined in this text, they are lands of the imagination.

The sorcerers who called the souls back from the four quadrates in the two summons poems of the *Chuci* are called *wu* 巫. This may be of significance. There has been much debate about whether such *wu* were what western anthropologists call 'shamans' and about whether shamanistic practices can be traced back to the Shang. This debate is beyond the purview of the present study, but the combination of the name which refers to the four quadrates in some oracle bone inscriptions and the role of the *wu* in these poems suggests that *wu* were originally specialist priests who could call souls and whose spirits could travel to these four uninhabitable lands.

The names of the four quadrates and their winds recorded in the two Shang inscriptions discussed above also appear in two later texts, the *Yaodian* 堯典 chapter of the *Shang shu* and the *Shanhaijing* 山海經.[16] This is important evidence of the continuation of Shang traditions after the fall of the dynasty, although, of course, the traditions were transformed with the changing times. The evidence is particularly powerful because the names are mentioned in context in these two texts and not given special prominance, so they are not a self-conscious resurrection of an earlier tradition.

In the *Yaodian*, the names of the four quadrates or those of their winds have been transformed into those of the people who inhabited the regions to the extreme north, south, east and west to which the Lord Yao ordered the brothers who are collectively called Xihe 羲和:

And then he ordered Xihe . . .

He separately commanded Xi Zhong 'Middle brother Xi' to dwell at Yuyi 嵎夷, which was called Yang gu 陽谷 and to respectfully receive the rising sun. . . . Its people were called Xi 析.

He also commanded Xi Shu 'Younger brother Xi' to dwell at the southern borders, called Ming Du 明都. . . . Its people were called Yin 因.

He separately commanded He Zhong 'Middle brother He' to dwell in the Western land, called Mei Gu 昧谷 . . . . Its people were called Yi 夷.

He also commanded He Shu 'Younger brother He' to dwell at Shuo fang 朔方, called You Do 幽都 . . . . Its people were called Ao 隩.[17]

Yang Gu is the Valley of the Sun: Mei 昧 (a sun on the tip of a branch) Gu, the valley at the foot of the Ruo Tree. Thus, as mentioned in Chapter 2, this passage is tied to the Mulberry Tree tradition by the names of the places to which the brothers went, as well as by the name Xihe. You Du

幽都 , here in the far north, was the name of the underworld in the *Zhao hun*.

In his study of the *Yaodian*, "*Légendes Mythologiques dans le Chou king*", Maspero, noting that Xihe was the mother of the ten suns in the *Shanhaijing* and other texts, took these four brothers as an example of how early Chinese writers transformed traditional myth into historical reality. Although I believe that Maspero's thesis of euhemerization is generally true—that ancient Chinese historians were rational men who, believing in the essential truth of their received tradition, excised its more fantastic elements—his explanation here is difficult to accept. That historians could have transformed a woman known by tradition to be the mother of the ten suns directly into four brothers is unlikely. Xihe may have been a collective or tribal name and the mythical mother of the ten suns might have had further sons, including the guardian spirits of the four quadrates.

Of more direct relevance to our problem herein, however, is that there are only four brothers, two *zhong* 仲 or 'middle brothers' and two *shu* 叔 or 'younger brothers'. Their names imply two further *bo* 伯 or 'elder brothers', six brothers altogether as discussed in the preceding chapter. Six was the number of the regions in the cosmology of the *Zhao hun*, that is above, below, and the four quadrates. The *Yaodian* also begins with the statement that the Lord "horizontally transversed the four extremes and reached to the (worlds) above and below." Possibly, the realms of the other two brothers were those of above and below.

The *Shanhaijing* is a complex work with many layers. It is probably a compendium of material from a variety of sources. The text cannot be discussed in detail herein, but its organization deserves note because it reflects a continuation of the tradition of four quadrates discussed above. The association of the mountains and regions in the north, south, east and west with strange and fabulous creatures may also be a continuation of this same tradition. The first section of the *Shanhaijing* includes five *jing* or books of mountains, in the north, south, east, west and center. This implies a world which has five parts and is *ya*-shaped. There follow four books of regions within the seas (*hainei* 海內) and four beyond the seas (*haiwai* 海外). Both sets are in the four cardinal directions. Finally, there are four books of the great outlands (*da huang* 大荒), again located in the four cardinal directions. The four 'outlands' (*huang*) are the outer regions of the four quadrates. Significantly, there are no books of the northeast, southeast, northwest or southwest in the *Shanhaijing*, as we would expect if the world were square and nine-parted.

The relationship of the regions within and beyond the seas and Great Outlands is not clear to me although I suspect the influence of Zou Yan's theory of supercontinents in the division into within and beyond the seas.

Furthermore, although the four seas occur in the earliest extant Zhou texts, I am not certain whether they belong to the configuration of beliefs which I am describing or whether they have a distinct origin. Nevertheless, the geographical plan of the *Shanhaijing* is cross-shaped.

I have argued above, primarily on the basis of the meaning of the four *fang* or quadrates that the Shang regarded the earth as a central square surrounded by four other squares, that is as having the shape of a cruciform or of the Chinese character *ya* 亞. Many archaeologists have previously observed the prevalence of the *ya*-shape in Shang Dynasty remains. I will briefly review its occurrences below and then discuss its meaning. Archaeologically, the *ya*-shape occurs:

1. as the shape of holes in the foot-rings of bronze ritual vessels.
2. as a symbol enclosing clan names and other ancestral dedications in the inscriptions cast on bronze ritual vessels.
3. as the shape of Shang royal tombs and of their wooden chambers.

There are also literary suggestions that Shang temples were constructed in this form, but these have not been confirmed archaeologically.

The *ya*-shaped holes in the foot-rings of bronze vessels are first found in the middle Shang period. From this period to the early Western Zhou, *ya*-shaped holes are frequently found on opposite sides at the top of the foot-rims of certain types of bronze vessels. Illustrations may be seen in figures 26 and 40. Most prominent are the *gu* 觚, *gui* 簋, *zun* 尊, *lei* 罍 and *pan* 盤, but any vessel with a footring may have such holes. In the late period, the cross is narrowed and so it is often said to resemble the Chinese character *shi* 十 rather than *ya* 亞, but the structure is the same.

These holes in the footrings of bronze vessels probably had a mechanical function in holding the core of the mould within the rings, as many scholars have suggested, but the *ya*-shape could not have been essential to that function because many such holes are either round or square, particularly in the middle Shang and early Yinxu period. Furthermore, vessel types, such as the *gu* 觚, in which the holes are normally found, are sometimes made without any holes at all. Thus, the hole must have had a decorative and not simply a functional purpose.[18]

This decorative purpose may also be seen in a pair of large *ya*-shaped holes found in the foot of a pottery *dou* 豆 excavated at Zhengzhou (see figure 13).[19] The size and shape of these holes are similar to those on a bronze *gu* from the same site and period.[20] Although pottery *dou* have a long history in neolithic China, to my knowledge they were not cast in bronze until the Yinxu period, and even then they are quite rare.[21] Thus, although the holes in the foot of the pottery *dou* are undoubtedly modelled

Figure 13 Pottery *dou* from Zhengzhou

From Henansheng Wenhuaju Wenwu Gongzuodui,
Zhengzhou Erligang, fig. 6.5

on those in the foot-rings of bronze vessels, the *ya*-shape had been isolated by the potter as a motif of symbolic importance when he transferred it to the pottery *dou* and gave it special prominence.

The *ya*-shape also occurs as a symbol enclosing a name or longer inscription in the ancestral dedications cast on bronze ritual vessels from the Yinxu period until the early Western Zhou dynasty. Some illustrations may be seen in figure 14. Similarly, a square seal was found at Yinxu in which a name was placed within a *ya*-shape made by marking off the four corners of the square seal (see figure 15).[22] *Ya* occurs as a character in bronze and oracle bone inscriptions where it is an official title or rank. I believe, however, that a distinction should be made between this character and the *ya* symbol. The symbol sometimes encloses a single character clan name and this may be the entire inscription. Sometimes a kinship term, such as *fu* 父, 'father' or *zu* 祖, 'grandfather' and one of the cycle of ten characters by which the Shang identified their ancestors (and which, I have argued, were the names of the ten suns) is added; this ancestral designation may be placed within the *ya* or it may follow on after it. Sometimes the inscriptions are even longer and these may also either follow on after the *ya* or be placed within it. In the early Western Zhou, there are examples of quite long inscriptions placed within a *ya*.[23]

In early Chinese writing, two characters which have a compound meaning are sometimes written as a compound character or *hewen* 合文. For example, the name of the ancestor Bao Yi 匚 (報)乙 is often written as 㔾. If the contents of the *ya* were restricted to a clan name or even to a clan name plus ancestral designation (such as 'Father Yi', it might be possible to regard the *ya*-shape and the characters placed within it as compound characters in which the *ya* was a character designating a title or rank. However, since completely unrelated characters can also be included within the *ya*,

Sandai 2.9a

Sandai 1.7a

Sandai 5.2b

Sandai 6.18a

Sandai 2.14b

Sandai 6.17b

Sandai 3.1a

Sandai 5.8a

Sandai 3.10b

Sandai 7.34b

Figure 14 Bronze inscriptions with the cruciform (*ya*) symbol

Figure 15 Bronze seal from Yinxu

From Hu Houxuan, *Yinxu fajue,* figure 87

the *ya* cannot be part of a compound character. It is a symbol, not a character. This does not exclude the possibility, however, that only people with
the rank or title of *ya* were entitled to use this symbol. There is a close
relationship between the names used in conjunction with the character in
the oracle bone and bronze inscriptions and those which appear within the
ya-shape and so this limitation is quite possible.

Scholars disagree about the precise meaning of the character *ya*,
although the *ya* were evidently a type of *hou* 侯 or 'lord'—the names which
are used with the title *ya* are also called *hou*, but not all *hou* are called *ya*.
Some, such as Tang Lan 唐蘭, have considered *ya* to be a rank; others,
such as Chen Mengjia, Guo Moruo 郭沫若 and Zao Ding 曹定, have
understood *ya* as an official title. Liu Jie 劉節, on the other hand, argues
that the *ya* were a maternal lineage (*bao zu* 胞族). Liu contrasts the usage
of the expression, the 'many *ya*' (*duo ya* 多亞) with that of the 'many *fang*'
(*duo fang* 多方) and argues that the 'many *ya*' were the Shang king's own
lineage, whereas the 'many *fang*' were lineages from outside regions,
foreigners.[24] This contrast between *ya* and *fang* coincides with my own
view, which I will discuss in the following, that the *ya* was used as a symbol
which signified centrality.

The *ya* symbol may be written as 亞 or as 卍. The first form resembles
a large square from which the corners have been removed and recalls the
seal mentioned above in which a *ya* was formed by marking off spaces in
the corners of the seal. It also recalls the shape of the piece mould used for
casting the base of a square (*fang*) *ding* vessel, with its indentations to
allow for the attachment of the four legs.[25] The second form more closely
resembles a small central square with four squares attached to its sides,
although either form can be seen either as a large square with spaces in the
corners or as five smaller squares. A central square with four other squares
in the cardinal directions is the form of a traditional Chinese temple in
which four side chambers adjoin a main hall or a central courtyard.

According to the Qing Dynasty scholar Ruan Yuan. "There are many *ya* shapes on ancient vessels. Since Song times, everyone has considered the *ya* to be a temple "[26] and this is still the prevalent view of the meaning of the *ya*.

Chen Mengjia argued on the basis of the names of the halls used to make sacrifices in the Shang oracle bone inscriptions that Shang temples were *ya*-shaped, that is that they were constructed as four halls surrounding a central open courtyard.[27] Gao Quxun 高去尋 also observed that the royal temples of the Xia, Shang and Zhou, the Shi Shi 世室, Chong Shi 重室, and Ming Tang 明堂, as reconstructed by Wang Guowei from later texts, most importantly the *Kao gong ji* 考工記, were *ya*-shaped and later temples patterned after the early Zhou Ming Tang 明堂 were of this shape. Unfortunately, none of the large building foundations excavated at Anyang, neither the foundations which the excavator Shi Zhangru 石璋如 thought were temples nor those which he supposed to be palaces, are *ya*-shaped (see figure 1). Gao argued that some of the foundations might be so reconstructed if it were not for the intrusion of other buildings, but this is merely supposition; there is no physical evidence.[28]

Although the building foundations excavated at Yinxu are not *ya*-shaped, the great tombs excavated there are. The temples and palaces were built to the south of the Huan River. To the north was the royal cemetary at Xibeigang (see figure 2). Eight large tombs were discovered in the western section of the site: seven with four tomb ramps extending in the cardinal directions and one without any ramps which was unfinished and unused. One large tomb with four ramps extending in the cardinal directions has also been discovered in the eastern sector, as well as two somewhat smaller tombs with two ramps (including the large tomb excavated at Wu Guan Cun in 1950) and two with a single ramp, including that from which the large *ding* dedicated to Simu Wu 司母戊, a wife of Wu Ding, is thought to have come. There are altogether nine kings from the time of Wu Ding 武丁 —the first king to whom oracle bone divination inscriptions can be attributed—and Zhou Xin 紂辛, the last Shang king who was overthrown and executed by Wu Wang 武王 of the Zhou dynasty. Thus, Yang Xizhang 楊希璋 has argued that only those tombs with four ramps are those of the Shang kings. The unfinished and unused tomb would, accordingly, be that of Zhou Xin who was overthrown and the smaller tombs, those of wives or other nobility.[29]

The four ramps of the great royal tombs lead down to earthern pits. These are *ya*-shaped in three of the tombs (1001, 1217 and 1400). In one tomb (1550), the top of the pit is rectangular, but the bottom is *ya*-shaped. The others are rectangular. Within each earthern pit, there was originally a wooden chamber which contained the most important grave goods and the

Figure 16 Tomb 1001, Houjiazhuang: Remnants of the wooden burial chamber

From Liang Siyong and Gao Quxun, *Houjiazhuang 1001-hao da mu*, v. 2, pl. XXVIII

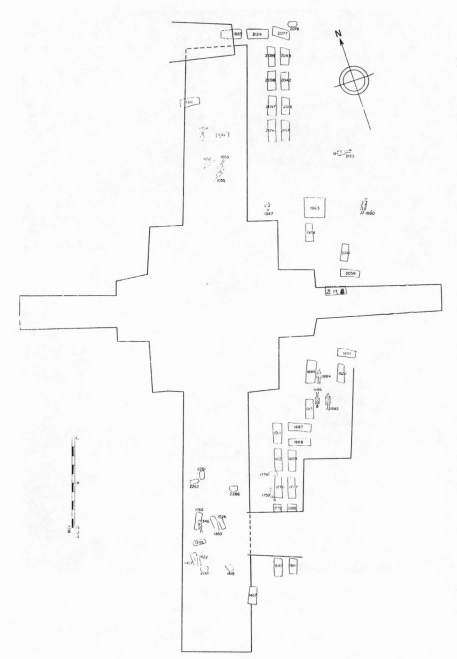

Figure 17a Tomb 1001, Houjiazhuang: Section of upper layer with small tombs on the Eastern side

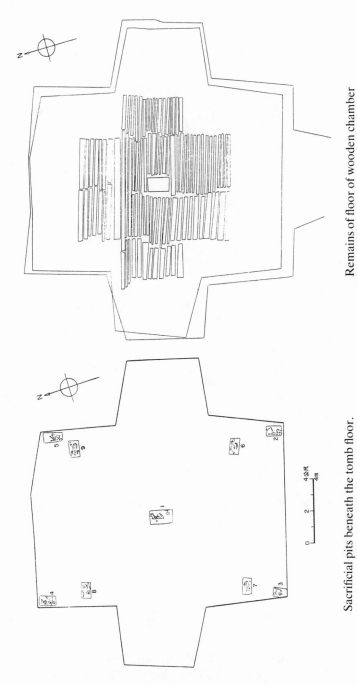

Remains of floor of wooden chamber

Sacrificial pits beneath the tomb floor.

Figure 17b Tomb 1001, Houjiazhuang

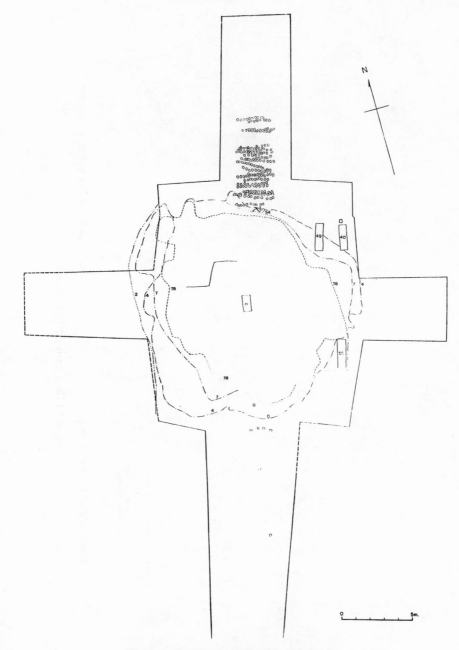

Figure 18a Tomb 1550, Houjiazhuang:
Cross section of the tomb showing sacrificial burials of skulls

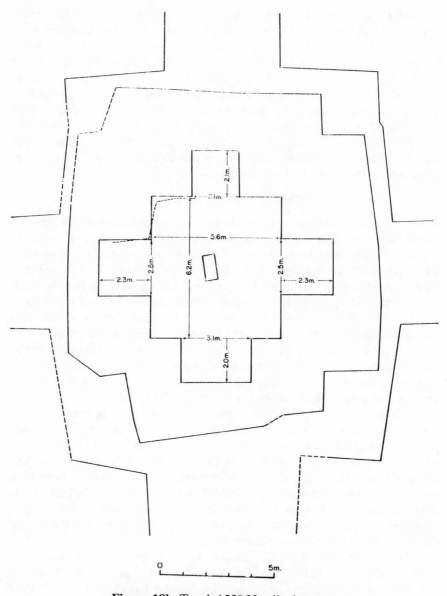

0   5m.

Figure 18b Tomb 1550 Houjiazhuang:
Reconstruction of the wooden burial chamber

From Liang Siyong and Gao Quxun, *Houjiazhuang 1550-hao
da mu,* figs 2 & 3

coffin of the deceased. In the four tombs in which the remains of the chambers could still be traced (1001, 1003, 1004 and 1550), the chambers were *ya*-shaped. Two examples are illustrated in figures 17 and 18. The chamber of one of these (1001) is a simple *ya* (see fig. 16). That of the other might more properly be described as a central square with side chambers attached, but since any *ya*-shape can also be so described, we may see it as a variation of the same basic structure. Besides these royal tombs, a large two-ramped tomb excavated at Hougang 後岡 also had a *ya*-shaped wooden chambers.[30] *Ya*-shaped earthen pits and wooden chambers were clearly awkward to construct and such labour would not have been undertaken unless the shape had a particular meaning.

THE SYMBOLISM OF THE CENTER

Mircea Eliade has written extensively about the significance of the symbolism of the center in the ritual of archaic religions. According to Eliade, the center is "preeminently the zone of the sacred, the zone of absolute reality", that is it is at this point alone that there is perfect access to and harmony with the spirit world. He further formulates a series of beliefs which are common to many archaic peoples. These include a belief in a sacred mountain (or giant tree) which is situated at the center of the world. This sacred mountain is the point at which the world originated and it is the meeting point of heaven and earth. The mountain is the axis of the world and all temples and palaces and, by extension, all cities and royal residences are symbolic representations of this axis and all of these may also be regarded as places where heaven, earth and hell meet.[31]

This formulation has many aspects which will immediately appear familiar to sinologists and I do not think it will be necessary to convince anyone with any acquaintance with the Chinese tradition of the importance of the symbolism of the center to the Chinese who, after all, still call their country *Zhongguo* 中國, the central country. The reason why there is so much resemblance between the beliefs of archaic peoples in different parts of the world is not, I believe, because of any common mental archetype or common inheritance but for structural reasons which are related to the dualism inherent in mythological thinking.

The human mind naturally tends to think in terms of contrasts: good implies bad; above, below; the sky, the earth; east, west, . . . Myths which are tales are necessarily linear. As Levi-Strauss has demonstrated, they proceed spirally, in a never-ending continuum of thesis, antithesis, and synthesis. In the Judeo-Christian tradition, such contrasts are usually defined as being in absolute opposition; in the Chinese tradition of *yin* 陽 and *yang* 陰, they are understood as complementary, but both traditions reflect a native tendency to think in binary terms.[32]

According to my earlier reconstructions, the Shang identified themselves with the ten suns which rose one by one on the ten days of the Shang ritual week from the branches of the Fu Sang tree in the far east of the world and flew as birds across the sky to set in the Ruo Tree in the far west. Mythologically, the Shang were associated with the suns, birds, the Fu Sang tree, fire, the sky, the east, and these motifs were in contrast to those traditionally associated with the Xia, that is moons, dragons, the Ruo Tree, water, the Yellow Springs, the west. This system provided the prototype for the dualism later described in terms of *yin* and *yang*. In terms of directions, east from which the suns rose was contrasted with the west where they entered the watery underworld.

Cosmologically, however, dualism is insufficient. East implies west, but east and west imply north and south. As man stands upon the apparent plane of the earth, he can only achieve a sense of harmony by standing at the center of a circle or at the axis of the four directions: at this point alone there is no contrasting position. It is the centrality of this axis, then which is implied by the *ya*, at the center of which the dead can rest in peace and offerings be received directly by the ancestral spirits. The dead were placed literally at the center of the axis in the *ya*-shaped tombs; and symbolically within the *ya* in the inscriptions on the bronze vessels. The symbolism of the *ya* on the footrings of the vessels is less specific, but these were, after all, offering vessels for the dead ancestors.

Eliade stressed the significance of the sacred mountain as the symbol of the center and place of the earth's origin. In some early civilizations, the central mountain is called the navel of the earth. Although models of a sacred mountain do not appear in the Chinese tradition until the late Warring States and Han times when bronze censors often depict such a supernatural mountain and a *ya* shape rather than the sacred mountain appears to have been used to symbolize centrality by the Shang, in China, too, there was a tradition of a mountain at the center of the earth. In Han astronomy, the central mountain was usually identified with Kunlun and Han astronomical calculations were based upon the supposition of this center.[33] However, Kunlun, on the borderland of Xinjiang province and Tibet, was far from the center of Shang civilization and possibly not even known to them. According to a competing tradition, however, one associated with ritual rather than astronomy, the central mountain was Song Mountain 嵩山 in Henan Province, the central peak (*zhong yue* 中岳) of the five sacred peaks.

In Shang oracle bone inscriptions, the *di* 禘 rite was performed to *Yue* 岳 (𛲢) (the Peak) and *He* 河 (𠂤) (the River) as well as to the four *fang* and the high ancestors. *He* is easily identified as the Yellow River. The identity of *Yue* is less certain, but I believe it to be Songshan. Anyang is

dominated by the Taihang mountain range to the west, but the area between Yanshi 偃師, the site of the first Shang capital and Zhengzhou 鄭州,
a capital of the middle period, is dominated by Songshan. Indeed, the importance of this site goes back much earlier than the Shang for a neolithic
city or castle wall (approximately 100 meter square) dating to the mid-third
millenium B.C. has been discovered in the foothills of Dengfeng,
Gaochengzhen 登封, 高城鎮.[34]

When this site at Dengfeng was first excavated, it was identified with
the Xia Dynasty because it was traditionally known as the place of Yu's
capital, Yangcheng 陽城 (the 'City of the Sun'). It was here that Yu's wife,
the lady of Tu Mountain, turned into a stone and gave birth to Qi, as
discussed in the previous chapter. This was later disputed because radiocarbon dating suggested an even earlier date than the Xia dynasty. I believe, however, that this traditional association of the site with Yu is significant,but that it may be better interpreted in terms of myth and ritual. The
story of Yu controlling the flooding waters is a type of creation story—
the creation of the first physical and political order in the world, if not of
the earth itself. As I discussed in Chapter 2, the same flood myth is also
reflected in the story of the Shang minister Yi Yin's birth when his mother
turned into the Hollow Mulberry after looking at the flooding waters. As I
observed therein, the Hollow Mulberry is a cosmic mountain and it is
also identified with the Yellow Emperor and other Xia ancestors. As Qi
Wenxin has demonstrated, Yin 尹 is a title and Yi 伊 the name of a state
located on the Yi River.[35] The name Yangcheng also suggests a relationship with the Mulberry Tree tradition in which, as I have argued, both
the Xia ancestors and the Shang were complementary parts. The identification of Song Mountain with the center and the myth of the flood may have
a neolithic origin and even then it may have been a cult center. This would
explain the walled enclosure which was too small in any case to enclose a
city.

Eliade described the central mountain of ancient cosmologies as the
meeting point between heaven and earth. That so many ancient peoples
should believe that a high mountain (or sometimes a giant tree) should
be a point of access from the earth to heaven is natural—mountains reach
up into the sky. Cosmologically, man must orient himself not only two-
dimensionally—with regard to the four directions—but also three-
dimensionally—with regard to above and below. Above and below may be
understood as either the sky above and the earth below or as the sky above
and an underworld below, and Eliade refers to the sacred mountain as both
the meeting point between heaven and earth and as that between heaven,
earth and hell.

In China there were also both orientations. Indeed, the problem is confused because *xia* 下, 'below' in the expression *shang xia* 上下, 'above and below' can mean either the earth (*di* 地), that is 'that under heaven' (*tian xia* 天下) or that which is below the earth, that is the Yellow Springs. In Shang ritual as recorded in the oracle bone inscriptions, there is a six pointed orientation implied in the offerings to the four quadrates, and to Yue 岳, the mountain reaching up the sky and He 河, the river descending beneath the earth and fed by springs. *Tian* 天, 'heaven' occurs only rarely in the inscriptions, if at all—some scholars would interpret the character in Shang inscriptions as *da* 大. *Di* 地 does not occur at all. Only in Zhou times is the ruler described as the son of heaven, ruling all-under-heaven. This suggests that the identification of above and below with heaven and earth occurred with the overthrow of the Shang by the Zhou and the identification of the Lord on high with the Zhou god 'Heaven'. Nevertheless, the Shang were aware, as are all men, that the sky surmounted the earth and both orientations of sky and earth and sky and underworld were undoubtedly present in their minds as they were in later times.

FIVE AND SIX

In the following, I will argue that the turtle was a model of the Shang cosmos, seen as the sky and the earth with four pillars in the northeast, southeast, northwest and southwest. Before turning to this argument, however, I will make a few remarks about the numbers five and six in the patterns already described. The literature about the development of Chinese numerology, especially *wu xing* theory, is very extensive and will not be dealt with herein, but the patterns described above have important implications to the understanding of this development which should be noted.[36]

The earth as symbolized by the *ya xing* had five parts: a center and four quadrates.[37] The number five is particularly important in the oracle bone inscriptions. There were five mountains 五山 and Shang Di 上帝 had five ministers 五臣. We do not know the function of these ministers. Some scholars have suggested that they represented the forces of nature, rain, wind, the clouds and lightning, because these forces received Di's orders just as the ministers did. Another possibility, however, is that they reigned over the five parts of the earth. Beginning in the second period, there was also a regular schedule of five rites. Furthermore divinations were frequently repeated five times, sometimes on a set of five shells, as I shall discuss again later on.

This suggests that the number five was already of importance in the Shang and that its primary image was geographical, the divisions of the earth represented by the *ya xing*. Guo Moruo's reconstruction of the calendar chart of the You guan 幼宮 (or Xuan gong 玄宮, as it should probably be titled) of the *Guanzi* 管子 takes the form of a *ya xing* (see Figure 19).[38] The *Yue ling* 月令 is closely tied to the Ming Tang 明堂, which also has this shape. Many scholars have supposed that this it was the result of a correlation between four seasons and a number theory based on five. The Shang, however, had only two seasons—spring 春 and autumn 秋. Summer 夏 does not appear in bronze inscriptions until the Spring and Autumn period.[39] (The first appearance of winter 冬 is less easily determined because the same character is used for 終). This suggests that the geographical division of the world into five parts was the *source* of the significance of the number five, not a later development.

Two-dimensionally, the earth was divided into five parts. When the cosmos was seen three-dimensionally, however, there were six divisions— *shang* above, *xia* below and the *si fang* in which *xia* might be understood as either the central region of the earth or as the land beneath the earth, the Yellow Springs. In Zhou texts, these six divisions were called the six *ji* 六極 poles, the six *he*, '六合'—as in the *Zhuangzi* 莊子, "Inside the six *he*, how did the birth of the ten thousand things come about?" (*Zeyang* 則陽, 8/58a–b), or the six *mo* 六謨 as in the *Chuci Yuan you* 楚辭. 遠游, "I toured the four outlands and travelled all around the six *mo*."[40]

In Zhou texts, schemes of six alternate with schemes of five before the systemization which took place at the end of the Warring States Period. The six *qi* 氣 were of particular importance, as in the *Zuozhuan* 左傳 (Zhao Gong 1):

> Heaven has six vapours (*qi* 氣) which descend and give birth to the five flavors, going out produce the five colors, are called up in the five tones, and in excess give birth to the six sufferings. The six vapours are called *yin*, *yang*, wind, rain, dark and light; separated, they make the four seasons and in sequence, the five degrees.

Here, the six *qi* include *yin* and *yang*. As Xu Fuguan 徐復觀 has demonstrated, these originally referred to sunshine and shade.[41] The six *qi* are correlated with sets of five and with the four seasons.

If my reconstruction of the cosmos is correct, then these schemes of six, as well as those of five and four, may derive from Shang cosmology. As I will discuss in this following chapter, the repetition of propositions on the oracle bones five or six times may also represent these divisions. There are also sets of six numbers on some bones which Zhang Zhenglang has related to the hexagrams of the *Yijing* 易經.[42] These sets of six numbers and the use of six lines in the hexagrams may also derive from these same divisions.

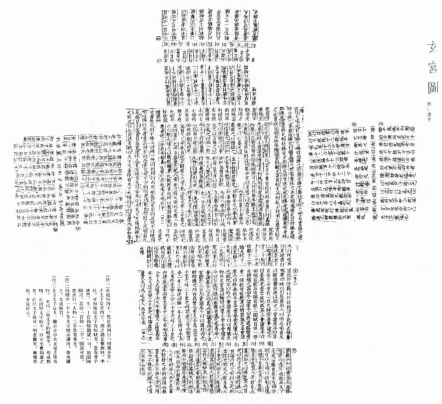

Figure 19 Plan of the Dark Palace (*Xuan Gong*)

From Guo Moruo, et al, *Guanzi jijiao*, p. 140

THE SHAPE OF THE TURTLE

Pyromancy—divination by fire—began in China in the fourth millennium B.C. and grew gradually in the sophisticated system of the late Shang Dynasty.[43] In neolithic times, various bones from different animals, including pigs, dogs, sheep and oxen, were used in divinations. These animals had already begun to be offered to the ancestors in ritual sacrifice and the idea of reading cracks on animal bones which had been produced by the deliberate application of heat may have derived naturally from accidental cracking when the sacrifices were burnt by fire.[44] By the late Shang period, however, the bones were carefully prepared before cracking, including the boring or scooping out of hollows at the points where the heat was to be applied, and divination was largely restricted to the scapulae of water buffalo or cattle (the two are difficult to distinguish from their bones) and turtle shells, particularly the plastron or undershell of the turtle. The oracle bone inscriptions record the offering of turtles in tribute to the Shang kings and these may have come from as far away as Burma.[45]

The reason for favoring the scapulae of water buffalo or cattle in divination is easily surmised: they had the largest flat surface of any common animal bone, a surface which was readily prepared for the inscriptions which were now engraved beside the divination cracks. When the spine was removed from the back side—that on which the hollows were made—and part of the socket was sawn off, the scapulae were also easily stacked. Turtle plastrons were also a flat surface, but they were more than that. They were, as I shall argue below, a model of the earth.

As many scholars have noticed, the turtle with its round, domed upper shell and flat undershell resembles the ancient Chinese concept of a round, domed sky and flat earth. That the turtle and the cosmos were identified, at least in Han times, is evident in the following myth in which the goddess Nü Gua 女媧 used the legs of a turtle to prop up the sky:

> In a time long ago, the four poles (*ji* 極) were decayed and the nine states, rent asunder. The sky did not cover everywhere and the earth was not filled in all around. Fire raged and flamed without dying out; water swelled and rose without dying down. Fierce beasts ate the vigorous and vultures snatched the old and weak. Then, Nü Gua smelted stones of five colors and patched up the azure sky and cut off the legs of a sea-turtle to stand up the four poles . . .
>
> *Huainanzi* 6/6b

The *Huainanzi* from which this passage was taken was compiled in the early second century B.C. The same story was recorded in almost identical language in the first century A.D. by the rationalist Wang Chong who argued, quite reasonably, that if there was a turtle big enough for its legs to hold up the sky, it would have filled the whole world and that its legs, being made of flesh and bone, would have quickly rotted.[46] The language of Wang Chong's account of this myth in the *Lun heng* 論衡 is so similar to that of the *Huainanzi* that it must either derive directly from that text or from a common source. In the *Lun heng* version of the story, however, its setting is the destruction caused by Gong Gong 共工 in his battle with Zhuan Xu 顓頊 to become Lord (*di* 帝). This story also appears in the *Huainanzi*, again in almost identical language, but divorced from the story of Nü Gua and in a different part of the text.

According to the *Huainanzi* (3/1a–b):

Previously, when Gong Gong fought with Zhuan Xu to become Lord, in his rage, he butted the Mountain which cannot be circumnavigated (*Bu zhou zhi shan* 不周之山). The sky's pillar was broken and the tie with the earth severed. The sky inclined to the northwest, and so the heavenly bodies move in that direction. The earth was not full in the southeast, and so the water and dust go there.

From these accounts in the *Huainanzi*, repeated in the *Lun heng*, we know that the likeness between a turtle and the cosmos was not a scholarly metaphor, but an ancient mythic identification. We also know that the legs of the turtle which held up the sky were not in the cardinal directions, but in the northwest, southwest, southeast and northeast.

The earliest references to this mythology are the cryptic references of the *Tian wen* or 'Heavenly questions' section of the *Chuci*. Nü Gua appears in the line, "Nü Gua had a form; who made and shaped it?" 女媧有體 孰製匠之 .[47] Although the commentators take this as a reference to Nü Gua's unusual form—in Han stone reliefs she is depicted with a human head and upper torso and a serpent's body, the primary point of the line is a reference to her role as a creator goddess. More to the point is a line which refers to Gong Gong, here called Kang Hui 康回: "When Kang Hui raged in anger, why did the earth slant in the southeast?" 康回馮怒何故以 東南傾 .[48] The *Tian wen* also asks, "Who knows the number of the many jigs and jags of the boundaries of Heaven's sections?" 幾天之際 安放安屬隅隈多有誰知其數 .[49] The meaning of 隅隈 is not at all clear, but these recall the sutures which join the sections of a turtle shell.

Léon Vandermeersch has argued that the turtle represents the totality of time rather than space and turtles were associated with longevity.[50] This association which is made in many cultures is evident from the *Shiji*: "When I went to Jiangnan, . . ., I heard of a turtle who perambulated on a lotus leaf for a thousand years." And, "In the south, an old man used turtles as the legs of his bed. When over twenty years later, the old man died, and they moved the bed, the turtles were still alive. Turtles can make their vital breath move and . . . ."[51] However, the cosmos was always assumed to be eternal before modern physics and so the longevity of the turtle would have contributed to rather than contradicted the association of the turtle with the physical cosmos.

Although many scholars have observed the resemblance of the turtle to the Chinese vision of the cosmos, they have not, to my knowledge, recognized the significance of the shape of the plastron. A turtle plastron, or undershell, is not square, the shape of the earth in later times, but roughly speaking, a cross or *ya*-shape, that of the earth as I have reconstructed it above (see Figures 23 and 24). As I observed previously, the *ya*-shape may be seen either as a large square from which the four corners have been removed or as a small square surrounded by four others, both of which could have provided the origin of the later theory of a square earth.

As a large square with its corners removed, the *ya* resembles the turtle plastron with its indentations for four legs and also the base of a square *ding* vessel, the piece mould of which was also *ya*-shaped before the legs were attached. If there were four legs—or mountains—in the northeast, northwest, southeast and southwest and a circle is drawn to represent the sky which the legs held up, the image is:

If the cross-shape is then extended so that it becomes a large square, then the shape is:

Significantly, this is the shape of the ritual jade object, the *cong* 琮, which occurs with the round *bi* 璧 disc, from neolithic times (see Figure 29) and is traditionally associated with the earth. The square then has nine parts, the number of states in the Zhou texts and there are also eight quadrates (八方) outside the central square.

Each of the eight quadrates had a pillar and the *Tian wen* enquires, "How were the eight pillars placed?" [52] Although the *ya*-shape has eight points where pillars could be placed to hold up a circular sky, these are usually assumed to be located in the eight directions and this is implied by the following line, "why is the southeast deficient?" However, the eight pillars could not be at the far points of the eight directions upon a square earth and hold up a circular sky. Thus they would appear to be the original four pillars of the northwest, southwest, southeast and northeast, to which pillars at the extremes of the cardinal directions have been added:

The pillars of the east and west are probably the Mulberry Tree and the Ruo Mu, to which two further pillars in the north and south have been added.

Besides using turtle shells for divination, the Shang made models of turtles in jade and stone, but the function of such models is not understood. Turtles also appear as a motif in Shang bronze art. There, they are among the few creatures which are always portrayed realistically as a single animal rather than as part of a composite. The upper shell of the turtle is always decorated with circles, the number of which is not consistent. Illustrations may be seen in Figures 20 and 22. Frequently, there is a central circle with a whorl motif and in some examples, there is only this central circle. This motif is identified with the character 囧 meaning fire.

The meaning of these circles is not known. In one early model, the back of the turtle has a grid pattern which suggested that the circles may represent the sections of the turtle shell.[53] However, the inconsistency of the number of circles and the use of the whorl suggest another possibility, that these are heavenly bodies. In Han tomb art, stars were conventionally represented as circles. Thus, these, too, might be stars. If this interpretation is correct, then the identification of the turtle with the physical shape of the cosmos in Shang times would be confirmed for the upper shell would clearly be the sky.

The positions of the turtle motif in Shang bronzes suggest that turtles were regarded as water animals. They are mostly frequently found in the middle position of the bowl on *pan* 盤 water basins (see Figures 20 and 22). This position is alternatively occupied by bottle-horned dragons (see Chapter 6, p. 162). Other *pan* motifs include fish and birds. This suggests that they are symbolic ponds, perhaps representing the *Xian chi* 咸池 (also

Figure 20a Turtle motifs on bronze vessels

a: Turtle and fish motifs from the inside of a *pan water basin*.

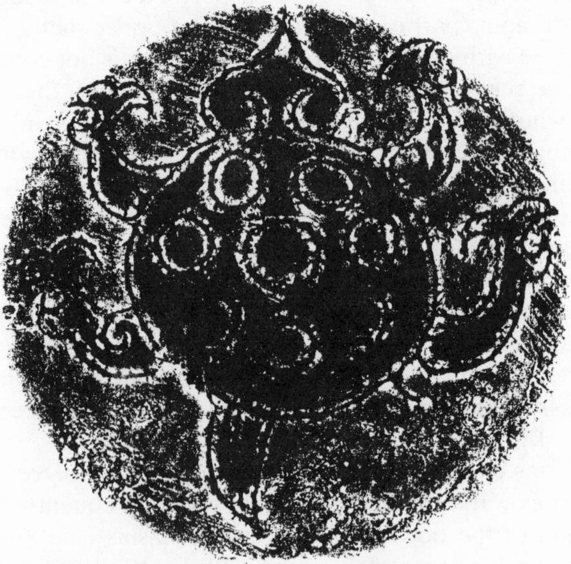

Figure 20b Turtle motif on the underside of a
pan water basin

a: From *Shaanxi chutu Shang-Zhou qingtong* qi, vol. I, p. 67

Figures 21a and 21b *Pan*-water basin with Bottle-horned
Dragon Motif

Courtesy of the Freer Gallery of Art, Smithsonian Institution, Washington, D.C.,
Accession number 56.26.

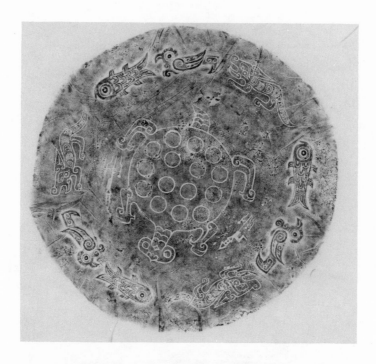

Figures 22a and 22b *Pan*-water basin with Turtle Motif

Courtesy of the Asian Art Museum of San Francisco (The Avery Brundage
Collection), Accession number B60 B1001

called the Tang 湯 or *Yang gu* 陽［崵］谷; see p. 64) and Yu Yuan 虞淵, the entries to the under world. Turtles are also found on the underside of vessels, where they also alternate with dragons (see Figures 15b and 29).

This association of turtles with water is consistent with the species of turtle used in Shang divination, almost all of which were water rather than land species. Furthermore, the oxen which were used in divination may have been water oxen.[54] In divination, a crack was made by applying a red hot hardwood poker to the shell or bone. Thus, in the case of the turtle, and possibly also in the case of oxen, fire was applied to water—the two primary cosmic forces identified with *yang* and *yin* were conjoined.

V

Divination and Sacrifice

Every divinatory rite, however simple it
may be, rests on a pre-existing sympathy
between certain beings, and on a
traditionally admitted kinship between a
certain sign and a certain future event.
Further, a divinatory rite is generally not
isolated, it is part of an organized whole.
The science of the diviners, therefore,
does not form isolated groups of things,
but binds these groups to each other. At
the basis of a system of divination there is
thus, at least implicitly a system of
classification.

Emile Durkheim and Marcel Mauss,
Primitive classification, p. 73

As I have discussed in the previous chapter, the turtle was a model of the
cosmos as it was envisioned by the Shang kings and their diviners and in
applying a red-hot poker to a turtle shell or the bone of a water ox, the
diviner combined the two cosmic forces of fire and water. The division of
the earth into five parts, the belief in lands above and below, and the use of
a cosmic model for divination suggest a new interpretation of Shang oracle
bone divination.

The ancient Greek philosopher Plato and the Roman Cicero distinguished two kinds of divination. The first, defined as an art, was inductive—
by studying omens. Such omens were signs which indicated good or bad
fortune to follow, such as extraordinary natural phenomena, lightning,
cloud movements, bird flight, unusual animal behaviour. The other, which
Plato considered a later and higher form of divination, could not be taught
for it was intuitive. Its mark was divine possession or ecstatic trance. The
oracles delivered by the priestess of Delphi and other shrines were state-

ments foretelling the future in enigmatic language produced by such possession.[1]

In China, there is clear evidence of the use of possession and trance in religious ritual, if not necessarily in divination, in later Chu culture. Although some scholars believe such practices can be traced back to the Shang,[2] divination using the so-called oracle bones did not involve trance or divine possession. Signs which indicated good or bad fortune were produced mechanically upon the bone. As discussed previously, such signs may originally have been produced naturally when the bones were burnt in rites of sacrifice. Later they were produced deliberately and by the late Shang period, the bones or shells were carefully prepared with hollows bored on the reverse side, allowing considerable control over the resulting *bu* ⼘ -shaped cracks. The turtle which was shaped like the cosmos also came to be a favored medium. These signs were omens which had come to be produced artificially rather than naturally and they were studied for signs of good or bad fortune.

If we thus regard Shang oracle bones as models for the cosmos upon which omens were produced by artificially combining the cosmic forces of fire and water, then we can begin to understand how Shang divination operated. I will argue below that this system was not an attempt to foretell the future, as commonly supposed, but to control it through ritual sacrifice. The acceptance of proferred sacrifices or the need for further sacrifice to prevent impending curses was indicated by the omens produced upon the bones. The Shang divination system was extremely complex; more than one school of diviners appear to have worked during the reign of each king and the system changed greatly over the two to three hundred year period during which Yinxu was the Shang ritual center. Nevertheless, I propose the following generalities about Shang divination in the belief that the principles which motivated Shang divination did remain the same—and in the expectation that the hypothesis outlined below will need further refinement.

Shang divination has certain enigmatic features which have not been adequately explained. These include:

1. The vast majority of divination inscriptions include only a charge or proposition, prefaced by the cyclical date upon which the crack was made and the name of the diviner who performed the ceremony, for example 'it will rain', 'it will not rain', 'the coming ten-day week will be without disaster', 'coming and going there will be no misfortune', 'we shall offer one cow to Father Yi', 'it is Mother Geng who is cursing us'. . . . Prognostications—in which the king interpreted

the crack and made a statement about its meaning (*zhan* 占)—were not usually recorded. Verifications in which it was recorded what really (*yun* 允) did happen are even more rare. This emphasis is so overwhelming that it cannot be accidental.

2. The divinations were inscribed *after* the crack was made; thus the charge was not inscribed in order to communicate it to the spirits, but as a matter of record that it had been made.[3]

3. Grammatically, the charges are normally recorded as statements rather than interrogatives, with a limited number of exceptions, primarily within the Shi 自 and Wu 午 diviner groups.[4]

4. The charges are often put in both affirmative and negative modes. For example, in *Heji* 合集 9950, illustrated in Figure 23, the inscription on the right side reads, "Cracked on the *bingchen* day, Que divining, we shall receive millet harvest" and that on the left, "Cracked on the *bingchen* day, Que divining, we shall not perhaps receive millet harvest". On turtle plastrons, such as this, the inscriptions often mirror one another and some of the characters are written in mirror form, as are the name of the diviner Que 殻 and the character for harvest, *nian* 年, in this example. The cracks (*bu* 卜) also mirror one another, as they do here, including the angle of the horizontal line.

5. The same charges are made repeatedly, normally five times.[5] Six and ten are also not uncommon. The repeated charges may be made on a single bone or shell, as on *Heji* 9950, on which the repetitions are simply indicated by the numbers one to five by the cracks on each side. They may also be made on a series of shells or bones, as on the set of five plastrons, *Heji* 6482–6486 (*Bingbian* 丙編 12–21), the third of which is reproduced in figure 24 On these shells, the same charges are recorded on each of five shells, albeit in somewhat abbreviated form in later examples. The number of the charge is also indicated beside the crack; thus all of the cracks on this example have the number three.

In order to understand why the charge rather than the prognostication was the focus of attention and why the charges were statements rather than questions, we must briefly review the contents of the charges. In *Sources of Shang History*, David Keightley lists some seventeen topics as the major areas of concern in Period I divinations. His list, which generally follows an earlier listing of Dong Zuobin, includes: sacrifices, military campaigns, hunting expeditions, excursions, the ten-day week, the night or the day, the weather, agriculture, sickness, childbirth, distress or trouble, dreams, settlement building, orders, tribute payments, divine assistance or approval,

and requests addressed to ancestral or nature powers. If we analyse the contents of the inscriptions, however, we find that they may be divided into three general categories:

(1) divinations about ritual offerings;
(2) divinations about the future; and
(3) divinations about calamities which had already befallen the king, his people, or the land.

(1)

Divinations about ritual offerings to the ancestors and nature spirits are the most common topic. The charge names the spirit or spirits to whom the offering(s) are addressed, the rite to be performed, and often specifies a type of animal or human sacrifice. *Heji* 6484, for example, includes the charge "Divining, we shall offer a *you* 出 -sacrifice of dog(s) to Father Geng and a cut-open sheep." Numbers of victims are often specified, for example "Crack-making on the *guihai* day, Que divining, we shall make a burning sacrifice to Shang Jia 上甲 of three sheep and a *you*-offering of ten beheaded humans and ten Qiang tribesmen and a pig." (*Hebian* 合編 162).

Although the precise nature of many of the rites is not understood, a large proportion of them involved the sacrifice of animals and people and such sacrifices have been confirmed by archaeological excavations. Grain and wine were also offered and ceremonies performed which included music and dance. In the first period, alternative offerings were sometimes proposed, such as *Yibian* 乙編 4747, "Cracked on the *gengxu* day, Bin divining, on the next *jiayin* day, we shall make a *you*-offering of five cows to Shang Jia", "Divining, on the next *jiayin* day, we shall make a *you*-offering of three cows to Shang Jia." However, the schedule of offerings quickly became standardized and by the fifth period the proposed offerings were simply validated on the last (*gui* 癸) day, before the start of a new ten-day week. As discussed in the second chapter of this work, the ancestors received sacrifices on the day of the sun with which they were classified.

(2)

The second category of charges are divinations about the future. The purpose of such charges was not to predict the future, as I will discuss further in the following, but to discover by the signs produced upon the shell or bone whether, *under present circumstances,* the king and his associates, land, etc., would meet with good or bad fortune in the future. The charges in this category may be further divided into three groups.

(a) Divinations about Nature

These divinations are primarily about fertility, either agricultural or human and include both harvest and childbirth. Death and birth are the two sides of man's life and in other early cultures, the desire for fertility is closely linked to the deliberate taking of life in ritual sacrifice. This was un-doubtedly also the case in China even though the divination system was such that charges concerning ritual sacrifice and charges concerning fertil-ity are discrete units. There is, however, an exception in the *qiu* 求 -rite, often translated as prayer which is made for harvest or rain and which may include animal sacrifices, for example, "We shall offer a prayer to Shang Jia for rain, one penned(?) sheep" (*Yibian* 2508). More commonly, howev-er, divinations such as 'we shall receive millet harvest' or 'Lady Hao's childbirth will be lucky' are only linked by implication to those concerning ritual sacrifice.

Divinations about the weather were also divinations about the harvest. When the Shang kings proposed 'it shall rain' or 'it shall not rain', his intention was not, I believe, to *find out* whether or not it would rain; he was *not* trying to prophesy a predetermined future. Nor was it a disinterested question. He either needed rain for the harvest or needed for it to stop. What he wished to discover was whether the spirits were pleased or dis-pleased and thus whether the harvest would be cursed or blessed—rain was itself a blessing or a curse, as were wind, storms, etc. This is evident both in alternative divinations that the Lord on High will 'order rain', 'send down drought', etc. and also in the third category of divinations which I will discuss below, in which the diviners attempted to discover which spirit was responsible for a curse upon the rain, harvest, etc.

(b) Divinations about Proposed Activities of the King and his Associates

Again the king wished to know whether such activities would be auspicious or not. It is often stated that the Yin kings divined about most of their activities. Although a comprehensive review has not been possible, pre-liminary study indicates that they divined only about a limited number of activities of ritual significance. The most common topics are hunting, war-fare and misfortune 'going and coming' (*wanglai* 往來), which may be an-other aspect of these same activities. As Walter Burkert has observed, "for the ancient world, hunting, sacrifice and war were symbolically inter-changeable'.[6] All three acts were demonstrations of the ruler's power to kill and, in the Chinese case at least, both animals and humans were captured for use in ritual sacrifice. Divinations about agricultural activities and the building of cities were also made but they too were of ritual significance.

We may also include in this category divinations about receiving tribute. Such divinations which state that a certain tribe or state will send in a certain number of turtles, Qiang tribesmen, horses, dogs, are clear evidence that the divinations were not intended to foretell the future—the king could not have been divining to *find out* whether so many turtles, Qiang, dogs, *would* be sent, but whether, if they were sent, it would be auspicious. Such tribute, we may reasonably assume, was primarily for ritual use, although the horses may have been for warfare. Similarly, in divinations about military campaigns, the king could not have divined to *find out* whether he or one of his commanders would follow another but, again, whether, if he did so, it would be auspicious.

(c) Divinations Which State that Misfortune Will Not Occur Within a Given Time Period, Such as an Evening or a Ten-day Ritual Week (*xun* 旬)

Divinations which state that misfortune will not occur within a given time period are always negative, that 'there will be no misfortune', never affirmative. In this they are similar to divinations about coming and going (*wang lai* 往來).

(3)

The third category of divinations concern misfortunes which have already happened rather than the future. These provide the clue to the relationship between the two other categories. The purpose of such divination was to determine the source of the misfortune or omen—the identity of the spirit who was cursing the king, his land, or his entourage—and alternative names were sometimes proposed in a series of divinations, for example 'Ancestress Jia is cursing the king', 'Ancestress Yi is cursing the king'. Such misfortunes might be visited upon the land ('the Peak [*Yue* 岳] is cursing the harvest', 'the Peak is not cursing the rain'. Or they might be visited upon the king personally or on his associates, for example "the king's bellyache, it is ancestress Ji who is cursing" (*Yibian* 7797). Dreams were also curses, and the identity of the responsible spirit was the subject of such divination, for example 'Divining, the king's dream—it is Da Jia' (*Yibian* 6638). (The problem is not, as sometimes imagined, who appeared in the king's dream but who sent it).

This category of offerings only occurs in the first period (during the reign of Wu Ding) in which there were also alternative proposals concerning the ritual sacrifices. This suggests that the purpose in determining which spirit was responsible for a curse was to rectify the offerings made to him. When the ritual schedule had become standardized, there are no longer such attempts to discover the cause of a particular calamity. Indeed, in the fifth period, when the offerings had become entirely routine, they simply divined, 'the coming ten-day week will be without misfortune', 'coming and going there will be no calamity'. Although such generalized divinations had replaced the more specific divinations, that it will or will not rain on a certain day, that the king should follow a certain commander, etc. and the system became conventionalized, the purpose was still to determine that the offerings would be accepted by the spirits and that they would not curse the king or his people.

Both Walter Burkert and René Girard have provided psychological explanations for the role of sacrifice in primitive communities, arguing that it served to direct the natural aggressive instincts inherent in any community upon selected victims and by the collective act of killing to establish a sense of social unity.[7] Another solution to the problem of sacrifice, however, is that it was not an attempt to direct aggression in the community, but the violence of the natural world which would otherwise randomly select its victims. Even in an early agricultural community no longer dependent upon hunting, man's aggressive instinct could still be directed against external enemies in warfare, but once he had begun the struggle to control his environment by sowing and reaping seasonally and had become sedentary, he was helpless in the face of the caprices of nature which might withhold rain or bring it in torrents, bring swarms of locusts to devastate a crop, or send disease to him or his livestock.

Burkert has observed that among the Greeks and Romans, the fire that burns the corpse is described as a beast of prey "tearing apart" the dead man with a "furious jaw".[8] K. C. Chang has also noted the importance of the open animal mouth as a symbol of passage to the other world in many early cultures,[9] and its importance as an image on the sacrificial vessels of the Shang will be discussed in the following chapter. Indeed, the world beyond must have seemed to early man like an ever hungry beast, randomly consuming men, animals and crops.

The heart of the agricultural revolution was a primitive recognition of the yearly cycle of growth and death in plants and an attempts to control and take advantage of that cycle. Yet there were still other forces or cycles not so easily perceived which might bring death and destruction. How could these forces be controlled? I do not know whether all sacrifice in early societies can be understood as an attempt to control and direct natural violence, but Shang sacrifice can be so understood. On the one hand, sacrifices were offered and their appropriateness determined by signs upon the bone or shell. On the other, future activities were proposed to determine whether blessings or misfortune would befall them. If, when the system was still flexible, misfortunes did happen, then the cause of the curse was determined in order that new offerings might be proposed. By providing meat, grain and wine, the kings and their diviners hoped that they and their harvest would not be taken by the unseen forces of the cosmos.

The duty of the diviner was to ensure that the appropriate offerings were made so that the future would be auspicious or, at least, so that calamity could be avoided by anticipating the needs of the spirits who would otherwise wreak havoc randomly. He thus proposed his offerings and cracked the bone. His statement stood for the intended act; the shell or bone, for the cosmos. He was not asking whether offerings should be made; he was stating that they would or would not be made in order to elicit a response—an omen of good or evil fortune. This is the reason that a statement was made rather than a question asked. Divinations about the future were the other side of this same system. They were an attempt to confirm that the spirits were satisfied with the offerings and that they had been received rather than an attempt to prophesy the future. A statement about what would happen was made in order to elicit a response. If the offerings were satisfactory, then the future would produce 'no misfortune'.

In the natural world, omens are unusual phenomena. So, too, on the oracle bones, and this is why the proposition is more important than the prognostication. Hollows were made on the back side of the bones and shells and the person who made the crack had such control over them that he could produce mirror images on the two sides of the bone. Normally, he must have expected that no unusual sign would be produced. When there was, there might be a prognostication stating that the divination was auspicious or inauspicious. In the first period, inauspicious prognostications were not rare. By the fifth, however, there was simply a conventional *ji* 吉 'auspicious' in response to a divination about the future—usually simply that there would be no calamity in the coming ten-day week—and then a statement of the offerings which would be made. Presumably, this is because omens of misfortune were no longer produced on the bone or shell— the divinations simply served to verify the sacrifices by communicating them to the spirits.

If we assume that the turtle or bone was meant to stand for the cosmos, then, in making the divination cracks, the diviner was attempting to replicate the forces of nature. I have mentioned above that fire was applied to water. Furthermore, the earth had five parts and there was a world above and below. The diviner hoped to perform his series of cracks without any sign to indicate misfortune and to encompass the entire cosmos in his divinations. Thus, the mirroring of the divination cracks and the propositions made in the affirmative and negative may have been intended to represent lands above and below. By putting the undesirable form of his proposition on the left side and reversing the direction of the cracks, he may have hoped to negate it. Conversely, he would hope to confirm the desirable form put on the other side. By a series of five propositions, the diviner might further hope to account for all parts of the world.

Heji 9950, illustrated in Figure 16, to which I referred previously, is an ideal example of this pattern with its positive and negative propositions, "Cracked on the *bingchen* day, Que divining, we shall receive millet harvest" on the right, and "Cracked on the *bingchen* day, we shall not perhaps receive millet harvest" on the left; a series of five cracks perfectly mirroring each other on each side, each series numbered one to five; and a prognostication on the back, "The king read the crack and said, 'fortunate, we shall receive harvest'." The series of cracks on the face also have the notation *er gao* 二告 'two reports'. This notation frequently occurs when there are such pairs of divinations and may possibly refer to the informing of spirits above and below.[10]

In *Heji* 9950, the charge was evidently repeated five times, in both positive and negative forms. This is indicated by the numbers one to five beside the cracks although the charge is only written out once. *Heji* 6482–6 (Figure 24) on the other hand, are a set of five plastrons on which more than one series of five charges were made. All of the charges on each plastron are numbered the same, three in the case of the plastron illustrated in Figure 24, and the charges are repeatedly inscribed, albeit with some abbreviations. Here, the king is concerned with two problems, whether in the spring(?) he should follow a certain Wang Cheng to attack the Xia Wei, in which case he will receive blessings, or whether (left-hand side) this spring he shall not follow Wang Cheng in attacking the Xia Wei and so will perhaps not receive blessings. He also proposes following a certain Zhi Guo, in two pairs of inscriptions. This might be an alternative, or refer to a different campaign. His other problem is a toothache and there are a pair of inscriptions in which a sacrifice is linked to a curse, "*you*-sacrifice a dog to Fu Geng and cut open a sheep" on the right and "When we make an invocation to stop the aching tooth, we will be favored" on the left; also "the sick tooth will be favorable" and "the sick tooth will not be favorable" again below. On the back are recorded a further series of divinations, probably associated with the cause of the king's toothache: "It is Father Jia", "It is not Father Jia", "It is Father Geng", "It is not Father Geng", "It is Father Xin", "It is not Father Xin", "It is Father Yi; it is not Father Yi."

On the reverse side there is also a prognostication stating that there will be a natural phenomenon 𤲞 (thunder?) and that if it is on the *wu* 戊 day on which there is such a phenomenon it will not be auspicious. (Other days are mentioned as fortunate or unfortunate on other plastrons in the series). Generally, prognostications which do more than indicate auspiciousness or misfortune specify either that certain days of the ten-day cycle would be fortunate or unfortunate, as in this case, or that misfortune will come from a certain direction. This suggests that the five cracks in a series (ten altogether and sometimes series of ten) may have been associated with direction (center and the four quadrates) and/or time (10-day week).

Heji 14295, discussed above (see Figure 11), is not in a typical form, but it can nevertheless be understood in the same manner. First, there were affirmative and negative propositions, on the right and left sides of the plastron, that, " . . . the Lord will order rain" and " . . . the Lord will not perhaps order rain." Then four propositions were put about offering the *di* 禘 -rite to each of the four quadrates. These are only put in the affirmative, but two are on the right and two on the left. All six propositions were cracked four times. In this case, the first two propositions may be taken as representing above and below and these are cracked four times for the four *fang* 方. The next four represent the four *fang* only.

In sum, Shang divination was an attempt to verify that the ritual offerings were received and satisfactory and that there would therefore be no curse. Thus they made a series of positive and negative statements which stood for parts of the cosmos and possibly also for time elements. Normally, the turtle simply confirmed the offerings, but sometimes, especially in the early Yinxu period, a sign was made to indicate unusual fortune. This theory is, of course, speculative. Few examples are as ideal as those which I have cited and a careful working out of the different styles of divination will be needed to validate it. This is planned for a further volume. Nevertheless, I put it forward as a new approach to the interpretation of the Shang divination which may prove fruitful if examined in greater detail.

VI

Art and Meaning

"Any interpretive theory aiming
to account for the meaning of the animal
design on Shang and Zhou bronzes
should explain all of the characteristics
and not just some of them . . . the issue of
the animal design involves . . a series of
questions: Why did the bronze makers of
Shang and Zhou use animal designs on
their decorations? What functions did
these designs serve in Shang ideology?
Why was there such variety? Why do the
figures often appear in pairs? Why do
they sometimes occur together with humans? Why do man and beast appear in
such distinct relationships?"

K. C. Chang,
Art, Myth and Ritual, p. 61.

The motive force of Chinese religion, as I discussed early on in this work, was ancestor worship—the belief that people continue to exist after death, to need food, and to exercise power over the living. Thus, grain offerings were placed in pottery vessels and buried with the dead already in neolithic times. In the late Shang, the ancestral cult dominated the lives of the Shang kings. They not only made offerings of grain and wine made from grain, they hunted other tribesmen and captured them in war or accepted them in tribute from vassal states, and both hunted and raised animals to assuage the hunger of the spirits. As discussed in the previous chapter, the elaborate process of divination which they recorded in the oracle bone inscriptions was in order to ensure that the appropriate offerings were made and received by the spirits.

These offerings were placed in bronze ritual vessels which are the supreme aesthetic and technological achievement of the Shang and the ener-

124

gies devoted to their manufacture are comparable to the vast energies devoted to the divination process. The power of their decoration, like that of much other primitive art, is readily apparent even without understanding. But what was the meaning of their motifs and how are they to be interpreted? Before we can understand the meaning of Shang art, we must turn to the problem of meaning in primitive or mythic art more generally; and if we are to understand the nature of mythic art, we must first return to the question of the nature of myth.

Myths characteristically breach the limitations of natural reality. People live for centuries, turn into animals or inanimate objects, become pregnant by swallowing bird eggs or stepping on footprints, shoot down the suns, pile up earth with a spade to make a mountain, butt a mountain with their head and cause the earth to tilt, walk on water, rise from the dead, become pregnant without sexual intercourse. . . . In myths, there are no limitations to the possible: *anything* not only can happen, but does.

Malinowksi described myths as a charter for social institutions and they often purport to tell the origin of institutions.[1] In a previous chapter, I also suggested that there was a connection between a myth of ten suns rising from the Mulberry Tree and the Shang ritual week in which the ancestors received sacrifices on the day of the week corresponding to the sun with which they were classified. Whatever their function, however, mythical narratives do not themselves express social norms. Just as the physical limitations of the natural world are routinely violated in myth, so too are social norms. Incest, bestiality, patricide, murder, theft, adultery and cannibalism are the very substance of mythical narratives (though more rigidly suppressed in later Chinese rationalizations than the violations of natural laws) and they frequently occur without any hint of moral sanction.

The great insight of Claude Levi-Strauss into the nature of myth was to see that myths have a logical structure, that they derive their meaning as part of a system and that their structural relationship can, to a certain extent, be decoded.[2] Yet this does not explain why they take such a peculiar form or why, in spite of their apparent irrationality, they are believed to be true. The Shang must have known that a woman cannot become pregnant by swallowing a bird egg, just as we know that man cannot walk on water. The problem is not one of the absence of scientific thinking as Levi-Strauss suggests, however, because the most sophisticated of modern space scientists often believe in the literal truth of the impossible events in biblical myths and even the most primitive of peoples could not survive if they did not have recourse to assumptions of cause and effect in the course of their daily lives and make elementary distinctions between the real and the unreal. The *point* of such stories is that they violate reality, that they are impossible in the profane world, and this is easily recognized.

As I have discussed in the second chapter of this work, there is no clearly distinguishable world of the supernatural in the early Chinese textual tradition nor were there gods who were distinguishable in kind from ancestors, dead men who continued to exercise power over the living. Certain stories are distinguishable in the historical tradition as myth not because they concern gods as opposed to men or take place in another sphere of existence, but because common sense tells us that they could not have happened. For this same reason, rationalist Chinese scholars who assumed the validity of the tradition corrected the texts or provided rationalistic glosses contrary to their apparent meaning.

Myths have been defined by Alan Dundes and others as 'sacred narratives', by which they mean that they are stories told in a religious context.[3] This context is, I believe, the key to understanding their meaning for myths are meant to represent that which is beyond this world, that which transcends ordinary reality, the religious dimension of our lives. For this reason, they violate ordinary reality both as a matter of course and as a matter of necessity. The violation of natural limitations is the sign that the stories are concerned with the sacred rather than the ordinary. In order to accept myths, we must suspend our sense of reality and we thus put ourselves on another plane in which ordinary logic does not apply. This does not mean that the myths do not have a logical structure or refer ultimately to the real world or to traditional social institutions, but they do not attempt to *portray* reality. The strange language which characterizes myth is their essential and defining feature and signifies their sacredness, that their truth is one of a world not bound by mundane restrictions.

If myth is thus regarded, as characterized by the breach of natural restrictions, then we can understand the meaning of the strange language which also characterizes the art of mythological societies. Primitive art is an expression of the same religious impulse as myth. Like myth, it alludes to reality, but breaches its norms and limitations. It is characterized by disjunction, distortion, illusion and transformation. Different animals or animals and people may be combined in a single image; necks may be longer than bodies or planes occur where the body is rounded; an image may be two things at once or a head have two bodies; a bird may become a dragon. . . . These characteristics are common to the religious art of so-called primitive peoples throughout the world, though the specific motifs differ and the societies have no common history. This strangeness is not because of a lack of technical sophistication; this may be very high and there are sometimes more representational images within the same culture. Nor is it because the people perceive the world differently than we do; their physical perceptions are surely the same.

As in myth, such breaches of normality are not accidental, but

Figure 25 The Chu silk Manascript

From Noel Barnard, *Scientific Examination of an ancient Chinese document*, p. 2

meaningful. They signify that the art is not of this world but 'other'. They are not illustrations, however, but transformations deriving from the same religious structure as the myths. Illustration is a later phenomenon associated with a developed literary tradition. In order to illustrate a myth, the artist must be able to externalize it and regard it intellectually as an entity. Although the Shang were literate, writing in China appears to have developed in connection with divination as I discussed in Chapter 1. Bamboo slips were used for writing in Shang times because the character *ce* 冊 occurs in the oracle bone inscriptions, but its usage in these inscriptions suggests a further means of communicating with the spirits. The earliest extant texts, the *Shang shu* 尚書 documents, are similar to bronze inscriptions of the Western Zhou period. The gradual development of this tradition can be seen in the gradually lengthening bronze inscriptions at the end of the Shang dynasty. Thus, although there are references to Yin texts in the Zhou documents,[4] the absence of any extant texts and the coalescence of the bronze and text tradition suggest that the use of writing was still severely limited in the Shang dynasty.

The difference between illustrative and mythic art can be seen by comparing the Shang motifs with the paintings on the Chu silk manuscript (see figure 25). Whereas those of the Shang are continually changing and impossible to define precisely, the illustrator of the manuscript has evidently begun with a description of a three-headed creature and then wrestled with the problem of representation. Similarly, when the Han artist wished to illustrate the relationship of the sun and the bird which in Shang times was one of totemic identity, he had to decide *how* the sun and the bird corresponded: he could put the bird in the sun (see figure 7) make the sun the bird's body, or simply represent the sun as a bird. This self-consciousness is not evident in the earlier representations.

SHANG BRONZE MOTIFS

The art with which I will be concerned herein is the decor on the bronze ritual vessels in which the Shang nobility made their ancestral offerings. The bronzes of the Yinxu period are extremely finely cast and beautiful works of art, but although their primary motifs, the so-called *taotie* 饕餮 or animal face (*shou mian* 獸面) and one-legged dragon or *kui* 夔 are well-known and easily recognized (see figures 30–38, 50–52 for illustrations), they have thus far presented an insuperable problem to those who would give them a symbolic rather than simply a formal meaning or relate them to Shang religion as it is known from oracle bone inscriptions. In *Sources of Shang History*, David Keightley recounts that he was once asked the significance of the *taotie* by a colleague who declared that "if you don't understand the *taotie*, you cannot understand the Shang", but, he argues, the *taotie* is "one of the numerous enigmas which the inscriptions have not solved."[5] The problem is that the *taotie* and other motifs on Shang bronzes are not representations of the ancestors or other spirits named in the oracle bone inscriptions. Indeed, although anyone acquainted with Shang art 'knows' that what is known as the *taotie* is its major motif and has no difficulty recognizing it, the motif is so constantly changing that it could not refer to any particular spirit.

To some, the problem of meaning has seemed impenetrable. Others have denied its relevance, regarding the motifs as designs, growing out of abstractions and thus assumed to have no more meaning than the abstractions from which they were supposedly derived. This position has been taken by Max Loehr and since it has had great influence through his own writings and those of his students, most prominently Robert Bagley, its theoretical basis is worth examining with some care. Loehr's theoretical position is taken from Susanne K. Langer. Thus, in *Ritual Vessels of Bronze Age China*, he quotes *Feeling and Form:*

> The fundamental forms which occur in the decorative arts of all ages and races—for instance the circle, the triangle, the spiral, the parallel—are known as *motifs* of design. They are not art 'works', not even ornaments, themselves, but they lend themselves to composition, and are therefore incentives to artistic creation. . . . [Actually, I think,] a comparative study of decorative art and primitive representational art suggests forcibly that *form is first*, and the representational function accrues to it.[6]

Loehr goes on to add with regard to Shang bronze design:

If the ornaments on Shang bronzes came into being as sheer design, form based on form alone, configurations without reference
to reality or, at best with dubious allusions to reality, then we are
almost forced to conclude, they cannot have had any ascertainable
meaning—religious, cosmological or mythological—*meaning at
any rate of an established literary kind*. (My italics)[7]

In spite of this last important caveat, Loehr clearly means to imply that
the ornament on Shang bronzes was, as he goes on to state, "iconographically meaningless, or meaningful only as pure form." He suggests, "we
must renounce attempts to explain these elusive images in terms of cosmology or religious lore"; and, "Not by choice, but of necessity, do all writings
on the subject of symbolism in bronze decoration depend on identifiable
images of real beasts. But the identifiable images are greatly outnum-
bered by the zoomorphs which are design merely, interesting solely on
formal grounds as 'pure art'."[8]

Langer, too, argues that although the decorative forms of archaic peoples are gradually "modified more and more to picture all sorts of objects",
they are nevertheless pure form. "Where designs include pictorial
elements . . . those images are simplified and distorted with perfect free-
dom to fit the rest of the pattern. Their graphic rendering is never a copy of
direct visual impressions, but formulation, shaping, defining of the impressions themselves according to the principle of expressiveness, or vital
form". Langer's thesis that 'form comes first' is, as her 'actually, I think'
(omitted by Loehr) indicates, based on supposition and would be difficult
to substantiate—figurative cave paintings occur extremely early.

Theoretically, however, even if one accepts the hypothesis that form
comes first, it does not follow that the motifs once developed were
meaningless. We know from this development only that the images are
not inspired by an attempt to represent the real world, but no art, as Langer herself effectively demonstrates, is truly concerned with visual representation. Its purport as she defines it is to "articulate visual form, and to
present that form—so immediately expressive of human feeling that it
seems to be charged with feeling—as the sole, or at least paramount object
of perception" and she stresses that it must present a visual unity.

Primitive or mythic art, however, is neither pure decoration nor representation. Like myth, it alludes to reality, but it does not depict it. It is not
meaningful in an established literary sense, that is it is not symbolic of
ideas which are verbally articulated, but its vocabulary is nevertheless
meaningful in the context of the religion of the people who have made it.
Though its allusions are not illustrations, they nevertheless refer to the

realities of the society and the belief system of the people for whom it is a ritual object.

Few who have contemplated the bronze art of Yinxu will doubt that it represents form charged with feeling and we can respond to its visual unity without understanding its vocabulary, but its vocabulary does not strike even the uninitiated viewer as simply decoration or as strange because it is unfamiliar. The motifs of Shang bronze art, like those of other such mythic art, are strange in themselves, a distortion of any reality. They are, in the original sense of the word, awful, inspired with a sense of the sacred. This effect is achieved by the deliberate breach of reality, on the one hand, and the sense of visual unity or harmony, on the other. The real world has been broken apart, but another harmony established for us.

If we are to understand the art of the Shang, or of other early societies, then we must recognize that the fantastic quality of primitive art is not accidental, but meaningful. The forms are not simply decorative, but neither are they a depiction or representation of myth or of reality, not even of an imagined reality or of a reality to which a symbolic meaning has been assigned. Their sense derives from the same religious structure which generates mythology, but the art forms are generated directly from that structure rather than derived from the mythology. Such art is religious and it derives its religious force—its sense of being sacred—from transformations which allude to, but do not represent—indeed, deliberately contradict—reality, which suggest another order beyond our logical comprehension, and from their sense of aesthetic harmony. The power of this harmony is all the greater because normality has been shattered.

Shang bronzes, which are my concern herein, were ritual vessels, that is they are vessels which were made to contain sacrifices—animals and humans (no distinction is made between the two in the enumerations of offerings in the oracle bone inscriptions), grain and wine—which were offered to the spirits. Such vessels are analogous to vessels used by the living and the living may have partaken of the feast of the dead from them, but their purpose was a singular one, to feed the spirits. They were thus decorated in the language of the spirit world so that the boundary between the living and the dead might be crossed and the sacrifice be received by those for whom it was intended. The motifs which were not of this world signify the crossing of this boundary.

The language of Shang bronze art, as I shall discuss below, is characterized by disjunctions, double images and transformations. By disjunctions, I refer to the conjoining of unrelated animals to form a composite. Even when one animal predominates, the suggested realism is usually contradicted by the addition or replacement of some part with that of a different animal. Double images, such as the two-bodied snake or the *taotie* which may be seen either as a single animal with two bodies or as two dragons facing one another, create a further sense of illusion. In this art, nothing is ever quite what it seems. Moreover, the motifs are continually transformed, each manifestation deriving from a previous one, but exhibiting new changes. Even parts of an established motif, such as the horns on a *taotie*, may be transformed into a new motif, such as dragons (see figure 36d), and take on a life of their own while still functioning as part of another whole.

By such means, the bronze motifs create a sense of the other, that which is not limited by the physical realities of this world and which can never be precisely defined. Not only are the motifs on Shang bronzes continually transformed, however, their primary allusions are to transformations of state—eating and sacrifice, the watery underworld of the dead, the dragon which is also a bird, the cicada which emerges winged from the earth, snakes which slough their skins, deer which shed their antlers, etc. In spite of this emphasis on change and transformation, however, the number of motifs on Shang bronzes is strictly limited and although the *taotie* and *kui* dragon are difficult to define because of their changes, their structural consistency is such that we have no difficulty recognizing them. The artist is not designing freely, but referring again and again to the same things.

THE TAOTIE

Although Max Loehr argued that Shang bronze motifs have their origin in pure design, even in the earliest example of his styles I and II equivalent to bronzes excavated from Erligang, Zhengzhou, Shang bronze decor is dominated by an early form of the *taotie* which is more than a decorative motif. Some examples are given in figure 32. See also figures 26–8. This motif alludes to an animal or other being although it makes no attempt at depiction or representation. It is characterized by two eyes and there is usually some further suggestion of a face, such as a reference to ears or horns and a nose. Lines to the sides may suggest bodies, but there is no separation of image from ground and the features of the body are not defined.[9] In its simplest form, this motif is reduced to two eyes, either two round, animal-like eyes, as in figure 32a or human-shaped eyes, as in figure 32b. In one example from Erligang, however, a sheephorned face is modelled realistically in three dimensions, although the body remains undefined (see figure 28 and figure 32i). In all of these examples, however, the two eyes alert us to the presence of a creature or being.

Some seven bronze *jue* 爵 are the only bronze vessels which have thus far been excavated from the earlier Shang site at Erlitou—discussed above in connection with the Xia. One example is illustrated in figure 5. This is

Figure 27 *Jia* (Zhengzhou Erligang period)

Reproduced by courtesy of the Trustees of the British Museum

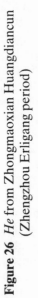

Figure 26 *He* from Zhongmaoxian Huangdiancun (Zhengzhou Erligang period)

From *Henansheng Bowuguan*, no. 7

Figure 28 *Lei* with ram-horned *taotie* face and
ya-shaped hole in footrim, from Zhengzhou city,
Baijiazhuang, tomb no. 2 (Erligang period)

From *Henansheng Bowuguan*, no. 3

probably an accident of excavation, but the *jue* may also have a particular significance. It is a vessel for pouring wine. Wine, drunk from *gu* 觚 -beakers which frequently accompany *jue* at later sites, was much used in Shang ritual and naturally suggests a change of mental state. Significantly, the name and shape of the vessel suggest the three-legged bird. *Jue* is the name of a small bird as well as of this ritual vessel and the connection is evident in the oracle bone character 爵 which is both a picture of a bird and one of a vessel. The *jue* from Erlitou, however, are undecorated except that, as Robert Bagley has observed, one example has a pattern of raised dots.[10]

Although the *jue* found at Erlitou are undecorated, a turquoise plaque with two staring eyes has been excavated from this same site.[11] Eyes and the suggestion of a face are also found on a jade *baton*.[12] This suggests that the motif was already known, if not utilized, on the still primitively cast bronze vessels. Many scholars have found the origin of the *taotie* design in jade *cong* 琮 —the square objects with a tubular center associated with the earth in later symbolism—from the Liangzhu 良渚 neolithic culture of the southeast coast (third millennium B.C.).[13] These are decorated with two eyes and a horizontal bar suggesting either a nose or a mouth (see figure 29). Although there is no direct line of development from this motif to the *taotie* as it appears at Zhengzhou, or even Erlitou, the *cong* itself was clearly introduced from this culture and so we may assume some cultural diffusion.

Eyes are themselves a powerful image, one which implies more than formal play. As an image, they suggest, even without elaboration, an unknown power, a reality which may be sensed but not depicted, which sees but cannot be seen. Thus although there is no pictorial image of an animal or other being in these early examples, the motif is nevertheless iconographically meaningful. Eyes are a universal image in primitive art and, as Ernst Gombrich has noted, they inspire fear and so frequently have an apotropaic function.[14] Although the descendants of the *taotie* which decorate tomb doors in Han times did have such a function, there is no obvious rationale for a function of averting evil on vessels intended for use in feeding the spirits, especially since there were not two classes of spirits, malevolent and benevolent, in Shang religion. Such eyes, however, may be readily understood as a suggestion of the sacred or other, that which sees but cannot be known, the world of the spirits to whom the offerings must pass, the contemplation of which inspires the living with a sense of awe or dread.

The simple imagery of the Zhengzhou Erligang period bronzes is increasingly elaborated until it becomes the sophisticated and complex imagery of the late Shang period. This increasing complexity and added detail parallels that of myths which also tend to be increasingly detailed and elaborate with the passage of time. The suggestion of an animal face in the

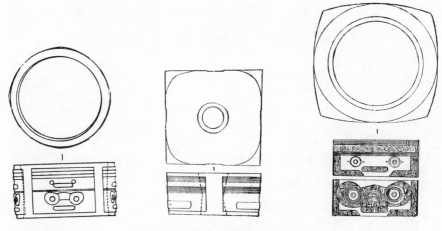

Figure 29a Neolithic *Jades*

a. Jade *cong*, Liangzhu culture, excavated at Sidun, Jiangsu

Figure 29b b. Jade dragons, Hongshan culture

a. from *Kaogu* 1988.3, p. 240; b. from Yeung, *Neolithic Jades*, pl. 25

early motif becomes explicit. Direct allusion is made to specific animals and, as I shall discuss below, to eating and sacrifice. Double imagery, disjunctions and continual transformation replace the vague suggestion of the earlier period, but the fundamental sense of the motif, the reference to the unknown and unknowable, remains the same. Furthermore, just as the early forms are not decorative patterns, the *taotie* of the late Shang period is not a representational image.

Scholars in search of a symbolic meaning for the *taotie* have attempted to identify it as a particular animal, such as the buffalo, or tiger, or, recognizing that it is not a real animal, argued that it is a 'mythological

Figure 30 *Hu* with *Taotie* motif

Reproduced by Courtesy of the Trustees of the British Museum.

Figure 31 *Hu* with tiger-eared and bovine-horned *Taotie* motifs (Yinxu period)

Reproduced by Courtesy of the Trustees of the British Museum

creature'.[15] However, the *taotie* cannot represent any single animal or, indeed, a mythological one, because the motif is in a continual state of transformation. Only the eyes which were its earliest feature remain as a constant in its many manifestations. In the Yinxu period characteristically, it also has horns, eyebrows, a nose, ears—which may replace the horns above the eyes, but are often human-shaped and placed to the sides, the horns remaining in place—and an upper jaw. Occasionally, a full mouth is included (for example, figures 34a–b). The lines drawn to the sides now refer explicitly to two bodies and frequently become a double image in which one animal with two bodies can also be seen as two animals facing one another (see, for example, figure 37a). In the later stages, these are often detached becoming two separate animals with a central face (for example, figure 37b, see also figures 34d, 35c). The animals thus alluded to usually—there are no constant rules in Shang art—have a single leg and tail and are conventionally known as *kui*-dragons; these will be discussed again below.

A limited number of examples of the *taotie* are included in figures 32–7. The variations are endless. Clearly, no one creature is depicted or represented, nor even a number of different creatures. Bernhard Karlgren and, more recently, K. C. Chang with the assistance of a computer, have attempted to classify its variations without success.[16] The problem in such an approach is that the Shang did not begin with a catalogue of real or mythological creatures which they chose to represent. Each vessel was a new creation, deriving from the forms which preceded it, but transforming them to make a new form and image. A structural identity remains, however, and it is this which allows us to recognize that, in spite of the variation, we are faced with the same motif.

Although the *taotie* is not representational, the image does nevertheless allude to real creatures, including the buffalo or ox, sheep, possibly the goat, deer, tiger, all of which were used in sacrifice. These allusions are most apparent in the shape of the horns/or ears. The renderings vary in their degree of stylization and although some horn types are easily identified, others are more uncertain. The horns represented in figure 34, for example, may be those of a goat, but this is uncertain. Those in figure 35 are ram horns (as in the example from Erligang, figure 32 and figure 28). The twisted horns in figure 36 are probably, as Elizabeth Childs-Johnson has also observed, those of a stag[17] because they are found on the stylized *taotie* on the inside of the leg of the large deer *ding* 鼎 from tomb no. 1004 (see figure 38c). On its pair, a large ox *ding* from the same tomb, ox horns are repeated on the inside of the legs. The horns in figure 37c are clearly bovine; the 'horns' of figure 37b, however, are probably ears, possibly those of a tiger, as in the tiger *you* 卣 illustrated in figure 42 (see also figure

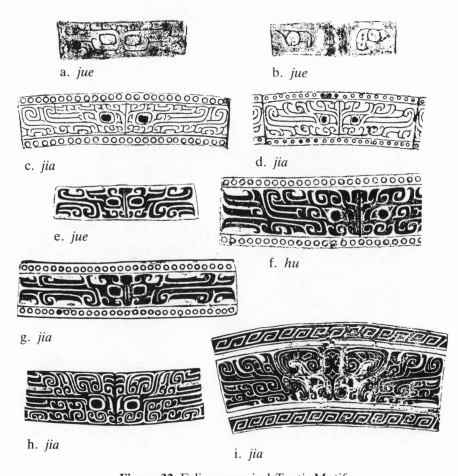

a. *jue*

b. *jue*

c. *jia*

d. *jia*

e. *jue*

f. *hu*

g. *jia*

h. *jia*

i. *jia*

Figure 32 Erligang period *Taotie* Motifs

From *Shang-Zhou qingtongqi wenshi,* 222, 223, 63, 64, 62, 154, 153, 4, 3

31 in which these two types of horns occur on similar faces). More conventionally, however, tiger-like animals are given round ears, as in figure 37a (see also figures 43a, 44a). The shape of these ears strangely resemble human ears, often placed to the side of the head (see figures 43b, 36c, d, also figure 37b). Reference to humans may also be seen in the frequent addition of eyebrows beneath the horns and in human-shaped noses.

Only rarely does the *taotie* refer explicitly to a single, real animal. Two examples are two enormous square *ding,* excavated from tomb no. 1004 at Xibeigang, one of which has a realistic deer head and the other, an ox (see

a. *gu*

b. *jue*

c. *hu*

d. *ding*

e. *zhi*

Figure 33 Development of the *Taotie* Motif in the
Yinxu period

From *Shang-Zhou qingtongqi wenshi,* 168, 169, 159, 160, 170

a. *jia*

b. *hu*

c. *ding*

d. *zun*

Figure 34 Goat (?) horned *Taotie* Motifs

From *Shang-zhou qingtongqi wenshi,* 85, 88, 81, 90

a. *you*

b. *you*

c. *zun*

Figure 35 Ram Horned *Taotie* Motifs

From *Shang-Zhou qingtongqi wenshi*, 31, 17, 61

a. *ding*

b. square *ding*

c. square *ding*

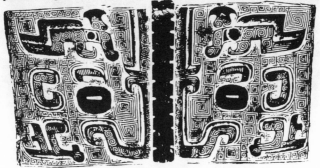

d. square *ding*

Figure 36 Stag (?) Horned *Taotie* Motifs

from Shang-Zhou qingtongqi wenshi 113, 112, 484, 141

a. *hu*

b. *you*

c. *ding*

Figure 37 Tiger and Bovine *Taotie*

From *Shang-Zhou qingtongqi wenshi,* 203, 205, 204

figure 38b, c).[18] The great size of these vessels suggests that they may have been used to offer whole animals. Normally, however, even when one animal predominates, its realism is contradicted by the addition of a contradictory element. For example, horns and clawed feet are added to the strikingly realistic human face on the large square *ding* excavated at Ningxiang in Hunan Province (see figures 40 and 36c). Similarly, the human-faced lid on the Freer Gallery *he* 盉 illustrated in figure 39 has bottle-shaped horns (these will be discussed again later) and a snake's body along its back.

In the late Shang period, the *taotie* face is often marked off distinctly from the two adjoining bodies and these may be detached entirely, becoming separate dragons, as mentioned above. This gives it a mask-like appearance. Jordan Paper and, more recently, Elizabeth Childs-Johnson have argued that it is a representation of a shaman's mask.[19] Masks may have been carved in wood in Shang times, but they are no longer extant.[20] If masks were used for such a purpose by the Shang, then their function would also have been to mark the sacred, to signify the transformation of the dancer or shaman and to allow him communication with the spirit world, just as the motif on the ritual vessels transformed the offering and allowed it to be received by the spirits. Although such a possibility cannot be discounted, the sequence of the development of the motif on the bronzes is such that a mask could not have been the *origin* of its development: only in the later stages of its development is the face of the *taotie* clearly marked off from the body. Furthermore, the *taotie* often appears on war helmets (see figure 38a). Its function there may be to signify the supernatural power of the warrior or the power of death which he holds, but it could not imply shamanistic trance.

The term *taotie* 饕餮 first occurs in the textual tradition in the *Zuo zhuan* 左傳, with reference to one of the four evil creatures of the world, a certain worthless son of the Jinyun 縉雲 clan, who lived in the time of the Yellow Emperor. Because of his insatiable greed and appetite, he was called *Taotie,* which, according to the commentators, means 'glutton'.[21] The term is associated with the bronze motif, however, because of a passage in the *Lüshi chunqiu* 呂氏春秋 (16/3a) which states: "Zhou *ding* were decorated with *taotie* which have a head but not a body. It devoured a man, but before it could swallow him, its own body was damaged." This text, written in the third century B.C., does not reflect Shang thought and there is no reason to suppose that the term *taotie* was known to the Shang. Certainly, the motif known by that name is not an illustration of a member of the Jinyun clan known for his gluttony. Nevertheless, it does reflect an ancient association between the motif and eating and this is significant since the motif was used to decorate vessels used for offering food sacrifices to the

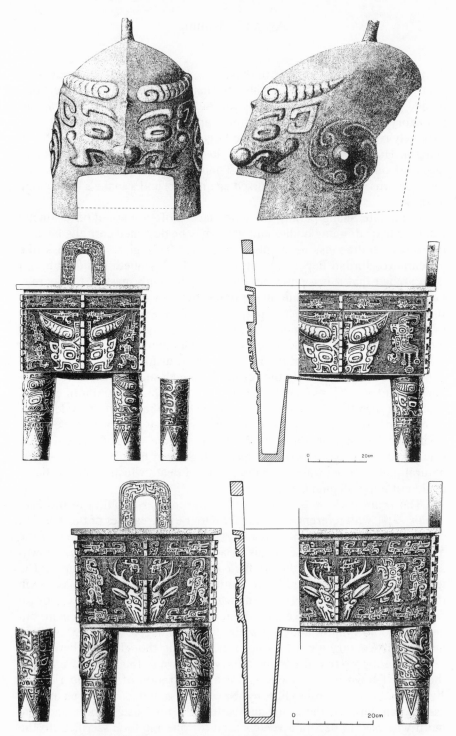

Figure 38 Bronzes Excavated from Tomb 1004, Houjiazhuang

From Liang Siyong & Gao Quxun, *Houjiazhuang 1004-hao
damu* Figures 119, 117, 110

Figure 39 *He* with Bottle-horned humanface *Taotie* Motif

Courtesy of the Freer Gallery of Art, Washington, D.C. Smithsonian Institution, Washington, D.C., accession number 42.1

Figure 40 Square *ding* with human face *Taotie* motif,
from Ningxiangxian Huangcun, Hunan Province
(Yinxu period)

From *Hunansheng bowuguan*, no. 11.

spirits of the dead whose appetite, as I have discussed previously, was insatiable.

Although the *taotie* has an upper mouth, it is normally lacking a lower jaw. This is traditionally understood as the open mouth of the gluttonous *taotie*. Some scholars have argued that the lack of a lower jaw is a representation of a splayed animal from which the jaw must be removed.[22] Such realism, however, is contrary both to the spirit of Shang art and to the development of the motif from a vaguely defined face surrounding two eyes and an unarticulated body.[23] The animals to which the motif alludes in its more explicit forms, however, do reinforce the theme of eating, for they are all used in ritual sacrifice, including the human being, even though they do not include the full complement of sacrificial animals. Furthermore, even at Zhengzhou Erligang, as discussed above, there is an example of a face with explicit ram horns, one of the major sacrificial animals (figures 28 and 32i).[24]

The jawless *taotie* occasionally takes a more explicit form, as a man or bird in an open animal mouth. This occurs in two contexts. In one, which is normally on the handles of bronze vessels, the animal holds a bird in its mouth. In the other, the animal takes the form of a tiger and a human is held in its mouth. The face of the human is realistically depicted. The significance of the tiger as the animal which holds a human being in its mouth is undoubtedly because tigers were the one animal traditionally regarded as a man-eater in ancient China. Divination inscriptions refer to hunting tigers and, as Walter Burkert has observed, the animal of prey is also the supreme animal of sacrifice.[25] Other creatures might eat birds and there is no such specification in the depiction of the animal which holds the bird in its mouth, but, as I discussed in Chapter 2, the Shang rulers identified themselves with the suns which were also birds. Thus the meaning of a bird in an animal mouth or a man in that of a tiger may be the same.

The most famous example of the motif of a man in a tiger mouth are on two almost identical *you,* one in the Sumitomo Kakkokan, Kyoto, and the other in the Musee Cernuschi, Paris (see figure 42).[26] Although neither of these vessels was scientifically excavated, tradition and style both suggest that they come from the south, probably Hunan Province. The man-in-tiger-mouth motif also occurs on another, somewhat earlier *zun* 尊, from Funan 阜南 in Anhui Province (see figure 41).[27] The tiger on this vessel has a double body and although it is relatively realistically portrayed, it has the rounded ears which are conventionally given to bronze tigers, rather than the more realistic pointed ears of the *you.* In its mouth is a human figure with his arms and legs bent and to his sides. The meaning of this position, which also occurs on white pottery from Yinxu and which may be traced back to painted pottery of the neolithic Yangshao culture, is not known, but it may be a schematization of the squatting posture of the man on the Cernuschi *you.*

Although these two *you* and the *zun* are all southern pieces, the motif is not specifically southern. At Anyang, it is found on the handles of the Simu Wu square *ding* (see figure 44b) and on the blade of a *yue* 鉞 -axe found in the tomb of Lady Hao (see figures 43a, 44a and 45).[28] In both examples, the double-bodied tiger has become two animals holding a single

Figure 41 *Zun* with human-in-tiger-mouth motif, from
Anhui Province Funanxian, Zhuzhairunhe.

From *Zhongguo Lishi bowuguan*, no. 29

Figure 42b Underside of *zun*

Courtesy of the Musée Cernuschi (MC 6155)

Figure 42a *Zun* with human-in-tiger-mouth motif

Courtesy of the Musée Cernuschi, Paris (MC 6155)

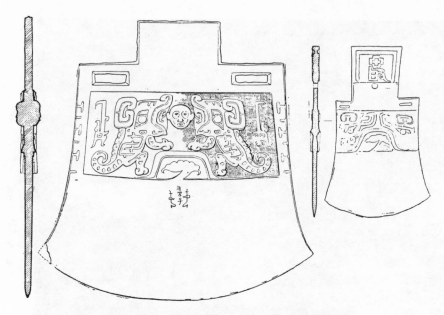

a. Axes from the tomb of Lady Hao

b. Axe from Yidu, Sufutun, Shandong Province

Figures 43a and 43b *Yue*-axes

a. From Zhongguo Kexuejuan Kaogu Yanjiusuo, *Yinxu Fu Hao mu*, p. 106, figure 66;

b. From *Shang-Zhou qingtongqi wenshi* 985

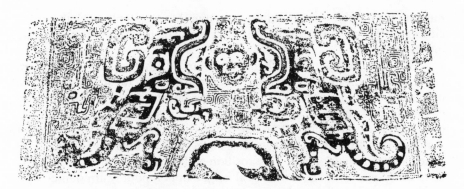

a. *Yue* from the tomb of Lady Hao

b. Decoration on handle of the Simu Wu *ding*

Figures 44a and 44b Man-in-tiger-mouth motif

a. From *Yinxu Fu Hao mu,* p. 106, fig. 67; b. From *Shang-Zhou qingtongqi wenshi* 589

human face in their open mouths. Although these examples lack the explicitness of the provincial examples, they nevertheless represent the same motif.

The *yue*-axe was used to behead human or other victims. A series of related motifs on such axes can serve to illustrate both the manner in which motifs are continually transformed and their power of reference. The motif of two tigers with a human head in their mouths is in an horizontal register on the Fu Hao *yue*. The bottom line of the register is also the upper part of a mouth with two cat-like fangs. This suggests the upper jaw of the *taotie* which is commonly found in this position and, indeed, another smaller *yue* from this same tomb has an identical fanged upper mouth surmounted by a *taotie* with the same round tiger ears (see figure 43a, number 2; cf. figure 46). In both examples, the blade extends from the upper jaw of the animal. Eating and sacrificial beheading are thus equated.

There are also *yue* which are decorated with a human face; two have been excavated from Yidu Sufutun 益都蘇阜屯 in Shandong Province (see figures 27b and 47) and another is in West Berlin.[29] Although the style of the face is like that of a *taotie*, the parts are all human. The Berlin *yue*, for example, has hair, nose, ears, eyebrows, and a full-toothed mouth including the lower jaw; the Sufutun example lacks hair. A further example in the British Museum (see figure 48) has a human face above the tiger-like fanged mouth. In light of the function of the axe and the blade which extends from the mouth to cut off the head, there can be no doubt that these motifs all refer to the passage of death or transformation from human world to that of the spirits. The art, however, only alludes to the theme of sacrifice. It does not illustrate it.

The tiger *you*, in spite of its exuberance and unusual degree of realism, also shows the same type of disjunctions and transformations with which we are familiar from Anyang. On the back of the vessel, for example, is a *taotie* with both bovine and sheep horns, human ears, eyebrows, and tusks, beneath which an elephant trunk extends to form a third leg for the vessel. To the sides of the tiger and man, there are two bottle-horned dragons, recalling the conventional placement of such dragons to the sides of an (often bodiless) *taotie*. There are more such dragons on the body of the vessels and other creatures including a pair of animals on the sides of the vessel with pointed ears and spots, perhaps leopards. The man in the tiger's mouth has serpents on his buttocks and legs and *kui*-dragons on his arms. Although there are indications of a costume, his body is also decorated with the squared spiral or *leiwen* 雷紋 pattern which covers the rest of the vessel and is a common background pattern for Anyang bronzes.

As K. C. Chang has observed, the open animal mouth occurs in many cultures as a symbol of passage to the other world. He further suggests that

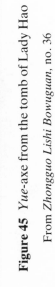

Figure 46 *Yue*-axe from Yin xu. From *Henan chutu Shang-Zhou qingtongqi*, v.1, no. 346 (C7 M15.4)

Figure 45 *Yue*-axe from the tomb of Lady Hao

From *Zhongguo Lishi Bowuguan*, no. 36

Figure 47 *Yue*-axe, from Yidu, Sufutun, Shandong Province, tomb no. 1

From *Zhongguo qingtongqi xuan*, no. 24

Figure 48 *Yue*-axe

Reproduced by Courtesy of the Trustees of the British Museum

the man held by the tiger is a *wu* 巫, a sorcerer or "shaman", as he interprets the term.[30] The appearance of this motif above the blade on a *yue*-
axe, however, suggests that the motif is not a representation of the shaman's passage to the other world, but an allusion to the passage of death,
the cult of which is, after all, the central concern of Shang ritual. If the man
has a specific reference, it is more likely to be to the ritual impersonators of
the dead, the *shi* 尸. This character is written in oracle bone script as 𠃌,
that is with the knees raised as on the *you* and the Funan *zun*.

In this light, the snakes and dragons which decorate the body or costume of the person in the tiger mouth and occur elsewhere on the vessel
can be understood; they are an allusion to the watery underworld of the
Yellow Springs.

THE DRAGON AND THE WATERY UNDERWORLD

The *taotie,* as we have seen, may often be seen as two dragons facing one
another. In its many transformations, the two bodies of the *taotie* may also
be separated and themselves become dragons. Horns, too, may change
into dragons and similar dragons are often depicted in bands of decoration
above and/or below the main relief. Since this motif usually has only a
single leg, the term *kui* which, according to the *Shuowen* 說文, means a
one-legged dragon has been used since the Song Dynasty to describe this
motif. Since the creature is only seen with one leg in profile, however, we
cannot be sure whether the artist intended it to be one or two-legged and,
unlike the term *taotie,* which was used in the third century B.C. to describe
bronze decoration, there are no early references which associate this term
with bronze decor.

Some examples of dragon motifs are illustrated in figures 49–52. As in
the case of the *taotie,* these motifs are so continually changing that they
cannot be a representation of any mythical figure, or, indeed, of a number
of different mythical figures for the variations on the motif cannot be distinguished as different creatures. Karlgren's attempts at cataloguing their
various forms have provided the art historian with a rich descriptive vocabulary, but they have been no more successful than those at cataloguing the
various forms of the *taotie* because each creation was a transformation created anew, not a representation of a finite creature which existed in the
imagination of the artist.

Birds often replace the *kui,* particularly in an upper band of decoration
above the main register (see figure 51b–e, cf. 49c). Furthermore the *kui*
itself frequently has the beak of a bird (see figure 51a). Although such
motifs are normally referred to as 'beaked dragons', following Karlgren's
terminology, such creatures are as much birds as they are dragons. As I
have discussed previously, however, although birds and dragons are

a. *pan* (Erligang period)

b. *pan* (mid-Yinxu period)

c. *pan* (mid-Yinxu period)

d. *pou* (mid-Yinxu period)

Figure 49 Single-eye motifs

From *Shang-Zhou qingtongqi wenshi*, 707, 352, 4977, 283

a. *gu*

b. *yue*

c. *gu*

d. *you*

e. square *yi*

f. *ding*

g. *gu*

h. *ding*

Figure 50 Dragon motifs

From: *Shang-Zhou qingtongqi wenshi* 288, 400, 281, 304, 145,
295, 267, 294

a. *ding*

b. *ding*

c. *gong*

d. square *ding*

f. *you*

e. *ding*

Figure 51 Beaked dragon and bird motifs

a, b, c, e, f. From *Shang-Zhou qingtongqi wenshi* 555, 575, 496, 578, 488; d. from *Yinxu Fu Hao mu,* 24

Figure 52 Dragons on the under side of *pan*-water basins

From *Yinxu Fu Hao mu*, figs 22, 21

opposed as symbols of sky and water, above and below, they are conjoined
in the motif of the sun-bird which descends into the watery underworld to
return to the other side of the earth. Although the beaked *kui* is not a
figurative representation of such a bird, it is a composite generated from
the same stock of ideas and images.

In some representations, particularly when it is seen from above, the
dragon motif has a serpent's body, often with a leg attached on each side,
and horns on its head, conventionally called 'bottle horns' because they
cannot be clearly identified with any animal and are shaped like old-
fashioned milk bottles. This is the dragon depicted in the oracle bone character 㞢, 㞢, the original form of the character *long* 龍,[31] the general term
for dragon in classical texts, although it does not occur in this sense in the
divination inscriptions.

Dragons, as I have discussed with regard to the myth of the Xia Dynasty, were water creatures who inhabited the Yellow Springs and the Shang
snake, as Tsung-tung Chang has observed, is a water creature.[32] The aquat-
ic nature of the *long* is suggested not only by its serpent's body, but also by
its two legs which suggest a creature which swims rather than walks. It is
also apparent in the frequent placement of this motif in the bowl of *pan* 盤
water basins and on the underside of some vessels. As discussed in Chapter
four, turtles often appear in these same positions. See figures 20–2.

Pan were not used to make offerings, but for ritual washing, as in the
story of Tang who washed and fasted before offering himself as a sacrificial
victim. The decoration on *pan*, primarily dragons or turtles, fish and birds
(either on top of the rim in relief or beneath it, perhaps interspersed with
fish), suggests ponds, such as those at the foot of the Fu Sang and Ruo Mu
trees in which the sun-birds bathed and which were the entrances to the
watery world of the Yellow Springs. On one *pan*, small snakes or perhaps
worms—who eat earth and drink from the Yellow Springs—take the
position beneath the rim where fish or birds and fish are more frequently
found. In another variation, tiger-like creatures are interspersed with fish
and birds.[33] Although this motif, unlike the others, does not imply water,
the tiger, as discussed above, is a man-eater and associated with the passage to the other world. Thus, just as food and wine were placed in ritual
vessels decorated in the language of the spirits, so too may the supplicant
be purified and transformed by washing in these basins which are also
sacred ponds.

The bottle-horned *long* is also often found coiled on the underside of a
vessel, frequently with a smaller *kui*, and sometimes accompanied by fish,
as on the underside of the tiger *you* (see figures 42b and 52). The use of
such motifs on the bottom of vessels again suggests their association with
the watery underworld. The *long*, however, is no more constant than other

Shang motifs. In a *he* in the Freer Gallery to which I have already referred (see figure 147), it has a human face and two clawed feet. Two further smaller *long* also face each other around the spout.

Snakes are a universal motif in primitive art. They may live in water or burrow beneath the ground, hibernate, and slough their skins in the spring; thus, they are a natural symbol of transformation or rebirth. They are often poisonous and their movement, as Balaji Mundkur has discussed in *The Cult of the Serpent,* causes a physiological reaction of fear and ambivalent awe in all higher primates including man.[34] They are also easily associated with the sacred or supernatural because of relatively common genetic aberrations in which they have either two heads or two bodies.[35] In Warring States folklore, a snake with two heads was said to cause the death of whoever saw it.[36] In Shang bronze art, a double-bodied serpent with or without bottle horns is a frequent motif and it may be traced back to the Erlitou period where it is found on a pottery fragment.[37] This suggests that although the double-bodied *taotie* is not clearly articulated in its earliest manifestations, it does refer at one level to a two-bodied animal. Such an animal in itself breaches the bounds of nature and can be regarded as sacred.

The association of snakes with death and sacrifice is also evident from oracle bone characters which include a snake element. Evil caused by the ancestors is commonly described by the verb 孑, that is, a foot stepping on the head of a snake (often transcribed as 祟 and translated as to curse). A common verb of sacrifice, also the term for a cult year of 360 days, is written as a snake and an altar: 禩 (*si* 祀). Some scholars have suggested that the snake in this character is simply phonetic, but we may reasonably assume that the choice of a snake to represent the sound is not entirely accidental.[38] Another more specific term of sacrifice is written as a hand holding a stake beside the head of a snake surrounded by dots representing drops of blood: 肂. Although the picture is of cudgelling a snake to death, the verb is performed on Qiang tribesman and the divinations propose an alternative of beheading (*fa* 伐) (*Bingbian* 7). Thus, it refers not to cudgelling a snake but a human to death—the snake representing death. This character, transcribed as *shi* 㢸, later meant to lay out a corpse.[39] A snake or wormlike parasite is depicted between the teeth: to represent toothache, caused by ancestral curse. Snakes or worms in a vessel: 蠱 (*gu* 蠱) further refer to the evil power which causes illness.

The *long* 龍, however, was not simply a snake. Reality, as is the norm in Shang art, is breached by the addition of horns. The so-called bottle horns have highly conventionalized markings (see figure 39) and often have the whorl circle design which refers to fire (☺) on top. Their meaning is not entirely clear, but as J. Leroy Davidson first observed, they may be deer horns before the antlers are grown, or after they have been shed.[40] In the late Anyang period and increasingly in the early Western Zhou, the bottle horn sometimes shows signs of a sprouting antler and, especially on the handles of *gui* 簋 and the lids of *gong* 觥, is often accompanied by deerlike ears and nose.

Antlers which are shed and grow anew each year, like snake skins which are sloughed every spring, are a natural symbol of rebirth. The association of deer and snake is also common in Siberian art and it is possible that the motif derives from this source. This possibility is all the greater because the earliest coiled dragons in China are jade objects from the Hongshan 紅山 neolithic culture in the far northeast of China (see figure 29b).[41] These dragons, however, do not have the bottle horn and the clear association of this motif with deer horns does not occur until relatively late in its development. The bottle horn is also reminiscent of the antennae of snails and slugs and the Hongshan dragons have a sluglike appearance so this may be a further reference. Unfortunately, I have not been able to find any references to snails or slugs in early texts or inscriptions and they do not appear to have played a significant role in early myth or folklore. It is possible, nevertheless, that the horns had more than one reference, the multiplicity of allusions increasing their power and interest.

OTHER MOTIFS

The *taotie* and the dragon (or dragon/bird) are the dominant motifs on Shang Dynasty bronzes, continually repeated in endless variation. There are also a limited number of animal motifs which are depicted in a relatively realistic form, such as the hare, elephant and rhinoceros. We know from oracle bone inscriptions that these animals were hunted by the king and they may be understood as further references to the themes of killing and sacrifice. Rhinoceros tusks and elephant trunks also appear intermixed with the *taotie* and dragon motifs. The elephant may have had some special meaning: the brother of Shun, who, as I have argued in Chapter three, is identifiable with Jun, the high ancestor of the Shang, was called Xiang 象, meaning 'elephant'. Elephants were buried sacrificially at Yinxu. I have noted above that the genetic aberration of the two-bodied or two-headed snake may have been regarded as supernatural. Similarly, the enormous size and strange trunk of the elephant are beyond the bounds of normal reality and may have given the animal a supernatural aura.

Finally, there are two other animals to which Shang bronze art frequently alludes: the owl and the cicada. Both of these have associations which reinforce our interpretation of death and transformation as the major themes of this art.

Some Shang vessels are shaped like owls. The motif is particularly

Figure 53 Owl *zun* from the tomb of Lady Hao

From *Henansheng bowuguan*, no. 12

prominent on bronzes from the tomb of Fu Hao, excavated in 1976, one example of which is illustrated in figure 53. Although this *zun* is shaped like an owl, its reality is once again contradicted by, for example, the snakes which are a part of its wings and the second owl face above the tail, surmounted by a *taotie*. A bird followed by a dragon also perches upon its head. The owl is both a night bird and a bird of prey and thus a symbol of death and an ill omen in many cultures including later Chinese folk tradition. In the *Fu niao fu* 鵬鳥賦 by Jia Yi 賈誼 (died 168 B.C.), the poet consults an oracle book about the meaning of an owl flying into his house, to be told that this omen means that the master will soon leave (that is die). Some scholars have wondered why owls which are unlucky in their associations should be cast as bronze vessels and placed in tombs, but the owl is unlucky to the living because it foretells death. For this same reason it is a suitable motif to decorated vessels intended to feast the dead.

The cicada is a less prominent but more frequent motif, though it is often highly stylized. For examples, see figure 54e, f, both from decoration on the bowls of vessels beneath a main register of decor. It, too, is a natural symbol of death and transformation. Its spectacular life cycle was described recently by Patrick Brogan in the *Observer*:

> The cicadas have returned to Washington after their 17–year sleep. . . Shedding their last skin, the fifth in their life cycle, they emerge nearly three inches long and deathly white with staring red eyes. Then they turn an elegant black and gold and start climbing the trees, rose bushes. . . When their wings are strong enough, they fly to the upper branches and start the mating call which sounds, for there are millions of them, like an equatorial storm falling mercilessly on the corrugated iron roofs of a vast African shanty-town. They are the very image of the locusts of biblical plagues, with this comforting difference—they do the vegetation no harm. . . . The females suck small quantities of sap from twigs before laying the eggs in slits in the bark. When the larvae emerge, they drop to the earth, burrow down to the roots, and stay there for 17 more years.

Although some cicadas have shorter life cycles—three, seven or thirteen years—it is difficult to imagine a more suitable symbol of transformation.

In sum, these ritual bronzes were food vessels for the ancestors. Thus, they were decorated in a sacred language, the language of the dead, so that their contents might be transformed and received by those for whom they were intended. Aesthetically, this sacred language, like the sacred lan-

a. *zun*

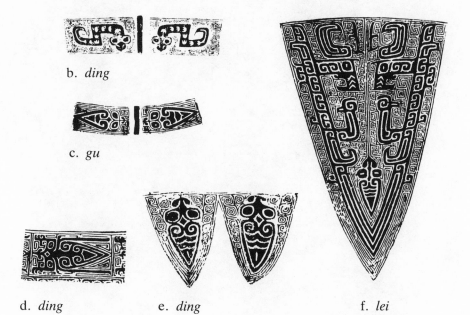

b. *ding*

c. *gu*

d. *ding*　　　　e. *ding*　　　　f. *lei*

Figure 54 Other Motifs

From *Shang-Zhou qingtongqi wenshi* 612, 617, 644, 643, 641, 571

Figures 55a and 55b Owl-shaped *You* with turtle motif
on the base

Courtesy of the Asian Art Museum of San Francisco (The Avery Brundage
Collection), Accession number B60 B336.

b

guage of myth, breaches the limitations of natural reality, signifying to the worshipper that it is an art of another world. This effect is achieved by such means as distortion, disjunction, the conjoining of different animals in a single image, double images which are both two images and one at the same time. . . . Furthermore, the images are continually transformed so that they cannot refer to any knowable entity.

Although the art of Shang bronzes is not representational, it is nevertheless iconographically meaningful and many of its references can be understood in light of the cult of ancestral sacrifice of which it was a part.

The themes are those of death and transformation and the world of the beyond: the *taotie* which is made up of animals and humans used in sacrifice, its open mouth, a passage to the other world, eating or killing; the dragon of the underworld and the bird of the spirit world above, often conjoined as a single image; snakes which slough their skins and signify death; deer which continually shed and regrow their antlers. . . .

VII

Conclusion

This book is intended as the first of a series in which I will trace the development of early Chinese patterns of thought. My concern in this volume has been with the Shang and I have attempted to build up a picture of Shang mythic thought by analysing it from different perspectives, those of its different manifestations. As I argued at the beginning of this work, Shang thought was mythic. By this I mean that Shang thinking had not yet been subjected to the self-awareness and conscious analysis inevitable with the growth of a literary tradition. Although writing was fully developed by the Anyang period from which we have the contemporaneous evidence of divination inscriptions, its uses were still limited. All of the extant transmitted texts are from the Zhou Dynasty or later and although we cannot be certain that the Shang had no literature at all, their thought had not yet been transformed by it.

In a mythic culture, myths, ritual, cosmology, divination, sacrifice, and art are all generated directly from a common religious structure rather than secondarily from a text. They share common patterns of organization, oppositions and motifs, but there is no sacred canon to be enacted in ritual or illustrated in art, nor a literature which could allow the people themselves to analyse and criticise their own beliefs. My analysis of Shang thought is necessarily speculative. Nevertheless, there are two tests by means of which my interpretations can be evaluated. The first is the coherence of my analyses of the different manifestations of Shang thought. The cosmology revealed in the myths, for example, should be the same as that in the divination system. However, my interpretations should not only make sense as a coherent whole for the Shang, they should also make sense in terms of the development of later Chinese beliefs and ideas. Thus, I have not only resorted to later texts as a matter of necessity, because there is no other way of understanding the Shang, I have attempted to explain how later patterns of thought can be understood as developments of Shang thought.

Some of my conclusions concerning Shang mythic thought are outlined below. Myth is most commonly defined as stories of the supernatural. The difficulty of applying this definition to the Chinese case is undoubtedly one reason why so many people have denied that the Chinese have myths. A better definition of myth, I believe, is that it is characterized by a breach of the limitations of the natural world. This breach of the limitations of mundane reality and common sense logic is not accidental, but necessary, a sign of the sacred. In chapter two, I hypothesized that the Shang had an origin myth in which they were born of the egg(s) of the black birds which were the suns. This myth had a number of different later manifestations, including the story of Di Ku and Jian Di, Jun and Xihe, and, in the historical tradition, Yao's appointment of Shun, having given him his two daughters in marriage. Since it could only be reconstructed with the aid of these later texts, the precise form of the Shang story was unclear, but the myth was confirmed by epigraphical evidence in the oracle bone inscriptions.

The belief that the Shang were fathered by a bird and there were ten sun-birds which rose alternately from the branches of a mulberry tree in the far east of the world has the hallmark of myth—an impossibility in the natural world. Though the myth continued at some level of society, its irrationality was recognized and, indeed, made explicit by the Han Dynasty rationalist Wang Chong who argued, for example, that the Mulberry Tree would have been burnt up by the heat of the suns and their fire extinguished when they bathed in the pond at the foot of the tree. At another level, that of the literati and historians, the problem of the irrationality of the ancient myths was dealt with by excising their more fantastic elements and regarding them as exaggerated history. This was the origin not only of the story of Yao's abdication to Shun, but of the Xia as a dynasty which preceded the Shang and the Yellow Emperor whose original role was lord of the underworld.

A belief in ten suns also provided the rationale for the Shang ritual schedule in which the Shang ancestors received offerings on the day on which the sun with which they were identified appeared in the sky. The importance of correlative thinking in primitive thought has been widely recognized since Durkheim and Mauss and, as Levi-Strauss argued, totemism is a system of classification, rather than an institution, in which a correlation is made between human society and the natural world. In the case of the Shang, the human society which was classifed into ten groups which corresponded to the ten suns was that of the dead spirits, rather than the living, though we cannot be certain that the classification of the ancestors did not also encompass their living descendants. Ten suns is also a cultural rather than a natural concept.

The ten suns with which the Shang ancestors were identified were also a class of their own in opposition to that of the twelve moons. The importance of binary thinking and dualism to the Shang is readily apparent. The class which included the Shang ancestors, the number ten, the suns, birds, black, the Mulberry Tree, the sky, east, above, and fire, was opposed to the number twelve, the moons, dragons and other water creatures, yellow, the Ruo Tree, the springs below the earth, the west, below, and water. In divining, days were defined in terms of both cycles of ten and of twelve and propositions were stated in both the affirmative and the negative.

Mythical narratives proceed in a never-ending spiral of thesis, antithesis and synthesis and are characterized by binary oppositions, but in cosmology, dualism is insufficient. East and west imply north and south. Harmony can only be achieved at the center of a circle or a cross, at which point there is no projected opposition, but perfect access to the spiritual worlds above and below. This, I argued in chapter four, is the reason for the prevalence of the motif of the world mountain or *axis mundi* in ancient religions, represented in the oracle bone inscriptions by Yue 岳, the 'Peak', which is identifiable with Songshan 嵩山, the central mountain in later five element theory, and Yangcheng 陽城 in the cosmogonic myths in which Yu controlled the great flood.

In Shang China, the earth was cross-shaped, a central square surrounded by four quadrates in the cardinal directions which were spirit lands from which the winds originated. The cross shape of the earth was replicated in the royal tombs and the dedicatory inscriptions on bronze vessels, so that the dead in the tombs and the offerings in the vessels might pass freely to the other world. Turtle plastrons, the favorite medium for oracle inscriptions, are also cross-shaped and the turtle with its domed, round upper shell and legs in the four corners perfectly represented the cosmos.

Although I have argued that the earth in Shang cosmology was cross-shaped rather than square as in the later texts, the Shang configuration leads naturally into the later beliefs. Not only was the central inhabited area a square, but, by extending the cross to include the four corners (the legs of the turtle or the four mountains which held up the sky), the earth became a square with nine parts, or eight surrounding a square center, as in later belief systems. The cross itself was five-parted, which may explain the tendency to repeat divinations five times, as well as provide an origin for later numerology based on the number five. Alternatively, from the point of view of the center, there were four regions outside and a land above and one below, six altogether, the number which competed with five for importance in early cosmology and divination.

Correlative thinking and primitive classification systems are not only a means of organizing and thus understanding human society and the natural world, they are also a means of exerting control over the cosmos by understanding the implicit relationships beyond man's immediate perceptions. Thus, I have argued, a correlation between turtle plastrons or ox scapulae and the physical world was the basis of Shang divination. By producing artificial omens on the shell or bone in response to proposals put as statements, the Shang attempted to determine the sacrificial offerings which would forestall the curses of the ancestral spirits and the Lord on High and thus to assume control of the violence in the natural world which would otherwise select its victims randomly.

By taking the breach of natural boundaries as the defining characteristic of myth, I was also able to provide a hypothesis by means of which the art of the Shang and other mythic cultures could be understood. Such art, like myth, is an expression of the religious structure. The function of the bronze vessels discussed in chapter six was to feed the ancestral spirits. Thus, they were decorated in an art which expressed their sacred function and which allowed their contents to pass to the spirit world. Their art does not illustrate myth, but it draws on the same stock of motifs and breaches the limitations of the natural world in a parallel manner to myth with such techniques as distortion; disjunction, in which different animals are combined in a single image; and double images which create a sense of illusion.

The primary motif on Shang bronzes is the *taotie*. It does not represent any deity and it is not representational since it is continually changing, but, I have argued, it is a meaningful image, characterized by two staring eyes and made up of various animals used in the sacrifical rites. An open mouth suggests the passage to the other world which the contents of the vessels must undergo: the double image, an animal which is neither one nor two, the illusion of the other world. Similarly, the dragons which may be part of the *taotie* or independant of them are neither real nor mythological creatures and in a constant state of transformation. However, the dragon form which derives from a water snake alludes to the watery underworld of the dead and when the dragon head is beaked, reminds us of the sun birds which return through the underworld springs when they set at the foot of the Ruo Tree. Owls and cicadas suggest death and rebirth.

With the development of a literary corpus at the beginning of the Zhou, thought—at least of those who could read—was transformed. Variant traditions were recorded and each record assumed a validity of its own, distinct from its origins which were usually unclear. Whereas unrecorded oral traditions changed imperceptibly over time, written records froze a single account as it was expressed in one time and place. That text then remained, to be read not only by contemporaries, but also by later generations, and to coexist with other variants of the same tradition and its own descendants. Although the relationships were sometimes observed by commentators, they were more usually forgotten. Texts influenced other texts and they allowed people to externalize and to think about their received traditions. On the one hand, the literati began to be skeptical about the received mythological tradition. On the other, they began to systematize and to theorize.

One solution when literate men become conscious of the irrationality inherent in myths is to recognize their sacred character and explain myths as another type of truth, allegorical or metaphysical rather than literal. This solution, preferred by the Sophists, is still popular among Christians. In China, however, the gods were ancestors and there was no clearly defined supernatural sphere. The Shang ancestors were divisible into the 'high ancestors' who were called by their personal names and had no clear chronological order and those after Wang Hai 王亥—above whose name a bird was often drawn—who were called by a combination of an epithet and one of the names of the ten suns. Nevertheless, these were all ancestors and they all received sacrifices from the Shang rulers in the same manner. The more obvious solution with such a structure was that which was offered in ancient Greece by Euhemerus—the assumption that the high ancestors were no different than the historical dead, but their deeds and personal features had been falsely exaggerated. Assuming a literal truth was concealed by the myth, the historians divested the stories of their more fantastic elements.

Pre-Shang 'history', from the Yellow Emperor to the founding of the Xia dynasty can all be understood as a later transformation and systematization of Shang myth. The story of Yao's abdication to Shun which first appears in the *Yaodian* chapter of the *Shang shu* was originally a story of the High Lord Di's appointment of the first Shang ancestor. Thus the cosmogonic events of the Zhou texts, such as the great flood and the butting of the northwestern mountain which caused the earth and sky to tilt toward one another, are normally placed in 'the time of Yao'—that historical period which had come to represent the mythical 'time long ago' of the high ancestors. The Xia were also the mythological opposites of the Shang, a watery people associated with death and the underworld, who were transformed into a political dynasty by the Zhou. By the Han, their ancestor, the Yellow Emperor, originally the lord of the underworld, had been transformed into an historical figure who, with his descendant Zhuan Xu, ruled before Yao.

The transformation of thought occasioned by the development of literature was, of course, uneven and myths continued to evolve and to be orally transmitted. These often entered the literature at a later date and in a different form. Certain texts, such as the *Shijing*, the 'Heavenly Questions' of the *Chuci*, and the *Shanhaijing*, consciously preserved orally transmitted forms without making them rational, but other texts also refer to certain myths, if only for literary effect. These are Zhou forms which have been polished by the literati, but they do give us a number of late variants. Thus, one of my methods of reconstruction has been to compare the differing accounts, including the historical versions, to posit a Shang origin which could account for the variation, and to test that hypothesis against contemporaneous Shang evidence. Conversely, by understanding the historical relationship of the Zhou variants, we can better understand their meaning.

Literature led not only to doubt, but also to theorization. Oppositions and patterns of organization which were implicit in Shang thought came to be recognized and made explicit. Correlative thinking was not abandoned, but systematized and made into a seemingly scientific system. Thus the oppositions of fire and water; sun, moon, etc. which were fundamental to Shang myth became the primary cosmological forces of *yin-yang* theory. The division of the earth into five parts and the magical importance of the number five led to the five element theory in which disparate natural classes, such as directions, seasons, parts of the sky, colors, elements of nature such as water, fire and earth, and finally political dynasties were correlated with one another.

Art was also transformed. I have compared Shang art with the figurative illustrations of the late Zhou and Han, but there was first a period in which the decoration of the bronze vessels became simply formal. At the same time, the inscriptions cast on the vessels lengthened. The word had come to take precedence over the image, but the images were not yet representations based on words. An analysis of this change must, however, await another volume.

Any reconstruction of Shang mythic thought must, because of the refractory nature of the evidence, be based upon a number of deductions. Proof can never be either complete or absolute. We are confronted with a jigsaw puzzle in which most of the pieces have been irretrievably lost and many questions can' never be answered. Readers, particularly those without a specialist knowledge of the materials, may wonder why I have concentrated on certain aspects of Shang myth and ignored others; why I have not attempted an orderly description of Shang theology. I have done so because these are the places where I could put together the pieces of evidence in a convincing manner. If my arguments are correct, then other scholars will be able to augment the picture which I have put together, but gaping holes will inevitably remain and we must recognize the limitations of our materials.

NOTES

CHAPTER 1

1. There are many variants of this famous story. The bones are sometimes said to have been discovered in 1899 and Wang Yirong's friend Liu E 劉鶚 has also been credited with being the first to recognize the writing. Li Xiandeng 李先登 ("Guanyu jiaguwen zui chu faxian qingkuang zhi bianzheng" 關於甲骨文最初發現情況之辨證, *Tianjin Shida Xuebao* 天津師大學報, 1984.5, pp. 51–2) has also argued cogently that the script was recognized in 1898 by Wang Xiang 王襄 and Meng Guanghui 孟廣慧.

2. See David N. Keightley, *Sources of Shang history: the oracle bone inscriptions of bronze age China*, Berkeley: University of California Press, 1978, pp. 3–27, for a description of the cracking process.

3. See S. Allan, *The heir and the sage: dynastic legend in early China*, San Francisco: Chinese Materials Center, 1981.

4. These are approximations of the traditional dates of the Xia and Shang dynasties. Recently, both David Nivison and his student David Pankeneier have attempted to provide more precise dates for the Zhou conquest of the Shang. In "The dates of the Western Chou," Harvard Journal of Asiatic Studies XLIII (1983), pp. 481–580, Nivison suggested 1045, later changed in his "1040 as the date of the Chou conquest," *Early China* VIII (1982–3), pp. 76–8. Pankeneier suggested 1046 in "Astronomical dates in Shang and Western Chou," *Early China* VII (1981–2), pp. 2–37. In "Mozi and the dates of Xia, Shang and Zhou: a research note," *Early China* IX–X (1983–5), pp. 179–81, Pankeneier suggests further dates for the beginning of the Shang (1576 B.C.) and even for the beginning of the Xia (1953 B.C.). I believe, however, that there are fundamental methodological problems in their approach to the Chinese texts.

5. See Shi Zhangru 石璋如, "Xiaotun C-qu de muzang qun" 小屯C-區的墓葬群 , *Bulletin of the Institute of History and Philology* XXIII (1951), pp. 447–87; see also Shi Zhangru, *Yinxu jianzhu yicun* 殷墟建築遺存, Taibei: Institute of History and Philology, Academia Sinica, 1959.

6. Miyazaki Ichisada 宮崎市定, "Chūgoku jōdai no toshi kokka to sono bochi – Shōyū wa doko ni attaka" 中國上代の都市國家とその墓地－商邑は何處にあつたか, *Tōyōshi Kenkyū* 東洋史研究 XXVIII (1970), pp. 265–82; "Hoi" 補遺, *Tōyōshi Kenkyū* 東洋史研究 XXIX (1970), pp. 147–52. See also K. C. Chang, *Shang civilization*, New Haven: Yale University Press, 1980, pp. 70–3.

7. Hsi-chang Yang, "The Shang Dynasty cemetery system," in *Studies of Shang archaeology*, K. C. Chang, ed., New Haven: Yale University Press, 1986, p. 52. See also Liang Siyong 梁思永 and Gao Quxun 高去尋, *Houjiazhuang* 侯家莊 , 7 vols. (Large Tombs 1001, 1002, 1003, 1217, 1004, 1500, 1550), Taibei, Institute of History and Philology, 1962–76.

8. Zhongguo Kexueyuan Kaogu yanjiusuo 中國科學院考古研究所, *Yinxu Fu Hao mu* 殷墟婦好墓, Beijing: Wenwu Press, 1980.

9. See Alexander Soper, "Early, middle and late Shang: a note," *Artibus Asiae* XXVIII (1966), 26–7; see also K. C. Chang, "Yin-hsü Tomb Number Five and the question of the P'an Keng/Hsiao Hsin/Hsiao Yi period in Yin-hsü archaeology," in *Studies of Shang archaeology*, p. 78.

10. Guo Baojun 郭寶鈞, "1950-nian chun Yinxu fajue baogao" 1950年春殷墟發掘報告, *Kaogu xuebao* 考古學報. 1951.5; "Anyang Yinxu nuli jisi keng de fajue" 安陽殷墟奴隸祭祀坑的發掘, *Kaogu*, 1977.1, pp. 20–36; Yang Xizhang 楊錫璋 and Yang Baocheng 楊寶成, "Cong Shangdai jisi keng kan Shangdai nuli shehui de rensheng"從商代祭祀坑看商代奴隸社會的人牲, *Kaogu*, 1977.1, pp. 13–19; Hu Houxuan 胡厚宣, "Zhongguo nuli shehui de renxun he renji *Xiabian*" 中國奴隸社會的人殉和人祭·下編 *Wenwu*, 1974.8, pp. 56–67. Hu also calculated another 1,145 oracle bone inscriptions mentioned human sacrifice without mentioning the number of victims.

11. For a summary of Shang archaeology at Zhengzhou with references to the original archaeological reports, see K. C. Chang, *Shang civilization*, pp. 52–5. For discussion of current debate about the cultural sequence, see An Chin-huai, "The Shang city at Cheng-chou and related problems," in K. C. Chang, ed., *Studies of Shang archaeology*, pp. 15–48.

12. See Li Xueqin 李學勤, "Tan Anyang Xiaotun yiwai chutu de you zi jiagu" 談安陽小屯以外的有字甲骨, *Wenwu*, 1956.11, p. 17 (illustrations in *Wenwu* 1954, opp. p. 8 and inside cover) for discussion of the Zhengzhou inscriptions.

13. Summaries of the Erlitou excavations may be found in K. C. Chang, *Shang civilization*, pp. 341ff., K. C. Chang, *The archaeology of ancient China*, 4th edition, New Haven: Yale University Press, 1986, pp. 309–16 (in the former, Chang identifies Erlitou finds with the Xia, but in the latter, he takes a more cautious approach). See also Yin Wei-ch'ang, "A re-examination of Erh-li-t'ou culture," in *Studies of Shang archaeology*, pp. 1–14, and the concise summary which he was written in Zhongguo Shehui Kexueyuan Kaogu Yanjiusuo 中國社會

科學院考古研究所 *Xin Zhongguo de kaogu faxian he yanjiu* 新中國的考古發現和研究, Beijing: Wenwu Press, 1984, pp. 211–8.

14. Reports on the Shixianggou excavations have been published in *Kaogu*, 1984.6, 1984.10, 1985.4 and 1988.2. Although the early reports mention a walled city, no detailed report of such a wall has yet appeared.

15. Summaries of these excavations may be found in *Shang civilization*, pp. 289–321 and in *Xin Zhongguo de kaogu faxian he yanjiu*, pp. 239–44.

16. Sichuansheng Wenwu Guanli Weiyuanhui 四川省文物管理委員會 and Sichuansheng Bowuguan 四川省博物館, "Guanghan Sanxingdui yizhi" 廣漢三星堆遺址, *Kaogu xuebao*, 1987.2; Chen Xiandan 陳顯丹, "Lun Guanghan Sanxingdui yizhi de xingzhi" 論廣漢三星堆遺址的性質, *Sichuan wenwu*, 1988.4, pp. 3–8; Sichuansheng Wenwu Guanli Weiyuanhui, etc., "Guanghan Sanxingdui yizhi erhao jisi keng fajue jianbao" 廣漢三星堆遺址二號祭祀坑發掘簡報, *Wenwu*, 1989.5, pp. 1–20; *Guanghan Sanxingdui Yizhi* 廣漢三星堆遺址 (Ziliao xuanbian, 資料選編), I, Guanghan, 1988.

17. Jack Goody and Ian Watt, "The consequences of literacy," in J. Goody, ed., *Literacy in traditional societies*, Cambridge: Cambridge University Press, 1968, p. 34. This important article is marred by lack of understanding of the Chinese writing system, corrected to some extent in *The interface between the written and the oral*, Cambridge: Cambridge University Press, 1987, pp. 36–7.

18. See Henansheng Wenwu Yanjiusuo 河南省文物研究所, "Henan Wuyang Jiahu xinshiqi shidai yizhi di er zhi liu ci fajue jianbao" 河南舞陽賈湖新石器時代遺址第二至六次發掘簡報, *Kaogu*, 1989.1, pp. 1–16.

19. *Duoshi* 多士, as translated by Bernhard Karlgren, "The book of documents," *Bulletin of the Museum of Far Eastern Antiquities* XXII (1950), p. 56.

CHAPTER 2

1. In Thomas A. Sebeck (ed.), *Myth: a symposium*, Bloomington: Indiana University Press, 1974, p. 3.

2. For a more extensive development of this thesis, see my article, "Shang foundations of modern Chinese folk religion," in S. Allan and Alvin P. Cohen (ed.), *Legend, lore and religion in China: essays in honor of Wolfram Eberhard on his seventieth birthday*, San Francisco: Chinese Materials Center, 1970, pp. 1–21.

3. See Sarah Allan, *The heir and the sage*.

4. Review in *Art Asiae* IX (1946), no. 4, pp. 355–67. See also Eberhard's own *Lokalkulturen in alten China* I (supplement to *T'oung Pao*, vol. 37, Leiden, 1942, trans. as *Local cultures in South and East Asia*, Leiden, 1968), II (*Monumenta Serica*, monograph III, Peking, 1942).

5. See "Drought, human sacrifice and the Mandate of Heaven in a lost text from the *Shang shu*," *Bulletin of the School of Oriental and African Studies* XLVII Part 3 (1984), pp. 523–39.

6. Other scholars who have related the Shang to a ten-sun myth include Akatsuka Kiyoshi 赤冢忠, *Chūgoku kodai no shūkyō to bunka: in ōchō no saishi* 中國古代の宗教と文化: 殷王朝の祭祀, Tokyo, Kadokawa Shoten, 1977 (see especially pp. 260, 443ff.), and Chang Tsung-tung, *Die Kult der Shang-dynastie im Spiegel der Orakelinschriften: eine palaographische Studie zur Religion im archaischen China*, Wiesbaden, Otto Harrassowitz, 1970, pp. 131–2, 202–3.

7. *Mengzi* 孟子 9/7a (5A.4). Also in the *Liji* 禮記 (*Zuantu huzhu liji* 纂圖互注禮記 6/4b, 15/13a, 20/16a). For ease of reference, citations will be given in this fashion, referring to the *juan*/page number of the Sibu Congkan 四部叢刊 editions published in Shanghai, whenever possible. Other editions have, of course, been consulted and will be cited where there are textual problems.

8. L. De Saussure, *Les origines de l'astronomie chinoise*. Paris, Maisonneuve, 1930; Henri Maspero, "L'astronomie chinoise avant les Han," *T'oung Pao* XXVI, 1929, p. 267; Joseph Needham, *Science and civilisation in China* III. Cambridge: Cambridge University Press, 1959.

9. *Lun heng jiaoshi* 論衡校釋, Huang Hui 黃暉 (ed.), Shanghai, Commercial Press, 1964, *juan* 11, p. 512.

10. In his 1962 edition of the *Ch'u Tz'u: songs of the south*, David Hawkes argued that the *Tian wen* could be dated to the fifth century B.C. and in an earlier article, "Sons of suns: myth and totemism," I followed this estimation which he has now revised. Although I continue to suspect an earlier date, without concrete evidence that the text predates Qu Yuan, we should perhaps err on the side of caution.

11. Yang Kuan 楊寬, "Zhongguo shanggu shi daolun" 中國上古史導論, in *Gushibian* VII, pp. 151–3. See also David Hawkes, *Ch'u Tz'u*, 1962, p. 45. In his 1986 edition Hawkes stressed the relationship between the Xia and Chu rather than the Shang. If, however, my argument in the following chapter that the Xia were the converse of the Shang in Shang myth is correct, then there is no contradiction.

12. K. C. Chang, *Shang civilization*, pp. 59–60, notes 198–204, gives a list of references to the Chinese sources concerning sites excavated in the south. Chinese excavators date Panlongcheng to the Erligang period, that is early or middle Shang, depending on the chronology adopted for the beginning of the dynasty.

13. *Kaogu xuebao* 考古學報, 1986.2, pp. 153–98.

14. Qi Wenxin 齊文心, "Guanyu Shangdai chengwang de fengguo junzhang de tantao" 關於商代稱王的封國君長的談討, *Lishi yanjiu* 歷史研究, 1985, no. 2.

15. *Shuowen jiezi gulin* 說文解字詁林, Shanghai, Yixue Shuju, 1928, pp. 2486.

16. The archaic reconstructions here and elsewhere in this paper are those of Bernhard Karlgren in *Grammata serica recensa, Bulletin of the Museum of Far Eastern Antiquities* XXIX, 1957.

17. ibid., 47 (102 v) glosses 榑 as 'a kind of tree', citing the *Lüshi chunqiu* as his source. *Lüshi chunqiu* (22/8b) does contain the line "Yu went east to the land of the Fu Tree", but this tree is the Fu Sang for it is also "where the suns emerge from the nine streams" and it is so understood by the commentator Gao You who refers to the Fu Sang tradition. I have not been able to find any examples in Zhou or Han texts where this character is used to refer to anything but the sun tree.

18. Marcel Granet, *Danses et legendes de la Chine ancienne*, I, Paris: Presses Universaires de France, 1959, p. 305.

19. The *Shizhou ji* 十州紀 as cited by Li Shan in his commentary to Zhang Heng 張衡, *Si xuan fu* 思玄賦 in the *Wenxuan* 文選 (15/8a). This interpretation is followed by Jean-Pierre Dieny in *Pastourelles et magnanarelles: essai sur un theme litteraire chinois*, Geneva and Paris, Librairie Droz, 1977, p. 58, but I have not been able to find any support for it in the description of the tree in other early texts.

20. See B. Karlgren, *Grammata serica recensa*, p. 46 (101f.).

21. *Huainanzi* 淮南子 3/9a, 14/8b.

22. *Gui zang* 歸藏, Changsha, Yu Han Shan Fang Jiyi shu 玉函山房輯佚書, 1884, 12a (*Qi wu pian* 契巫篇).

23. *Shang shu Yaodian* 尚書 · 堯典, as cited in the *Zhongwen da cidian* 中文大詞典, Taipei. Hua Gang Chubanshe, 1976, III, p. 4431, but none of the editions I have consulted gives this form.

24. Guo Pu's comment is 湯谷也. Similarly, M. Granet, *Danses et legendes*, p. 437, calls it "le Val des Eaux chaudes et bouillantes".

25. See S. Couvreur, *Dictionnaire de la langue classique chinoise*, Taipei, World Book Co., 1963 (facsimile of 1904 edition), pp. 423, which defines it as "la principe de la lumiere", and *Zhongwen de cidian*, IV, pp. 6482, which equates it with 暘 and 陽.

26. M. Eliade, *Shamanism: archaic techniques of ecstasy*, London, Routledge & Kegan Paul, 1964.

27. A very rare character 曊 is used here which is interpreted by the commentator Gao You as *you zhao* 猶照 'like shining'. I suspect, however, that it is related to 拂 which is used with reference to the sun mounting the Fu Sang and which M. Granet, *Danses et legendes*, p. 435, relates to 扶.

28. See p. 86 for a discussion of the term *di*. Another collective use of the term occurs in the *Zuozhuan* 左傳 (*Zhao Gong* 昭公 29, *fu* 4)—*Chunqiu Zuozhuan jin-zhu jinyi* 春秋左傳今注今譯, Taipei: Taiwan Commercial Press, 1970, p. 1300,

which refers to *you di* 有帝. For this use of *you*, see David S. Nivison, *Early China*, III, 1977, pp. 1–18.

29. "Myth of the Xia", p. 10.

30. *Chuchi*, 3/4a, b. (Hawkes, line 15). See also the *Huainanzi*.

31. *Shanhaijing* (*Haineijing*) 18/85a.

32. See M. Granet, *Danses et Legendes*, p. 435.

33. Mizukami Shizuo 水上靜夫, "Soju shinkō ron" 桑樹信仰論, *Nippon Chūgoku gakkaihō* 日本中國學會報 XIII, 1961, pp. 5–6, and "Jakuboku kō" 若木考, *Tōhōgaku* 東方學 XXI, 1961, pp. 1–12 (for the *ruo mu* as a mulberry). See also the Qing dynasty commentary of Duan Yucai 段玉裁 in *Shuowen jiezi gulin*, 2267b, and Guan Donggui 管東貴, "Zhongguo gudai shi ri shenhua zhi yanjiu" 中國古代十日神話之研究, *BIHP* XXXIII (1962), p. 301.

34. See the funerary pendants excavated from Changsha Mawangdui tombs no. 1 (*Changsha Mawangdui yihao Han mu* 長沙馬王堆一號漢墓, Peking: Wenwu Press, 1973, II, pl. 77) and no. 3 (*Wenwu* 1974.7, pl. 5) and Shangdong Linyi Jinqueshan 山東臨沂全雀山 (*Wenwu* 1977.11, inside cover).

35. *Yin Gong* 隱公 1 (Li Zongtong 李宗桐, ed., *Chunqiu Zuozhuan jinzhu jinyi*, 春秋左傳今注今譯, Taibei, Commercial Press, 1970, p. 4).

36. *Mengzi* 6/15a (3b.10); *Xunzi* 荀子 1/10a; *Huainanzi* 3/5a. This belief may extend to snakes which may explain the prominence of snakes in both oracle bone characters for curses and disasters and in the bronze vessels for making ritual offerings to the ancestors of the Shang period.

37. *Lun heng jiaoshi, juan* 13, p. 207.

38. *Zhuangzi* 6/26b (*pian* 17). See also *Huainanzi* 19/6a, "if it is not the top of the nine-layered sky, it is the bottom of the Yellow Springs."

39. For examples, see Kate Finsterbusch, *Verzeichnis und Motivindex der Han-darstellungen*, Wiesbaden, Harrassowitz, 1966 (I) and 1971 (II).

40. *Changsha Mawangdui yihao Han mu* 長沙馬王堆一號漢墓, I, 39; II, pl. 72.

41. This problem is discussed by Michael Loewe in *Ways to paradise: the Chinese quest for immortality*, London: George Allen and Unwin, 1979, pp. 50–2. I agree with Loewe that the nine suns are associated with the power called Di, but I believe the nine suns (*jiu yang* 九陽) of the *Yuan you* in the *Chuci* are similarly those suns in the underworld awaiting their turn. See Hong Xingzu 洪興祖, *Chuci buzhu* 楚辭補注, p. 125, Shanghai: Commercial Press, for an interpretation of *yang* as sun. Also Guan Donggui, "Zhongguo gudai shiri" p. 291.

42. See *Shanbei Dong Han huaxiang shike xuanji* 陝北東漢畫象石刻選集. Peking: Shaanxisheng Bowuguan, 1959, pl. 8 (K. Finsterbusch, p. 392); R. C. Rudolph, *Han tomb art of West China*, Berkeley and Los Angeles, University of California Press, 1951, pl. 55 (Finsterbusch, p. 152); "Shandong Anqiu Han huaxiang shi mu fajue jianbao" 山東安丘漢畫象石墓發掘簡報, *Wenwu*, no. 4, 1964, p. 40, fig. 10; E. Chavannes, *La sculpture sur pierre en Chine au temps des deux dynasties Han*, Paris: Ernest Leroux, 1893, pl. 20. In the Shanbei and Wu Liang Shrine (Chavannes) reliefs, a horse and chariot are tied to the Fu Sang Tree. I suspect that these may represent Qu Yuan in the *Li Sao*.

43. See Wu Shan 吳山, *Zhongguo xinshiqi shidai taoqi zhuangshi yishu* 中國新石器時代陶器裝飾藝術, 1982, p. 121; *Meishu* 美術, 1983.8.

44. Izushi Yoshiko 出石誠彥, *Chūgoku shinwa densetsu no kenkyū* 中國神話傳說の研究, Tokyo: Chūō Koronsha, 1943, pp. 75–82; Michael Loewe, *Ways to paradise*, p. 129.

45. *Gui zang*, 12a.

46. H. Maspero, "Legendes mythologiques," p. 8. See also Zhang Xincheng 張心澄, *Weishu tongkao* 偽書通考, Shanghai: Commercial Press, 1954, pp. 19–24. For other references, see pp. 35–6, notes 84, 85, 86.

47. *Shanhaijing (Dahuangxijing)* 16/76a.

48. Izushi, *Chūgoku shinwa*, p. 589; Yuan Ke 袁珂, *Zhongguo gudai shenhua* 中國古代神話, Shanghai: Commercial Press, 1957, p. 179.

49. Chen Mengjia 陳夢家, "Shanghai de shenhua yu wushu" 商代的神話與巫術, *Yanjing xuebao* 燕京學報, 20, December 1936, p. 490; Wolfgang Munke, *Die klassische chinesische Mythologie*, Stuttgart: Ernst Klett Verlag, 1976.

50. *Shanhaijing (Dahuangnanjing)* 10/68b.

51. *Shanhaijing (Haineijing)* 13/88a.

52. Chen Mengjia, "Shangdai shenhua," p. 490.

53. *Diwang shiji jicun* 帝王世紀輯存, Xu Zongyuan 徐宗元 (ed.), Peking: Zhonghua Shuju, 1964, p. 39.

54. *Diwang shiji jicun*, p. 29.

55. Wang Guowei 王國維, "Yin buci zhong suojian xian gong xian wang kao" 殷卜辭中所見先公先王考 in *Guantang jilin* 觀堂集林, Wu Cheng, Zhejiang, Mi Yun Lou of the Jiang family, 1923, Ch. 9 (*Shi lin* 1), 2a–3b; see also his "Yin buci zhong suojian xian wang xu kao", 18a–19a.

56. For studies which identify Di Jun, Di Ku and Shun, see Izushi Yoshiko, pp. 582–4; Guo Moruo 郭沫若, *Zhongguo gudai shehui yanjiu* 中國古代社會研究,

Peking: Renmin Chubanshe, 1959, pp. 247–8; Chen Mengjia, "Shangdai shenhua," pp. 488–9; Shirakawa Shizuka 白川靜, *Chūgoku no shinwa* 中國の神話, Tokyo, 1975, p. 165; Yuan Ke, *Zhongguo gudai shenhua*, p. 142. Since these works give detailed textual references in support of the identifications, I have not repeated them here.

57. *Guoyu* 國語 (Luyu 魯語) 4/8b.

58. *Liji* 禮記 (Jifa 祭法) 23/1b.

59. *Chuci buzhu*, pp. 20–1. Cf. David Hawkes, *Songs*, p. 28, II. 96–9. Hawkes's translation follows Wang Yi's Interpretation that Xihe was the 'charioteer of the sun' (日禦也). This accords with Wang Yi's interpretation that the Lord of the east' who drove a chariot across the sky in *Dong jun* 東君 of the *Nine songs* was the sun itself (*Chuci buzhu*, p. 50) which Hawkes also follows. However, there is a logical inconsistency between the idea that the suns were birds and their having chariots to drive them across the sky. Guan Donggui, p. 292, has argued that this tradition derives from a misinterpretation of the meaning of *ri yu* which was later the name of an official in charge of delineating the suns' movements. In any case, who the speaker is in *Dong jun* is unclear—it may be the poet-shaman himself whose spirit chariot is following the sun—and there is no other early reference to the sun being driven by a chariot.

60. *Chuci buzhu*, p. 100. Cf. Hawkes, line 18.

61. *Chuci buzhu*, p. 172. Cf. Hawkes, 1.22b.

62. Wang Yi substituted *bing* 並 'together' for *dai* 代 'alternately', presumably because he thought it was a reference to the myth of Archer Yi, but the ten suns coming out together only happened once. More logically, and in accordance with the original text, this refers to the great heat of the suns in the East as they awaited their turn to go out. Wen Yiduo 聞一多 (*Gudian xinyi* 古典新義 in *Wen Yiduo quanji* 聞一多全集, Shanghai, Kaiming Shudian, 1948, II, p. 453) and Hawkes, p. 104, follow Wang Yi, but see Guan Donggui, p. 291, and Izushi Yoshiko, p. 80.

63. *Chuci*, 3/4b. Cf. Hawkes, 11.15–16.

64. *Chuci*, 3/4b. Cf. Hawkes, 1.56. I have translated 揚 as 'risen'; Hawkes, as 'stirred'. The *Shuowen* definition is 飛舉 'fly up' and an alternative text, according to Hong Xingzu's commentary, gives 陽. This suggests that this character, like others with an 昜 element, is connected with the sun which rises in our terminology or flies up as a bird in the Fu Sang tradition.

65. *Chuci*, 3/12b. Cf. Hawkes, 1.56. See also *Gui zang*, 9b (*Zheng mu jing*) which refers to Yi shooting the suns in similar language.

66. See Izushi Yoshiko, *Chūgoku Shinwa*, p. 589; Wolfgang Munke, *Die Klassische Chinesische Mythologie*, p. 117.

67. Yi also appears as a trouble-maker in myths associated with the Xia Dynasty (see Ch. 3). It is not clear to what extent Xia Yi is the same as the sun-shooting Yi. See Eberhard, *Local cultures*, pp. 80–7.

68. *Chuci*, 3/12b.

69. *Zhuangzi jishi* 莊子集釋, Guo Qingfan 郭慶範 (ed.), Taipei, Heluo Tushu Chubanshe, 1974, p. 22 (1/9b).

70. *Zhuangzi jishi*, p. 89 (1/37b).

71. *Lunheng jiaoshi, juan* 11, p. 509.

72. *Guben zhushu jinian jijiao dingbu* 古本竹書紀年輯校訂補, Fan Xiangyang 祥雍 (ed.), Shanghai: Xin Zhishi Chubanshe, 1956, p. 14.

73. *Shiji* 史記, Peking: Zhonghua Shuju, 1959, p. 91 (*juan* 3).

74. See H. G. Creel, *Studies in early Chinese culture*, Baltimore, American Council of Learned Societies, 1937, p. 51; and H. G. Creel, *The origins of statecraft in China*, Chicago, University of Chicago Press, 1970, I, pp. 493–506, for *tian* as a Zhou deity.

75. See Chen Mengjia, "Shangdai shenhua," p. 490.

76. For this motif, See S. Allan, *The heir and the sage*, pp. 87, 108, 134.

77. There is a bird called the *wu yan* 烏燕 (see Jia Zuzhang 賈祖璋, *Niao yu wenxue* 鳥與文章, Shanghai 1931, p. 5) the 'crow-swallow' which may have contributed to the confusion. Guan Donggui, "Zhongguo gudai shi ri," pp. 295–6, also identifies the sun raven with the *xuan niao*. He further cites Hu Houxuan 胡厚宣, "Chu minzu yuan yu dongfang kao" 楚民族源於東方考, *Shixue luncong* 史學論叢 I, 1923.

78. *Mozi jiangu* 墨子間詁, Sun Yirang 孫詒讓 (ed.), Shanghai: Commercial Press, 1936, *juan* 8, p. 8 (*Ming gui, xia*): *Chunqiu Zuozhuan jinshi jinyi*, 1228 (*Zhao Gong* 28).

79. "Zhongguo shanggushi daolun," *Gushi bian*, vol. 7, p. 102.

80. E. Chavannes, *Le Tai chan: essai de monographie d'un culte chinois*, Paris, 1910, pp. 474–5; Marcel Granet, *Danses et Legendes*, p. 147.

81. *Shuoyuan*, 1/15b.

82. "Drought, human sacrifice and the mandate of Heaven in a lost text from the *Shang shu*," see esp. pp. 523–4. References to this text may be found in the *Lunyu* 10/9AB (堯曰), *Mozi* 4/14b (兼愛下), *Guoyu* 1/15A (周語上), *Lunheng* 5/14A–15 (感虛), *Sou shenji* 搜神記, p. 67 (捲 8), *Lüshi chunqiu* 9/38–49 (順民), *Huainanzi* 9/4a (主術訓), *Shangshu da zhuan* 尚書大傳 2/14a, *Xunzi* 19/15a–b

(大略), *Shuoyuan* 1/15b (君道). The extant *Tang gao* 湯誥 is based upon this same text but does not include the references to human sacrifice. The *Diwang shiji* includes six versions. That quoted here (*jicun*, p. 65) is the most complete. Although the language has been modernized, it appears to be based on an early version of the *Tang gao* from which the other references also derive. For a detailed textual comparison, see "Drought," p. 535–9.

83. "Drought", p. 527; Qiu Xigui 裘錫圭, "Shuo buci de fen wuwang yu zuo tulong" 說卜辭的焚巫王與作土龍, *Jiaguwen yu Yin-Shang shi* 甲骨文與殷商史 I, Shanghai, Guji chubanshe, 1983, pp. 21–35 (trans. by Vernon K. Fowler in *Early China* IX–X, (1983–5), pp. 290–306.

84. For discussion of this theme, see S. Allan, "The identities of Taigong Wang in Zhou and Han literature," *Monumenta Serica* XXX (1972–3), pp. 89–98.

85. "Some dualistic phenomena in Shang society," *Early Chinese civilization: anthropological perspectives* (Harvard-Yenching Institute Monograph Series XXIII, 1976), p. 100.

86. Qi Wenxin, "The case for Yi Yin and Huang Yin being two persons" in S. Allan et al, *Oracle bone collections in Great Britain*, part II (forthcoming).

87. *Chuci*, 3/24b–5a; cf. Hawkes, p. 53. See also August Conrady, *T'ien wen* (Asian Major Library, no. 2), Leipzig: 1931, p. 135. Ying 媵 which Wang Yi glosses as *song ye* 送也 appears to mean sent in the entourage of the bride, as a dowry present.

88. See Chen Bingliang (Chan Ping-leung) 陳炳良, "Zhongguo gudai shenhua xinshi liang ze" 中國古代神話新釋兩則, *Qinghua xuebao* 清華學報 VII, 2, 1969, pp. 209–10; M. Granet, *Danses et legendes*, pp. 433ff.

89. *Gui zang* (*Qi wu pian*), 12a. See also M. Granet, p. 9. The 'eight extremes' are presumably the 'eight pillars' of *Tian wen* (II.9–10), *Chuci*, 3/3b.

90. *Gui zang*, 14a.

91. See Chen Bingliang, p. 210, who gives a list of references to the *kong sang* and *qiong sang*. See also chapter 3, pp. 100–1.

92. *Guanzi zuangu* 管子纂詁, An Jingheng 安井衡 (ed.), Taipei: Heluo Tushu Chubanshe, 1976, p. 8 (*juan* 3), includes a reference to *xuan di* which is interpreted as *tian di* 天帝, but the epithet is very rare (I have not found any other references). The story of Confucius's birth comes from the *Chunqiu Kong yan tu* 春秋孔演圖 which is quoted in the *Taiping yulan* 太平禦覽, Tainan, Ping Ping Chubanshe, 1975, 4793 (955), and the *Yiwen leiju* 藝文類聚, Shanghai: Zhonghua Shuju, 1965, 1519 (88).

93. M. Granet, p. 435.

94. In the *Shiji, juan* 4, p. 6, Huang Di is described as going west as far as Kong Tong. Kong Tong was also the name of the north gate of the state of Song— see *Chunqiu Zuozhuan jinzhu jinyi*, 1513–14 (*Ai Gong* 26 and note) in which a corpse is brought in from Kong Tong. I suspect that the western symbolism of death in the east/west scheme has been transferred here to the north in a four-directional scheme.

95. *Shiji, juan* 3, pp. 99; *Guben zhushu jinian*, pp. 18–19.

96. *Chuci*, 3/25a; cf. Hawkes, e. 125.

97. Mori Yasutaro 森安太郎, *Zhongguo gudai shenhua yanjiu* 中國古代神話研究 (tr. Wang Xiaolian 王孝廉), Taibei, Di Ping Xian Chubanshe, 1974, p. 14.

98. For a list of scholars who view his name as Xian, see D. N. Keightley, *Sources*, p. 207, n.(a).

99. *Jiu gao* 酒告. B. Karlgren, *The Book of documents, Bulletin of the Museum of Far Eastern Antiquities* XVII, 1950, 45(9), translates *xian* as 'all', but see Hu Houxuan 胡厚宣, "Yin buci zhong di Shang Di he Wang Di" 殷卜辭中的上帝和王帝, *Lishi yanjiu* IX (1959), pp. 89–90.

100. This definition derives from Claude Levi-Strauss, *Totemism*, Rodney Needham (tr.), London, Merlin Press, 1964, and *The savage mind*, Chicago: University of Chicago Press, 1966. It should be noted, however, that 'man' in this case is represented by the ancestors. The relationship between the classification of the ancestors and social groups among the living is still an open question. Furthermore, although ten is a number with natural origins and the suns a natural object, the classification of ten suns is as much a cultural category as the ten groups of ancestors.

101. In a paper delivered at the School of Oriental and African Studies, November 1978, David Nivison, by assuming all the inscriptions on a single shell (*Bingbian* 334, p. 5) to be related, demonstrated a connection between the king's illness and weather phenomena. If he is correct, this could provide a precedent for Cheng Tang's offering.

102. See D. Keightley, "Late Shang divination: the magico-religious legacy," in Henry Rosemont, Jr., ed., *Explorations in early Chinese cosmology*, Chicago, California, scholars Press, 1984, esp. p. 18.

103. D. Keightley, *Sources*, p. 89, estimates that some three million man-hours were devoted to pyromancy in the historical period.

104. Wen Yiduo, *Gudian xinyi*, II, pp. 565ff.

105. For sun worship in the inscriptions, see pp. 52–6 and note 138 below.

106. *Shuowen jiezi gulin*, p. 2653.

107. For collections of the opinions of Chinese and Japanese scholars, see Li Xiaoding 李孝定, *Jiagu wenzi jishi* 甲骨文字集釋, Nangang, 1965, 2029 and Zhou Fagao 周法高, *Jinwen gulin* 金文詁林 and *Jinwen gulin bu* 金文詁林補, 6–0782. Although the clan name 🐟 which occurs in bronze inscriptions is often taken as 東, I see no evidence for this identification, as the character 'east' is never written in this manner.

108. This is discussed in my article, "On the engraving of oracle bone inscriptions" in S. Allan, etc., *Oracle bone collections in Great Britain*, Part II, forthcoming.

109. *Yingcang*, 2252.

110. See B. Karlgren, *Grammata serica recensa*, p. 118 (重, 腫, 踵, 鍾, 衝, etc.).

111. "Remarks on the evolution of Archaic Chinese," *Harvard Journal of Asiatic Studies* II, 3, 1937, pp. 347–9; L. C. Hopkins, "Archaic Chinese characters," *Journal of the Royal Asiatic Society* XIV, 1937 pp. 29–31. See also the rebuttal by H. G. Creel, "On the ideographic element in ancient Chinese," *T'oung Pao* XXXIV.4 (1939), pp. 278–81.

112. *Shuowen jiezi gulin*, pp. 5288.

113. Wang Guowei 王國維, "Yinxu buci zhong suojian xian gong xian wang kao," *juan 9, shilin* 史林 1, pp. 2a–3b (see also "Yinxu buci zhong suojian xian gong xian wang xu kao," 17b–18a). The arguments for various transcriptions are summarized by Shima Kunio, *Sōrui*, pp. 238–40, and Li Xiaoding 李孝定, *Jiagu wenzi jishi* 甲骨文字集釋, pp. 1905–8 and references given therein, and I will not therefore give detailed citations in the following discussion.

114. See K. C. Chang, "T'ien Kan: a key to the history of the Shang," in *Ancient China: studies in early civilization*, D. T. Roy and T. H. Tsien (ed.), Hong Kong, Chinese University Press, 1978, p. 37.

115. See Li Xiaoding, p. 2787.

116. Wu Qichang 吳其昌, "Buci zhong suojian xian gong xian wang san xu kao" 卜辭中所見先公先王三續考, *Yanjing xuebao* 燕京學報 XIV, 1933, p. 8.

117. See Yin Shun Fashi 印順法師, *Zhongguo gudai minzu shenhua yu wenhua zhi yanjiu* 中國古代民族神話與文化之研究, Taibei, Hua Gang Chubanshe, 1975, pp. 99–101.

118. *Shuowen jiezi gulin*, p. 4418; *Er ya Xia* 爾雅. 下, 9b(16). Also in the *Mu tianzi zhuan (Song ben)* 穆天子傳, 1/4b. See also Yin Shun Fashi, 102, who discusses the various animals which have been identified with the *suan*, other than the lion which was unknown in Shang and Zhou times. I suspect that the monkey pictograph of *Xiaotun di'erben: Yinxu wenzi: jia bian* 小屯第二本: 殷墟文字: 甲編

(repr. Institute of History and Philology, Academia Sinica, Taipei, 1971), no. 2336, which Shima Kunio 島邦男 includes in *Inkyo bokuji sōrui* 殷墟卜辭綜類, Tokyo, Kyuko Shoin, 1971, p. 211, under the same classification, is not the same character. The ear, eyebrow and nose are unique to this form. The inscription also includes a tiger and a horse over fire which implies that it may refer to a monkey used in sacrifice. There is little evidence but the general shape to tie it to the other forms of this character.

119. Akatsuka, *Chūgoku kodai*, p. 143.

120. For example Yuan Ke, p. 141; and p. 145, notes 3, 4. Yuan cites Wang Guowei's identification of Jun and Nao in *Gushi xin zhengshi* 古史新證釋 and Wu Qichang's identification of Nao and Jun. I do not think, however, that it is possible to justify this series phonologically as the characters do not belong to the same rhyme group.

121. Another common transcription among Chinese scholars although not among Western sinologists, is 离, a alternative form of Xie 契. This character has the advantage over Nao and Kui in a link with the Shang, but it is very rare and difficult to justify graphically. Scholars who use the transcription Jun, as I do, include, Yuan Ke, p. 141, Izushi Yoshiko, p. 582–3, Munke, p. 130, Yin Shun Fashi, pp. 99–101.

122. Akatsuka Kiyoshi, *Chūgoku Kodai*, pp. 443ff., see esp. p. 453.

123. Chen Mengjia, *Yinxu buci zongshu*, p. 574.

124. *Yinxu buci zongshu* and Chang Tsung-tung, p. 202, also make this identification. Akatsuka Kiyoshi, however, identifies Yi Jing 義京 (Shima Kunio, *Inkyo bokuji sōrui*, 356.3) with Xihe (and also E Huang). Since all the inscriptions by Shima refer to the same rite performed to Yi Jing, they may be a group. It is also possible the Eastern Mother is named in the inscriptions, but there is no means of relating the inscriptions.

125. See Shima Kunio, *Inkyo bokuji kenkyū*, p. 244, for a summary of viewpoints; also Li Xiaoding, pp. 3637–9. Akatsuka (see n. 118) identifies E with Nu Ying, Shun's second wife besides E Huang. Another view expressed by Chang Tsung-tung, p. 39, is that E was not a remote ancestor but the sister of Wu Ding. In this regard, it is possible (see below) that the name was also used with reference to later wives of Shang kings.

126. Shima Kunio, *Kenkyū*, p. 244, notes an apparent alternation in the periods in which Wang Hai and E were worshipped as well as their similar powers and suggests an identity. This seems unlikely since E has the female element and Wang Hai was Shang Jia's father. She is more likely Wang Hai's mother (that is E Huang). It also seems possible that *wo* meaning 'I' or 'we' derives its meaning from this first female ancestor, that is 'we descendants of E'.

127. See Yu Xingwu 于省吾, "Lue lun tuteng yu zongjiao qiyuan he Xia Shang tuteng" 略論圖騰與宗教起源和夏商圖騰, *Lishi yanjiu* 歷史研究 X (1959), pp. 66–7, whose interpretations I follow. The inscriptions may also be found in Luo Zhenyu 羅振玉, *Sandai jijin wencun* 三代吉金文存, Pojuezhai, 1936.

128. Shima Kunio 島邦男, *Sōrui*, 469.3.

129. *Sōrui*, 137.4 (probably also the first two characters of 138.1).

130. *Sōrui*, 138.1.

131. The totemic significance of this bird is discussed extensively by Hu Houxuan 胡厚宣 in "Jiaguwen Shangzu niao tuteng de yiji" 甲骨文商祖鳥圖騰的遺跡, *Lishi luncong* 歷史論叢 I (1964), pp. 133–59, and in "Jiaguwen suojian Shangzu niao tuteng de xin zhengju" 甲骨文所見商祖鳥圖騰的新證據, *Wenwu* 文物 1977.2, pp. 84–7.

132. In this context, Yu and Di Ku are parallel as the supernatural progenitors of human ancestors. Hou Ji was also fathered by Di Ku–when his mother stepped on Ku's footprint.

133. See Chen Mengjia, *Yinxu buci zongshu*, p. 337. Guo Moruo, *Zhongguo gudai shehui yanjiu*, p. 251, identifies this figure with both Xie and Zhi whom he identifies with one another and Hu Houxuan, 'niao tuteng', p. 135, follows him. Although the two figures are related, I believe that Zhi, Di Ku's son by Chang Yi, is better identified as Wang Heng 王恆 in the Shang inscriptions. The relationship is there because they are dual manifestations deriving from the same structure, not because they were originally the same figure. The same is true of Xihe and Chang Xi whom Guo also identifies.

134. *Chunqiu Zuozhuan jinzhu jinyi*, p. 1105. For other examples of *shi ri* referring to the *jia yi*, see *Huainanzi* 3/11b, 4/5b, *Guoyu* 18/3b.

135. *Lun heng jiaoshi, juan* 25, p. 1027 (Alfred Forke, *Lun heng*, New York: Paragon Book Gallery, 1962, II, p. 412).

136. See Chen Mengjia, *Yinxu buci zongshu*, pp. 499–500; Akatsuka Kiyoshi, Chūgoku, p. 803; and Léon Vandermeersch, *Wangdao ou la voie royale: Recherches sur l'esprit des institutions de la Chine archaique*, Paris: Ecole Francaise d'Extreme Orient, 1977, I, p. 340, for other discussion of these inscriptions. The original provenance of the weapons appears to be confused (see Chen), but they are at present in the Liaoning Provincial Museum in Shenyang where I was told they had been received from Luo Zhenyu. (See also his *Sandai jijin jicun*, 19.20–21.)

137. See "T'ien kan," pp. 17–20, for one version of Chang's argument. Other theories include that of Dong Zuobin 董作賓, "Lun Shangren yi shengri wei ming" 論商人以生日為名, *Dalu zazhi* 大陸雜誌 II.3 (1951), pp. 6–10, that these were death dates (see also Vandermeersch, pp. 284–94) and Chen Mengjia, *Zongshu*,

pp. 404–5, that they represented the order of sacrifices determined by the order of birth, enthronement and death.

138. See Chen Mengjia, *Zongshu*, pp. 573–4.

139. Shang Chengzuo 商承祚, *Yinqi yicun* 殷契佚存, Nanjing, Jinling Daxue Zhongguo wenhua yanjiusuo congkan jia zhong, 1933, p. 871.

140. *Xiaotun di'erben: Yinxu wenzi: bing bian*, Taibei, 1957, p. 392. Grammatically, this could also be translated as Shang Jia's sun, but it is difficult to understand the meaning.

141. See Shima Kunio, *Inkyo bokuji kenkyū*, p. 201.

CHAPTER 3

1. *Science and civilisation*, III, p. 177.

2. "Legends and cults," p. 264.

3. *Shiji, juan* 1, p. 14.

4. *Shanhaijing (Zhongshanjing)* 5/52a. Shima, *Inkyo bokuji sōrui*, 58.4, 㚖 is identified by Li Xiaoding, p. 4011, as *yao* 堯 but there is only one occurrence of this character in the oracle bone inscriptions. I suspect that Da Rao 大橈, credited with inventing the cyclical characters (*jiazi* 甲子) in *Lüshi chunqiu* 17/10a, is the same person since the name Da Rao does not occur in any other context and through these cyclical characters he is tied to the ten-sun tradition.

5. Guo Moruo, *Zhongguo gudai shehui yanjiu*, p. 251, suspects Tang Yao of *being* Tang but I think this an oversimplification.

6. For Di Dan Zhu, see *Shanhaijing (Haineinanjing)* 10/49b, *(Haineibeijing)* 12/56a.

7. Chapter 2, note 74.

8. The text to which I will be referring is that in B. Karlgren, *The Book of documents, Bulletin of the Museum of Far Eastern Antiquities* XXII, 1950, but in some cases I have revised his translations, as here, where I follow Karlgren in taking Yao rather than his virtue as the subject (see B. Karlgren, *Glossen on the Book of documents, Bulletin of the Museum of Far Eastern Antiquities* XX, 1948, 46, but take *heng* 橫 more literally as 'horizontally' in contrast with 'above and below'.

9. See Karlgren, "Legends and cults," p. 264.

10. Karlgren's translation, *The Book of documents*, p. 3, par. 3.

11. "Legends and cults," p. 264.

12. See Shima, *Inkyo bokuji sōrui*, 163.4.

13. Chen Mengjia, *Yinxu buci zongshu*, p. 590. Chen who argues that niao is *wu* 烏 meaning suddenly and *xing* 星, a verb referring to the night sky gives 彝 for the west in the Yaodian but I follow Karlgren and other *Guwen* editions. See also Yin Shun Fashi, p. 127–9.

14. *Shanhaijing (Dahuangdongjing)* 14/64b.

15. See, for example, Yin Shun Fashi, p. 433.

16. *Science and civilisation*, III, p. 245.

17. Karlgren, *The Book of documents*, p. 3, par. 9.

18. *Shuowen jiezi gulin*, p. 2451.

19. Karlgren, *The Book of Documents*, p. 3, par. 11.

20. *The Book of Documents*, p. 4, par. 12, but I take *xia* 下 literally.

21. *The Book of Documents*, p. 4, par. 12, Karlgren's translation.

22. *The Book of Documents*, par. 13, Karlgren's translation.

23. Henri Maspero, "Legendes mythologiques dans le Chou King", *Journal Asiatique* CCIV (1924), pp. 1–100; Gu Jiegang 顧頡剛, ed., *Gushibian* 古史辯, 7 vols., Peking and Shanghai: 1926–41; see also Wolfram Eberhard, *Lokalkulturen im Atlen China*.

24. Chen Mengjia, "Shangdai de shenhua yu wushu" 商代的神話與巫術, *Yanjing Xuebao* 燕京學報 XX (Dec. 1936), p. 291.

25. Xu Xusheng 徐旭生, "1959 nian yu xi diaocha 'Xia Xu' de chubu baogao" 1959年預西調查 "夏墟" 的初步報告, *Kaogu* 1959.11, pp. 592–600; "Henan Erlitou yizhi fajue baogao" 河南偃師二里頭遺址發掘報告, *Kaogu* 1965.5, pp. 215–224; "Henen Yanshi Erlitou zao Shang gongdian yizhi fajue jianbao" 河南偃師二里頭早商宮殿遺址發掘簡報, *Kaogu* 1974.4, pp. 234–48; "Henan yanshi Erli-tou yizhi san ba qu fajue jianbao" 河南偃師二里頭遺址三八區發掘簡報, *Kaogu* 1975.5, pp. 302–9.

26. For a sympathetic summary of the new attributions see K. C. Chang, *Shang civilization*, New Haven: Yale University Press, 1980, pp. 335–55. In the 4th edition of his *Archaeology in China* (New Haven, Yale University Press, 1987), however, K. C. Chang takes a more cautious approach, adopting the now popular and ambiguous term 'Erlitou culture' for the disputed sites. See esp. pp. 309–16.

27. E.g., the *Shao Gao, Duo Shi* and *Duo Fang*. See *The heir and the sage*, p. 4.

28. For discussion of the development of the theory of a changing mandate of Heaven, see also S. Allan, "Drought, human scrifice and the mandate of Heaven in a lost text from the *Shang shu*."

29. Peking, Zhonghua shuju, 1959, *juan* 2, p. 49.

30. *Gushibian*, v.7, p. 196.

31. See *The heir and the sage*, p. 6.

32. "Shangdai de shenhua yu wushu," p. 323.

33. The character 熊 may be read as *xiong*, 'bear', or *nai*, a three-legged tortoise or dragon, the gloss given to the creature into which Gun and Yu turned—see note 60 below. As Chen Mengjia, "Shangdai de shenhua", p. 323, observed, Han Yuan is the name of the heavenly tortoise and in some versions of the Yu myth, the mountain through which he passed before turning into a *nai*. Thus, *nai* should also be the reading for Huang Di's clan name.

34. *Gushibian* VII, p. 196.

35. *Shijing* 12/4b (song 192, *Xiao Yu, Zheng Yue*), 16/2b (241, *Da Ya, Huang Yi*).

36. See the *Nineteen Old Songs*, no. 16 (*Gushi yuan* 古詩源 Taiping Shuju, Hong Kong: 1966, p. 91).

37. *Shanhaijing jiaozhu* 山海經校注, Yuan Ke 袁珂 ed., Shanghai: Guji Chubanshe, 1980, p. 446 (*Haineijing*). These identifications are also made by Chen Bingliang (Chan Ping-leung), *Zhongguo gudai shen hua*, p. 212.

38. See, for example, *Huainanzi* 9/1b.

39. *Jinzhu jinyi*, p. 1112.

40. See Shima Kunio, *Sorui*, 149.4.

41. cf. *Shanhaijing* (*Dahuangbeijing* 17/81b); *Huainanzi* 15/1a–b; *Lüshi chunqiu* 7/3a.

42. *juan* 1, p. 10; *juan* 2, p. 49.

43. *Shanhaijing* (*Haineijing*) 18/84b.

44. *Shanhaijing* (*Haineijing*) 18/84b.

45. *Guben zhushu jinian jijiao dingbu* 古本竹書紀年輯校訂補, Shanghai: Xin Zhishi Chubanshe, 1956, pp. 5–6. The identification Han Liu and Han Huang was first made by Guo Pu, see note 44.

46. *Shanhaijing jiaozhu* (*Dahuangxijing*) 16/78a–b.

47. *Zhuangzi* 9/38b.

48. *Dahuangxijing* 16/74a.

49. See *Huainanzi* 4/11a for the yellow clouds which rise from the Yellow Springs; see also *Zuozhuan jinzhu jinyi* (*Shao Gong* 17, p. 1192) for Huang Di's emblem as clouds.

50. See William G. Boltz, "Kung Kung and the flood: reverse euhemerism in the *Yao Tien*," *T'oung Pao* LXVII 3–5 (1981), p. 141.

51. *Chuci* 3/7b (lines 35–6, David Hawkes' translation, *Ch'u Tz'u: songs of the south*, New York: Beacon, 1962).

52. For discussion of Yi Yin as a mythical figure, see "Sons of suns," pp. 306–7, 313; for the drought at the beginning of the Shang, see my article, "Drought and human sacrifice in a lost text from the *Shang shu*."

53. For this identification, see "Sons of suns", pp. 322–3.

54. B. Karlgren, *The Book of documents*, *BMFEA* XXII (1950), pp. 2–3, 11.

55. *Chuci* 3/6b–7a (1.31–2).

56. W. Boltz, pp. 150–3. I disagree, however, with Boltz's interpretation of Gong Gong as a personification of the flood. There are water spirits in ancient Chinese texts (and rivers were worshipped in the oracle bone inscriptions), but there is no pattern of personifying phenomena such as flooding as opposed to natural objects such as rivers and mountains, though there appears to be in Indian mythology. Although the *Yaodian* states that Gong Gong "swelled up to Heaven" (*tao tian*), the text may be corrupt—elsewhere he is described as causing the *waters* to swell up to Heaven and the *Yaodian* appears to have many textual layers of different periods. In any case, this one line is insufficient evidence upon which to establish a mythical system.

57. *Chuci* 3/6a (1.25–6). In a painting found in tomb no. 1 at Mawangdui (see note 20), owls and turtles are depicted in the underworld, flanking large fishlike creatures in the center.

58. *Haineijing*, 18/88b; see also *Liji* 14/4a for the damming up of the waters by Gun. The meaning of *xi xiang* is uncertain. The *Huainanzi* (5/15a) refers to the states in Kunlun's eastern range (in the far west of the central region) where the "swelling mould dams up the flooding waters." Cf. *Huainanzi* 4/2a which refers to Yu rather than Gun damming up the waters with the swelling mould.

59. For the story of Gun's punishment by Yao, see *The heir and the sage*, pp. 35–6, 206.

60. This character is glossed in the *Erya* as a three-legged turtle and may also be written as 能, as in the *Guoyu* 14/14b (*Jin yu* 8). According to some accounts, it was once written with three dots, but I have not found any extant examples. Some commentators have alleged that it is an error for *long* 龍 'dragon', but the consistent use of the character 熊 in various contexts makes this interpretation less likely. The three legs of the turtle recall those of the sun-bird.

61. *Chuci* 3/6a–b (*Tian wen* pp. 27–8, pp. 73–4, based on Hawkes' translation).

62. *Gui zang* 歸藏, Changsha, Yu han shan fang jiyi shu, 1884, 12b (*Qi shi bian*).

63. See p. G17, Pt 2 above.

64. *Huainanzi* 7/7a.

65. See the commentaries of the *Shiji*, juan 2, p. 51, and the *Diwang shiji jicun* 帝王世紀輯存, Xu Zongyuan 徐宗元, ed., Beijing: Zhonghua Shuju, 1964, p. 52.

66. *Chuci* 3/15a (*Tian wen*, p. 66).

67. From a citation of the *Sui chaozi* 隨巢子 as cited in the *Yi shi*, see *Shanhaijing jiaozhu*, p. 210.

68. *Chuci* 3/15a (*Tian wen* 1.65), 1/11b (*Li sao*, 1.74).

69. *Shanhaijing* (*Dahuangxijing*) 16/78a. See also 2/40a (*Haiwaixijing*) and the *Gui zang*, 9a (*Zheng Mu*) for this story. For the *Jiu shao*, see *Guben zhushu jinian*, p. 9 (in which Qi danced the *Jiu shao* in the ninth year), and *shanhaijing* 16/78a. The *Shiji*, juan 1, p. 43, describes Yu as the creator of this music.

70. *Shiji*, juan 2, pp. 85–6.

71. The earliest references to this story are in the *Chuci*, 3/15b–16b, 18b–19a, lines 67–62, pp. 85–90.

72. VII, pp. 282–92.

73. Yang Junshi 楊君實, "Kang Geng yu Xia hui" 康庚與夏諱, *Dalu zazhi* 大陸雜志 XX.3 (1960), pp. 83–88.

74. *Guoyu* (*Luyu* 魯語, *shang* 上) 4/9a.

75. *Jijiao dingbu*, p. 14.

CHAPTER 4

1. 11/6a. See A. C. Graham, *Later Mohist logic, ethics and science*, Hong Kong: Chinese University Press, 1978, pp. 471, 226.

2. 14/11b. My translation follows that of A. C. Graham, *Chuang-tzu; the seven inner chapters and other writings from the book of Chuang-tzu*, London, Allen and Unwin, 1981, p. 284.

3. The *Shi Su fangding* 史速方鼎, "Jiashanxian Jingdanggongshe Hejiacun Xihao Zhou mu" 山縣京當公社賀家村西壕周墓, *Wenwu*, 1972.6, p. 26, fig. 3.

4. *Jikan* 集刊, vol.2, pt.1, pp. 17–8 ("Lei si kao" 耒耜考) as cited in *Jiaguwen jishi* VIII, p. 2777. See also Zhou Fagao, *Jinwen gulin* and *Gulinbu*, 8.1159.

5. Tōdō Akiyasu 滕堂明保, *Kanji gogen jiten* 漢字語源辭典, Tokyo: Gakutosha, 1967, p. 112; Kang Yin 康殷, *Wenzi yuanliu qian shuo* 文字源流淺說, Beijing, 1979, p. 140.

6. Gao Ming 高明, *Guwenzi leibian* 古文字類編, Beijing, Zhonghua Shuju, 1982, p. 364.

7. *Jiaguwen jishi*, 5, pp. 1539–4.

8. *Jingjin* 京津 2974, *Jimbun* 人文 B.3221, *Jiabian* 甲編 216 (*Shi* diviner group); *Ninghu* 寧滬 76, *Duoyi* 掇一 448, *Cuibian* 粹編 1268, *Cuibian* 1036, *Shiduo* 拾掇 1.1 (Li diviner group).

9. *Zhixu* 撫續 91, *Jimbun* 人文 B.2298 (Li diviner group).

10. David S. Nivison also noticed a relationship between 方 and 中 in "A new study of Xiaotun Yinxu Wenzi Jiabian 2416," paper presented to the International Conference on Shang culture, Anyang, China, September 1987.

11. *Jiaguwen jishi*, pp. 0025–31.

12. See *Inkyo bokuji sōrui*, p. 74.

13. Gao Hongjin 高鴻縉 as cited in *Jinwen gulin* 8.1159; Edward Shaughnessy (夏含夷), "Shi Yu fang" 釋禦方, *Guwenzi yanjiu* 9 (1984), pp. 97–110.

14. See Hu Houxuan 胡厚宣, "Shi Yindai qiu nian yu si fang feng de jisi" 釋殷代求年於四方和四方風的祭祀, *Fudan xuebao* 復旦學報 (Renwen kexue 人文科學) 1956.1, pp. 49–86.

15. *Chuci* 9/2b–6a.

16. See chapter 2, p. 88.

17. I have followed Bernhard Karlgren's emended *Guwen* 古文 text of the *Yaodian* 堯典, as published in *BMFEA* XXII (1950).

18. Noel Barnard, *Bronze casting and bronze alloys in ancient China*, Tokyo, 1961, p. 116, also takes this view.

19. See *Zhengzhou Erligang* 鄭州二里岡 (Henansheng Wenhuaju Wenwu Gongzuodui 河南省文化局文物工作隊) Beijing, Science Press, 1959, pl. 7.4.

20. See "Zhengzhoushi Baijiazhuang Shangdai mu fajue jianbao" 鄭州市白家莊商代墓發掘簡報, *Wenwu* 1955.10, fig. 42. *Pan* 盤, *lei* 罍 and *zun* 尊 excavated at Zhengzhou also have *ya*-shaped holes; see Henansheng Wenwu Yanjiusuo 河南省文物研究所, Zhengzhoushi Bowuguan 鄭州市博物館, "Zhengzhou xin faxian Shangdai caocang qingtongqi" 鄭州新發現商代操藏青銅器, *Wenwu* 1983.3, pp. 49–59, "Zhengzhou bei Erqilu xin faxian sanzuo Shang mu" 鄭州北二七路新發現三座商墓, *Wenwu* 1983.3, pp. 60–77.

21. Hayashi Minao 林已奈夫, *In Shū jidai seidoki no kenkyū* 殷周時代青銅器の研究 , Tokyo: Kobunkan, 1984, v.1, p. 160, includes only 2 *dou* 豆 from the late Shang period.

22. Hu Houxuan 胡厚宣, *Yinxu fajue* 殷墟發掘, Shanghai: Xuexi Shenghuo Press, 1955, fig. 87.

23. See Zhongguo Shehui Kexueyuan Kaogu Yanjiusuo 中國社會科學院考古研究所 , *Yin-Zhou jinwen jicheng*, Beijing: 1985, vol.5, 2725.

24. See *Jiaguwen jishi* 14.4165–72; *Jinwen gulin* and *Gulinbu* 14.1833.

25. *Zhongguo gudai zongzu yizhi shilun* 中國古代宗族移殖史論, pp. 14–5, as quoted in *Jinwengulin* 14.1833 (p. 7865).

26. *Jinwen gulin* 14.1833 (p. 7850).

27. *Yinxu buci zongshu*, p. 481.

28. Gao Quxun 高去尋, "Yindai da mu de mushi ji qi hanyi zhi tuice" 殷代大墓的木室及其含義之推測, *BIHP* XXXIX (1960), pp. 75–188.

29. Yang Xizhang 楊錫璋, "Anyang Yinxu Xibeigang da mu de fenqi ji youguan wenti" 安陽殷墟西北岡大墓的分期及有關問題, *Zhongyuan Wenwu*, 1981.3, pp. 47–52; "The Shang Dynasty cemetery system" in K. C. Chang, ed., *Studies of Shang archaeology: selected papers from the international conference on Shang civilization*, New Haven: Yale University Press, 1982, pp. 49–64.

30. Shi Zhangru 石璋如 "Henan Anyang Hougang de Yin mu" 河南安陽後岡的殷墓, *BIHP* XIII (1947), pp. 21–48.

31. See *The myth of the eternal return*, London: Routledge and Kegan Paul, 1955.

32. See *The savage mind*, Chicago, University of Chicago Press, 1962.

33. See Marcel Granet, "Right and left in China" in Rodney Needham, ed., *Right and left: essays on dual symbolic classification*, Chicago, University of Chicago Press, 1973.

34. "Dengfeng Wangchenggang yizhi de fajue" 登封王成岡遺址的發掘, *Wenwu*, 1983.3, pp. 21–36.

35. "The case for Yi Yin and Huang Yin being two persons in S. Allan, Qi Wenxin, *Oracle bone collections in Great Britain*, Part II, Beijing, Zhonghua shuju, in press.

36. Recent studies of the origin of *wuxing* 五行 theory which also summarize previous research include A. C. Graham, *Yin-yang and the nature of correlative thinking*, Singapore: The Institute of East Asian Philosophies, Occasional Paper

and Monograph Series, no. 6, 1986; Li Deyong 李德永, "Wuxing tanyuan" 五行探源, *Zhongguo zhexue* 中國哲學, no.4, Beijing: 1980, pp. 70–90.

37. Guo Moruo 郭沫若, *Zhongguo gudai shehui yanjiu* 中國古代社會研究, Renmin Press, Shanghai: 1955, and Hu Houxuan 胡厚宣, "Lun wu fang guannian ji 'Zhongguo' chengwei zhi qiyuan"論五方觀念及'中國'稱謂之起源 *Jiaguxue Shangshi congchuji* 甲骨學商史叢初集 II, Chengdu, Jilu daxue yanjiusuo, 1945.

38. *Guanzi jijiao* 管子集校, Guo Moruo 郭沫若, Wen Yiduo 聞一多, Xu Weiyu 許維遹 ed., Science Press, Beijing, 1856, facing p. 140. See also W. Allyn Rickett, *Guanzi: political, economic and philosophical essays from China*, v.1, Princeton, 1985.

39. See *Guwenzi leibian*, p. 93.

40. *Chuci tongshi*, p. 113; see also David Hawkes, *Ch'u Tz'u*, p. 198 (11.163–4) whose translation of *huang* 荒 as 'outland' I adopt.

41. *Zhongguo renxing lunshi: Xian Qin bian* 中國人性論史・先秦編, Taizhong, 1963, appendix 2; "Yinyang wuxing ji qi youguan wenxian de yanjiu" 陰陽五行及其有關文獻的研究, pp. 509–86.

42. Zhang Zhenglang 張政烺, "Shi shi Zhou chu qingtongqi mingwen zhong de yigua" 試釋周初青銅器銘文中的易卦, *Kaogu xuebao* 考古學報 1980.4, pp. 403–15.

43. See David N. Keightley, *Sources of Shang history: the oracle bone inscriptions of bronze-age China*, Berkeley: University of California Press, 1978, p. 3.

44. This has previously been suggested by David N. Keightley.

45. See Keightley, *Sources*, Appendix I, "Identification of the inscribed turtle shells of Shang" by James F. Berry, p. 160, n.4, and *Oracle bone collections in Great Britain*, pt.2, appendix I. *Bingbian* 丙編 184 and *Yingcang* 1313 are Geochylene (Testudo) Emys which occur natively from Burma to Indonesia.

46. *Lunheng* 論衡 11/1a–3a.

47. *Chuci* 楚辭 3/20b.

48. *Chuci* 3/7b.

49. *Chuci* 3/3b.

50. *Wangdao ou la voie royale*, Paris, Publication de l'Ecole Francaise d'Extreme-Orient, vol.II, 1980, p. 290.

51. *Juan* 128, p. 3225.

52. *Chuci* 3/3b.

53. See Hayashi Minao, *In Shū jidai seidoki no kenkyū*, p. 294 (10–111). Erliton culture (Sammenxia Qilipu).

54. See Keightley, *Sources*, p. 7 and note 18 for discussion of the difficulty in differentiating water buffalo from other cattle bones.

CHAPTER 5

1. See Robert Flaceliere, *Greek Oracles*, London, Elek Books, 1965.

2. See, for example, K. C. Chang, *Art, myth and ritual: the path to political authority in ancient China*, Cambridge: Harvard University Press, 1983.

3. See S. Allan, "On the engraving of oracle bone inscription" in S. Allan et al, *Oracle collections in Great Britain*, Part II.

4. Rao Zongyi 饒宗頤, *Yindai zhenbu renwu tongkao* 殷代貞卜人物通考, Hong Kong, 1959, was the first to notice that the oracle bone sentences are not normally interrogative. See also Leon Vandermeersch, *Wangdao ou la voie royale* II, p. 289; David S. Nivison and David N. Keightley have both discussed this question in unpublished papers: for a summary of Nivison's "The Question question," See *Early China*, supplement I, 1986.

5. See David N. Keightley, *Sources*, pp. 38, 120.

6. Walter Burkert, *Homo Necans: the anthropology of ancient Greek sacrificial ritual and myth*, Berkeley: University of California Press, 1983, p. 47.

7. Walter Burkert, *Homo Necans*. Rene Girard, *Violence and the sacred*, Baltimore: Hopkins University Press, 1979.

8. See Burkert, p. 52.

9. K. C. Chang, *Art, myth and ritual*, p. 73. Chang also cites Nelson Wu, *Chinese and Indian architecture*, New York: Prentice-Hall, 1973.

10. See *Early China* IX–X (1983–5), pp. 20–37, D. N. Keightley, "Reports from the Shang: a corroboration and some speculation" and following comments for some inconclusive discussion of the meaning of 二告.

CHAPTER 6

1. Bronislaw Malinowski, *Myth in primitive psychology*, London: 1926.

2. *Mythologiques* I: *Le cru et le cuit* (Paris: Plon, 1964) [*The raw and the cooked* (London: Jonathan Cape, 1970)]; II: Du *Miel aux cendres* (Paris: 1967) [*From honey to ashes* (London, 1973)]; III: *L'Origine des manieres de table* (Paris: 1968) [*The origin of table manners* (London: 1978)]; IV: *L'homme nu* (Paris: 1971) [*The naked man* (London: 1978)]. This series of works contains the most extensive working out of Levi-Strauss theories which are, of course, also stated in other works (see bibliography).

3. See the introduction to Alan Dundes, ed. *Sacred narrative: readings in the theory of myth*, Berkeley: University of California Press, 1984.

4. *Shang shu Duoshi* 尚書. 多士, 1.19.

5. p. 137.

6. Susanne K. Langer, *Feeling and form*, New York: Charles Scribner & Sons, 1953, pp. 69–70; quoted by Max Loehr in *Ritual vessels of bronze age China*, New York, Asia House, 1968, pp. 12–3.

7. M. Loehr, *Ritual vessels*, p. 13.

8. M. Loehr, *Ritual vessels*, p. 13. See also Robert W. Bagley in Wen Fong, ed., *The great bronze age of China*, London, Thames and Hudson, 1980, p. 101, who states that "the history of the motif [*taotie*] suggests that Shang decoration is an art of pure design, without any specific symbolism attaching to particular motifs. The later versions of both dragon and *taotie*, with their protean shapes and incessant permutations, would seem to bear out this suggestion, which was first made by Max Loehr."

9. See Robert W. Bagley, *Shang ritual bronzes in the Arthur M. Sackler collections*, Cambridge: Harvard University Press, 1987, who states that "Although the taotie alludes to the animal world, it is not a proper picture because the arrangement of lines in the frieze unit contains inconsistencies which defeat any attempt to find a coherent image. . . . In other words the draftsman has not visualized an animal and sketched its contours or silhouetted it against a background. *The creature exists less on the bronze than in the imagination of the viewer* who, acting on the hint of some animal presence, forms an impression of a face and two bodies despite the impossibility of any consistent pictorial reading." Although Bagley denies a symbolic meaning for the *taotie* because it is not representational, like Loehr who argues that the *taotie* does not have any meaning of an established literary kind, he appears to recognize that the *taotie* may nevertheless provoke an image in the mind of the viewer which is of a face and two bodies. I agree that this art is not literal, but I believe that the creature evoked in the imagination of the viewer is no less meaningless because it has not been visualized as a concrete image by the artist.

10. *Henan chutu Shang Zhou qingtongqi* 《河南出土商周青銅器》, Beijing: Wenwu Press, 1983.3, pp. 203–10, p. 278.

11. *Zhongguo meishu quanji* 中國美術全集 IV, *Qingtongqi Shang* 青銅器. 上 (Li Xueqin 李學勤, ed., Beijing: Wenwu Press, 1985), no.3.

12. *Kaogu* 考古, 1976.4, pls. 6.2, 10.3–4; p. 229 fig. 1.2. Also illustrated in Kin-fong Yeung (Yang Jianfang 楊建芳) *Jade carving in Chinese archaeology* (*Zhongguo chutu gu yu* 中國出土古玉), pls. 3.1, 30.1A–1B), and R. W. Bagley, *Shang ritual bronzes*, p. 21.

13. Examples of Liangzhu *cong* are illustrated in Kin-fong Yeung, *Jade carving*, pl. 1, nos.9–13 and pls.27–8. Similar ornament is also found on a *gui* excavated at Dachengshan, Tangshan 唐山市大城山, Hebei Province, a Longshan culture site (pl.26.5). Cf. examples of late Shang *cong*, pls.27–8. The relevant excavation reports are cited by Yeung. See also R. W. Bagley, *Shang ritual bronzes*, p. 19 and figs. 19–21 (who argues that only the image of paired eyes was taken from Liangzhu) and Jessica Rawson, *Chinese bronzes: art and ritual*, London: British Museum, 1987, p. 13.

14. E. H. Gombrich, *The sense of order: a study in the psychology of decorative art*, Oxford: Phaidon, 1979, pp. 264ff. See also William Watson, *Style in the arts of China*, Harmondsworth, Penguin, 1974, p. 29.

15. H. G. Creel, *Birth of China*, Ungar, N. Y.: 1937, p. 117, identified the *taotie* with a buffalo; Florence Waterbury, *Early Chinese symbols and literature*, New York: E. Weyhe, 1952, with a tiger. See Hugo Munsterberg, *Symbolism in ancient Chinese art*, New York: Hacker, 1986, for a discussion of symbolic interpretations of the *taotie*.

16. Bernhard Karlgren, "Yin and Chou in Chinese bronzes," *BMFEA* VIII (1936), pp. 9–156; "New studies on Chinese bronzes", *BMFEA* IX (1937), pp. 1–117. Zhang Guangzhi 張光直 (K. C. Chang), *Shang Zhou qingtongqi yu mingwen de zonghe yanjiu* 商周靑銅器與名文的綜合研究, Monographs of the Institute of History and Philology, Academia Sinica, LXII, Taibei, Academia Sinica, 1972.

17. Elizabeth Childs-Johnson, "The ancestor spirit and animal mask in Shang ritual art," paper presented to the International Symposium on the Yin-Shang Culture of China, 10–14 September 1988, Anyang, China.

18. Liang Siyong 梁思永 and Gao Quxun 高去尋 *Houjiazhuang* 後家莊, v.5 (*Xibeigang 1004 hao da mu* 西北岡1004號大墓, pls. 107 and 113.

19. Jordan Paper, "The meaning of the 't'ao-t'ieh," *History of religions* XVIII (1978), pp. 18–41; Elizabeth Childs-Johnson, "The ancestor spirit and animal mask in Shang ritual art."

20. Liang Siyong and Gao Quxun, *Houjiazhuang*, II (*Xibeigang M1001*), pp. 56–61 describe the remains of wood carvings in tomb 1001. This suggests that wood *might* have been used for making masks, but none have been excavated. To my knowledge, there are no *taotie* masks in bronze.

21. *Wen Gong 18* 文公十八年, *Chunqiu jingzhuan jijie* 春秋經傳集解 9/15a.

22. See H. G. Creel, *Birth of China*, p. 248.

23. See R. W. Bagley, *Shang ritual bronzes*, p. 56, n. 114, who also rejects this solution in terms of the formal development of the motif.

24. See *Wenwu*, 1955.10, for the excavation report; see also William Watson, *The genius of China: an exhibition of archaeological finds of the People's Republic of China*, no. 70.

25. *Homo necans*, p. 43.

26. Vadime Elisseeff, *Bronzes archaiques Chinois au Musee Cernuschi*, L'Asiatique, Paris, 1977, I, no. 46; Kaizuka Shigeki 貝冢茂樹, *Sekai bijutsu zenshū* 世界美術全集 XII no. 28, Tokyo: 1962.

27. See "Anhui Funan faxian Yin-Shang shidaide qingtongqi 安徽阜南發現殷商時代的青銅器, *Wenwu*, 1959.1.

28. Zhongguo shehui kexueyuan kaogu yanjiusuo 中國社會科學院考古研究所, *Yinxu Fu Hao mu* 殷墟婦好墓, Beijing: Wenwu Press, 1980, pp. 105–6, figs. 66–7, color pl. 13.1.

29. "Shandong Yidu Sufutun yihao nuli xunzang mu" 山東益都蘇阜屯一號奴隸殉葬墓, *Wenwu* 1972.8, pp. 17–30; Staatliche Museen Preussischer Kulturbesitz, Museum für Ostasiatische Kunst, *Ausgewahlte Werke Ostasiatischer Kunst*, Berlin-Dahlem, 1970, no. 1.

30. *Art, myth and ritual*, p. 73.

31. See Jessica Rawson, "Dragons in Shang and Zhou bronzes," paper delivered to the Early China Seminar III (1984), abstract in *Early China* 9–10 (1983–5), pp. 371–3.

32. *Der Kult der Shang-dynastie*, p. 204.

33. Gustav Ecke, *Fruhe Chinesche Bronzen aus der Sammlung Oskar Trautmann*, Beijing, 1939, p. 7 (also in Rong Geng 容庚, *Shang Zhou yiqi tongkao* 商周彝器通考, Beijing: Harvard-Yenching Institute, 1941, fig. 823).

34. Albany, State University of New York Press, 1983.

35. B. Mundkur, pp. 77; see also B. Mundkur, "The bicephalous 'Animal Style' in Northern Eurasian religious art and its Western hemisphere analogues," *Current Anthropology* XXV no. 4 (—Oct. 1984), pp. 451–82.

36. The *Xin xu* 新序 1/16 recounts the story of Sun Shu'ao who saw a two-headed snake, killed and buried it, and went home crying. When his mother asked why, he replied that he had heard whoever sees a two-headed snake will die.

37. See *Kaogu*, 1965.5, pl. 3 ("Henan Yanshi Erlitou yizhi fajue jianbao" 河南偃師二裡頭遺址發掘簡報 215–27).

38. See *Jiaguwenzi jishi* 甲骨文字集釋 0067–70.

39. See *Jiaguwenzi jishi* 1049–52.

40. J. Leroy Davidson, "The riddle of the bottle horn," *Artibus Asiae*, vol. 22 (1959), pp. 15–22.

41. See *Wenwu*, 1984.6, pp. 1–5; *Wenwu*, 1984.11, pp. 1–11; *Kaogu*, 1986.1, pp. 497–510; *Wenwu*, 1986.8, pp. 1–17.

ORACLE BONE AND BRONZE INSCRIPTION COLLECTIONS CITED BY AN ABBREVIATION

Bingbian: Zhang Bingquan 張秉權. *Xiaotun di'erben: Yinxu wenzi, Bingbian* 《小屯第二本：殷廢文字‧丙編》. Taibei: Vol. I. pt.1 (1957), pt.2 (1959); Vol. II pt.1 (1962), pt.2 (1965); Vol. III pt.1 (1967), pt.2 (1972).

Buci: Rong Geng 容庚, and Qu Runmin 瞿潤緡. *Yinqi buci*《殷契卜辭》. Beijing, 1933.

Houbian: Luo Zhenyu 羅振玉. *Yinxu shuqi houbian*《殷虛書契後編》. n.p., 1916.

Cuibian: Guo Moruo 郭沫若. *Yinqi cuibian*《殷契粹編》. Beijing: 1959.

Hebian: Zeng Yigong 曾毅公. *Jiagu zhuihebian*　《甲骨綴合編》. n.p., 1950.

Heji: Guo Moruo 郭沫若, ed. *Jiaguwen heji*《甲骨文合集》. 13 vols. Beijing, 1982.

Jiabian: Dong Zuobin 董作賓. *Xiaotun di'erben: Yinxu wenzi, Jiabian* 《小屯第二本：殷虛文字‧甲編》. Taibei, 1977 (reprint of Nanjing, 1948).

Jimbun: Kaizuka Shigeki 貝塚茂樹. *Kyōto daigaku jimbun kagaku kenkyūjozō kōkotsu monji*《京都大學人文科學研究所藏甲骨文字》. 2 vols. Kyoto, 1959. *Shakubun*《釋文》. Kyoto, 1960. *Sakuin*《索引》. Kyoto, 1968.

Jingjin: Kyoto, 1968 Hu Houxuan 胡厚宣. *Zhanhou Jingjin xinhuo jiaguji* 《戰後京津新獲甲骨集》. Shanghai, 1954.

Jinzhang: Chalfont, Frank H., and Britton, Roswell S. *The Hopkins collections of inscribed bone*. New York, 1939.

Kufang: Chalfont, Frank H., and Britton, Roswell S. *The Couling-Chalfont collection of inscribed oracle bone*. Shanghai, 1935.

Ninghu: Hu Houxuan 胡厚宣. *Zhanhou Ninghu xinhuo jiaguji* 《戰後寧滬新獲甲骨集》. Beijing, 1951.

Sandai: Luo Zhenyu 羅振玉. *Sandai jijin wencun*《三代吉金文存》. Pojuezhai, 1936.

Shiduo: Guo Ruoyu 郭若愚. *Yinqi shiduo*《殷契拾掇》. Vol. I: Shanghai, 1951; Vol. II: Beijing, 1953.

Tunnan: Xiao Nan 肖南. *Xiaotun nandi jiagu* 《小屯南地甲骨》. Pt. I (2 vols.).: Beijing, 1980; Pt II (3 vols.): Beijing, 1983.

Xubian: Luo Zhenyu 羅振玉. *Yinxu shuqi xubian*《殷虛書契續編》. n.p., 1933.

Yibian: Dong Zuobin 董作賓. *Xiaotun di'erben: Yinxu wenzi, Yibian* 《小屯第二本: 殷墟文字‧乙編》. Pt.I: Nanjing, 1948; Pt.II: Nanjing, 1949; Pt.III: Taibei, 1953.

Yingcang: Allan, Sarah (艾蘭), Li Xueqin 李學勤, and Qi Wenxin 齊文心. *Yingguo suocang jiaguji*《英國所藏甲骨集》. Pt.I (2 vols.): Beijing, 1985.

Zhixu: Li Yanong 李亞農. *Yinqi zhiyi xubian*《殷契摭佚續編》. Beijing, 1950.

SELECT BIBLIOGRAPHY

(In the text and footnotes, the Sibu Congkan 四部叢刊 editions of primary texts, published by the Commercial Press, Shanghai, have been cited wherever possible. These are not listed in the bibliography.)

Ackerman, Phyllis. *Ritual bronzes of ancient China*. New York: Dryden Press, 1945.

Akatsuka Kiyoshi 赤冢忠. *Chūgoku kodai no shūkyō to bunka: In ōchō no saishi* 中國古代の宗教と文化: 殷王朝の祭祀. Tokyo: Kadokawa Shoten, 1977.

Allan, Sarah. "Drought, human sacrifice and the Mandate of Heaven in a lost text from the *Shang shu*." *Bulletin of the School of Oriental and African Studies* XLVII Part 3 (1984), 523–39.

———. *The heir and the sage: dynastic legend in early China*. San Francisco: Chinese Materials Center, 1981.

———. "The identities of Taigong Wang in Zhou and Han literature", *Monumenta Serica* XXX (1972–3), 57–99.

———. "The myth of the Xia dynasty." *Journal of the Royal Asiatic Society* (1984, no. 2), 242–56.

———. "Sons of suns: myth and totemism in early China." *Bulletin of the School of Oriental and African Studies* XLIV Part 2 (1981), 290–326.

———, and Cohen, Alvin P., ed. *Legend, lore and religion in China: essays in honor of Wolfram Eberhard on his seventieth birthday*. San Francisco: Chinese Materials Center, 1980.

———; Li Xueqin; and Qi Wenxin. *Oracle bone collections in Great Britain* (*Yingguo suocang jiaguji* 英國所藏甲骨集) Part I (1985), Part II (forthcoming). Beijing: Zhonghua Shuju.

An Jingheng 安井衡, ed. *Guanzi zuangu* 管子纂詁. Taibei: Heluo Tushu Chubanshe, 1976.

206

"Anhui Funan faxian Yin-Shang shidaide qingtonqi." 安徽阜南發現殷商時代 的青銅器, *Wenwu* 1959.1, 1.

Bachhofer, Ludwig. "The evolution of Shang and Early Zhou bronzes." *Art Bulletin* XXVI (1944), 107–16.

———. "Reply to Maenchen-Helfen", *Art Bulletin* XXVII (1945), 243–6.

Bagley, Robert W. "P'an-lung-ch'eng: a Shang city in Hupei", *Artibus Asiae* XXXIX (1977), 165–219.

———. *Shang ritual bronzes in the Arthur M. Sackler collections*. Cambridge: Harvard University Press, 1987.

Barnard, Noel. *Bronze casting and bronze alloys in ancient China, Monumenta Serica* monograph XIV. Tokyo: 1961.

Bidney, David. "The concept of myth." *Theoretical Anthropology* (1953), 286–326.

Boltz, William G. "Kung Kung and the flood: reverse euhemerism in the *Yao Tien*." *T'oung Pao* LXVII. 3–5 (1981), 141–53.

Boodberg, Peter A. "Remarks on the evolution of archaic Chinese." *Harvard Journal of Asiatic Studies* II.3 (1937), 29–31.

Burkert, Walter. *Homo necans: the anthropology of ancient Greek sacrificial ritual and myth*. Berkeley: University of California Press, 1983.

Cammaan, Schuyler. "The magic square of three in old Chinese philosophy and religion." *History of Religions* I (1961), 37–80.

———. "Old Chinese magic squares." *Sinologica* VII (1963), 14–53.

———. "Some early Chinese symbols of duality", *History of Religions* XXIV.3 (1985), 215–57.

Chan Ping-leung (Chen Bingliang 陳炳良). "Zhongguo gudai shenhua xinshi liang ze" 中國古代神話新釋兩則. *Qinghua xuebao* 清華學報 II (1969), 206–32.

Chang, K. C. *The archaeology of ancient China*. 4th edition. New Haven: Yale University Press, 1986.

———. *Art, myth and ritual: the path to political authority in ancient China*. Cambridge, Mass.: Harvard University Press, 1983.

———. *Early Chinese civilization: anthropological perspectives*. Harvard-Yenching Institute Monograph Series XXIII. Cambridge, Mass.: Harvard University Press, 1976.

———. *Shang civilization*. New Haven: Yale University Press, 1980.

———. (Zhang Guangzhi 張光直). "Shang Wang miaohao xinkao" 商王廟號新考 *Bulletin of the Institute of Ethnology* X (1963), 125–205.

———. (Zhang Guangzhi 張光直). *Shang Zhou qingtongqi yu mingwen de zonghe yanjiu* 商周青銅器與名文的綜合研究 Monograph of the Institute of History and Philology LXII. Taibei: Academia Sinica, 1972.

———. "Some dualistic phenomenon in Shang society." *Journal of Asian Studies* XXIV (1964), 45–61.

———. (Zhang Guangzhi 張光直). "Tan Wang Hai yu Yi Yin de jisi bing zailun Yin-Shang wangzhi." 談王亥與伊尹的祭祀並再論殷商王製. *Bulletin of the Institute of Ethnology* XXXV (1973), 111–27.

———, ed. *Studies of Shang archaeology: selected papers from the international conference on Shang civilization*. New Haven: Yale University Press, 1982.

Chang Tsung-tung. *Der Kult der Shang-Dynastie im Spiegel der Orakelinschriften: eine palaographische Studie zur Religion im archaischen China*. Wiesbaden: Otto Harrassowitz, 1970.

Chavannes, E. *La sculpture sur pierre en Chine au temps des deux dynasties Han*. Paris: Ernest Leroux, 1893.

———. *Le Tai chan: essai de monographie d'un culte chinois*. Paris: Annales du Musee Guimet, 1910.

Chen Bingliang: see Chan Ping-leung.

Chen Mengjia 陳夢家. "Shangdai de shenhua yu wushu" 商代的神話與巫術. *Yanjing Xuebao* 燕京學報 XX (1936), 485–576.

———. "Wu xing zhi qiyuan" '五行之起源'. *Yanjing xuebao* 燕京學報 XXIV, 35–53.

———. *Yinxu buci zongshu* 殷墟卜辭綜述. Beijing: Science Press, 1956.

Chen Pan 陳磐. "Huang Di shiji yanbian kao 黃帝事跡演變考. *Guoli Zhongshan Daxue yuyan lishi yanjiusuo zhoukan* 國立中山大學語言歷史研究所週刊 III (1925), 921–35.

Chen Xiandan 陳顯丹. "Lun Guanghan Sanxingdui yizhi de xingzhi" 論廣漢三星堆遺址的性質, *Sichuan wenwu* 四川文物 1988.4.

Cheng Te-k'un. *Archaeology in China,* Vol. I (1966); Vol. II (1960); Vol. III (1963). Cambridge, Eng.: W. Heffer & Sons.

Childs-Johnson, Elizabeth. "The ancestor spirit and animal mask in Shang ritual art", paper presented to the international Symposium on the Yin-Shang Culture of China, 10–14 September 1988, Anyang, China.

Cohen, Percy. "Theories of myth." *Man* (1969.IV), 337–53.

Conrady, August. *T'ien wen*. Leipzig: Asia Major Library (no.2), 1931.

Couvreur, S. *Dictionnaire de la langue classique chinoise*. Taibei: World Book Co., 1963 (facsimile of 1904 edition).

Creel, H. G. *The birth of China*. New York: Ungar, 1937.

———. "On the ideographic element in ancient Chinese." *T'oung Pao* XXXIV.4 (1939), 278–81.

———. *The origins of statecraft in China*. Vol. I: *The Western Chou empire*. Chicago: University of Chicago Press, 1970.

———. *Studies in early Chinese culture*. Baltimore: American Council of Learned Societies, 1937.

Cullen, Christopher. "A Chinese Eratosthenes of the flat earth: a study of a fragment of cosmology in *Huainanzi*." *Bulletin of the School of Oriental and African Studies* XXXIX Part I (1976), 106–27.

Davidson, J. Leroy. "The riddle of the bottle horn." *Artibus Asiae* XXII (1959), 15–22.

De Saussure, L. *Les origines de l'astronomie chinoise*. Paris: Maisonneuve, 1930.

"Dengfeng Wangchenggang yizhi de fajue" 登封王成崗遺址的發掘, *Wenwu* 1983.3, 21–36.

Dieny, Jean-Pierre. *Pastourelles et magnanarelles: essai sur un theme litteraire chinois*. Geneva and Paris: Librairie Droz, 1977.

Dong Zuobin 董作賓. *Dong Zuobin xueshu lunzhu* 董作賓學術論著. Taibei: Shijie Shuju, 1979.

———. "Jiaguwen duandai yanjiuli" 甲骨文斷代研究例. *Zhongyang Yanjiuyuan Lishi Yuyan Yanjiusuo jikan waibian* 中央研究院歷史語言研究所集刊外編 I.1 (1933), 371–488.

———. "Lun Shangren yi shengri wei ming" 論商人以生日為名. *Dalu zazhi* 大陸雜誌 II.3 (1951), 6–10.

Dundes, Alan, ed. *Sacred narrative: readings in the theory of myth*. Berkeley: University of California Press, 1984.

Durkheim, Emile and Mauss, Marcel, *Primitive classification*. Translated by Rodney Needham. Chicago: University of Chicago Press, 1963.

Eberhard, Wolfram. *Local cultures in South and East Asia*. Translated by Alide Eberhard. Leiden: E. J. Brill, 1968.

———. *Lokalkulturen in alten China* I (supplement to *T'oung Pao* IIIVII, Leiden, 1942); II (*Monumenta Serica*, monograph III, Beijing, 1942).

————. Review of *Legends and cults,* by Bernhard Karlgren. *Art Asiae* IX.4 (1946), 355–67.

Ecke, Gustav. *Fruhe Chinesche Bronzen aus der Sammlung Oskar Trautmann.* Beijing: 1939.

Eliade, Marcel. *The myth of the eternal return.* London: Routledge & Kegan Paul, 1955.

————. *Shamanism: archaic techniques of ecstasy.* London: Routledge & Kegan Paul, 1964.

Elisseeff, Vadime. *Bronzes archaiques Chinois au Musee Cernuschi.* Paris: L'Asiatique, 1977.

Evans-Pritchard, E. E. *Magic, witchcraft and oracles among the Azande.* Oxford: Clarendon Press, 1976.

Fan Xiangyong 范祥雍, ed. *Guben zhushu jinian jijiao dingbu* 《古本竹書紀年輯校訂補》. Shanghai: Xin Zhishi Chubanshe, 1956.

Finsterbusch, Kate. *Verzeichnis und Motivindex der Han-darstellungen.* Wiesbaden: Harrassowitz, 1966 (I) and 1971 (II).

Flaceliere, Robert. *Greek oracles.* London: Elek Books, 1965.

Fontenrose, Joseph. *The ritual theory of myth.* Berkeley: University of California Press, 1966.

Forke, Alfred. *Lun heng.* New York: Paragon Book Gallery, 1962.

Gan Bao 干寶, *Soushenji* 搜神記. Shanghai: Commercial Press, 1957.

Gao Ming 高明. *Guwenzi leibian* 古文字類編. Beijing: Zhonghua Shuju, 1982.

Gao Quxun 高去尋. "Yindai da mu de mushi ji qi hanyi zhi tuice" 殷代大墓的木室及其含義之推測 *Bulletin of the Institute of History and Philology* XXXIX (1969), 75–188.

Girard, Rene. *Violence and the sacred.* Translated by P. Gregory. Baltimore: Hopkins University Press, 1979.

Gombrich, E. H. *The image and the eye: further studies in the psychology of pictorial representation.* Oxford: Phaidon, 1982.

————. *The sense of order: a study in the psychology of decorative art.* Oxford: Phaidon, 1979.

Goody, Jack. *The domestication of the savage mind.* Cambridge: Cambridge University Press, 1977.

————. *The interface between the written and the oral*. Cambridge: Cambridge University Press, 1987.

————. ed. *Literacy in traditional societies*. Cambridge: Cambridge University Press, 1968.

Graham, A. C. *Chuang-tzu: the seven inner chapters and other writings from the book of Chuang-tzu*. London: Allen and Unwin, 1981.

————. *Later Mohist logic, ethics and science*. Hong Kong: Chinese University Press, 1978.

————. *Studies in Chinese philosophy and philosophical literature*. Singapore: Institute of East Asian Philosophies, 1986.

————. *Yin-yang and the nature of correlative thinking*. Singapore: Institute of East Asian Philosophies (Occasional Paper and Monograph Series, no. 6), 1986.

Granet, Marcel. *Danses et légendes de la Chine ancienne*. Paris: Presses Universaires de France, 1959.

Gu Jiegang 顧頡剛, ed. *Gushibian* 古史辨. 7 vols. Beijing and Shanghai: 1926–41; reprint ed., Shanghai: Shanghai Guji Chubanshe, 1982.

Guan Donggui 管東貴. "Zhongguo gudai shi ri shenhua zhi yanjiu" 中國古代十日神話之研究 *Bulletin of the Institute of History and Philology* XXXIII (1962), 287–330.

Guanghan Sanxingdui yizhi 廣漢三星堆遺址 (Ziliao xuanbian 資料選編) I. Guanghan: Sichuansheng Guanghanshi Wenhuaju, 1988.

Gui zang 歸藏. Changsha: Yu Han Shan Fang Jiyi shu 玉函山房輯佚書, 1884. Guo Baojun 郭寶鈞. "1950–nian chun Yinxu fajue baogao 1950 年春殷墟發掘報告. *Zhongguo Kaogu xuebao* 中國考古學報 V (1951), 1–61.

————. "Anyang Yinxu nuli jisi keng de fajue" 安陽殷墟奴隸祭祀坑的發掘. *Kaogu* 1971.1, 20–36.

————. *Shang Zhou tongqiqun zonghe yanjiu* 商周銅器群綜合研究. Beijing: Wenwu Press, 1981.

Guo Moruo 郭沫若 *Xian Qin Tian dao guan de yanjin* 先秦天道觀的演進, Shanghai, Commerical Press, 1934.

————. *Zhongguo gudai shehui yanjiu* 中國古代社會研究. Beijing: Renmin Chubanshe, 1954.

Guo Moruo 郭沫若; Wen Yiduo 聞一多; and Xu Weiyu 許維遹, ed. *Guanzi jijiao* 管子集校. Beijing: Science Press, 1956.

Guo Qingfan 郭慶範, ed. *Zhuangzi jishi* 莊子集釋. Taibei: Heluo Tushu Chubanshe, 1974.

Hawkes, David. *Ch'u Tz'u: songs of the south.* New York: Beacon, 1962; revised ed., Harmondsworth: Penguin, 1985.

Hayashi Minao 林己奈夫. *In Shū jidai seidoki no kenkyū*《殷周時代青銅器の研究》. Tokyo: Yoshikawa Kobunkan, 1984.

――――. *Iwayuru tōtetsumon wa nani o hyō shita mono ka*《所謂饕餮紋は何を表したものか》. Tōhō Gakuhō 東方學報 LVI (March 1984), 1–97.

Henan Wenwu Gongzuodui Diyidui 河南文物工作隊第一隊. "Zhengzhoushi Baijiazhuang Shangdai mu fajue jianbao" 鄭州市白家莊商代墓發掘簡報, *Wenwu* 1955.10, 3–23.

"Henan Yanshi Erlitou yizhi fajue baogao" 河南偃師二里頭遺址發掘報告. *Kaogu* 1965.5, 215–24.

"Henan Yanshi Erlitou yizhi fajue jianbao" 河南偃師二里頭遺址發掘簡報. *Kaogu* 1965.5, 215–27.

"Henan Yanshi Erlitou yizhi san ba qu fajue jianbao" 河南偃師二里頭遺址三八區發掘簡報. *Kaogu* 1975.5, 302–9.

"Henan Yanshi Erlitou zao Shang gongdian yizhi fajue jianbao" 河南偃師二里頭早商宮殿遺址發掘簡報, *Kaogu* 1974.4, 234–48.

Henansheng bowuguan 河南省博物館 (*Zhongguo bowuguan* 中國博物館, VII), Beijing: Wenwu Press, 1983.

Henansheng Wenhuaju Wenwu Gongzuodui 河南省文化局文物工作隊. *Zhengzhou Erligang* 鄭州二里岡. Beijing: Science Press, 1959.

Henansheng Wenwu Yanjiusuo 河南省文物研究所. *Henan chutu Shang Zhou qingtongqi* 河南出土商周青銅器. Beijing: Wenwu Press, 1981.

――――. "Henan Wuyang Jiahu xinshiqi shidai yizhi di er zhi liu ci fajue jianbao" 河南舞陽賈湖新石器時代遺址第二至六次發掘簡報. *Wenwu* 1989.1, 1–14.

――――. "Zhengzhou bei Erqilu xin faxian san zuo Shang mu" 鄭州北二七路新發現三座商墓, *Wenwu* 1983.3, 60–78.

――――, and Zhengzhoushi Bowuguan 鄭州市博物館, "Zhengzhou xin faxian de Shangdai caocang qingtongqi" 鄭州新發現的商代操藏青銅器. *Wenwu* 1983.3, 49–59.

Henderson, John B. *The development and decline of Chinese cosmology.* New York: Columbia University Press, 1984.

Hentze, Carl. *Die Sakralbronzen und ihre Bedeutung in den fruehchineschen Kulturen.* 2 vols. Antwerp: Die Siktel, 1941.

Ho Ping-ti. *The cradle of the East.* Hong Kong: Chinese University of Hong Kong, 1975.

Hong Xingzu 洪興祖, ed. *Chuci buzhu* 楚辭補注. Beijing: Zhonghua Shuju, 1983.

Hopkins, L. C. "Archaic Chinese characters." *Journal of the Royal Asiatic Society* XIV (1937), 27–32.

Hu Houxuan 胡厚宣. "Chu minzu yuan yu dongfang kao" '楚民族源於東方考'. *Shixue luncong* 史學論叢 I (1923).

———. "Jiaguwen Shangzu niao tuteng de yiji" 甲骨文商祖鳥圖騰的遺跡. *Lishi luncong* 歷史論叢 I (1964), 131–59.

———. "Jiaguwen suojian Shangzu niao tuteng de xin zhengju 甲骨文所見商族鳥圖騰的新證據. *Wenwu* 1977.2, 84–87.

———. *Jiaguxue Shangshi luncong* 甲骨學商史論叢. Chengdu: Jilu Daxue, 1944 (Vol. I); 1945 (Vol. II).

———. "Shi Yindai qiu nian yu si fang he si fang feng de jisi" 釋殷代求年於四方和四方風的祭祀. *Fudan xuebao* 復旦學報 (Renwen kexue 人文科學) 1956.1, 49–86.

———. "Yin buci zhong de Shang Di he Wang Di" 殷卜辭中的上帝和王帝. *Lishi yanjiu* 1959.9, 23–50; 1959.10, 89–110.

———. *Yinxu fajue* 殷墟發掘. Shanghai: Xuexi Shenghuo Press, 1955.

———. "Zhongguo nuli shehui de renxun he renji Xiabian" 中國奴隸社會的人殉和人祭. 下編. *Wenwu* 1974.8, 56–67.

———, ed. *Jiagu tan shi lu* 甲骨探史錄. Beijing: Sanlian Shudian, 1982.

———, ed. *Jiagu yu Yin-Shang shi* 甲骨與殷商史. Shanghai: Guji Shudian, 1983.

Huang Hui 黃暉, ed. *Lun heng jiaoshi* 論衡校釋. Shanghai: Commercial Press, 1964.

Huang Zhanyue 黃展岳. "Woguo gudai de renxun he renxing" 我國古代的人殉和人性. *Kaogu* 1974.3, 153–70.

Hubert, Henri, and Mauss, Marcel. *Sacrifice: its nature and function.* Chicago: Chicago University Press, 1984.

Hunansheng Bowuguan 湖南省博物館 (*Zhongguo bowuguan* 中國博物館, II), Beijing: Wenwu Press, 1981.

Hunansheng Bowuguan 湖南省博物館 and Zhongguo Shehui Kexueyuan Kaogu Yanjiusuo 中國社會科學院考古研究所, *Changsha Mawangdui yihao Han mu* 長沙馬王堆一號漢墓. Beijing: Wenwu Press, 1973.

Izushi Yoshiko 出石誠彥. *Chūgoku shinwa densetsu no kenkyū* 《中國神話傳說 の研究》. Tokyo: Chūo Koronsha, 1943.

Jia Zuzhang 賈祖璋. *Niao yu wenxue* 鳥與文學. Shanghai: 1931.

"Jiashanxian Jingdanggonshe Hejiacun Xihao Zhou mu" 山縣京當公社賀家 村西壕周墓. *Wenwu* 1972.6.

Kaizuka Shigeki 貝冢茂樹. *Sekai bijutsu zenshū* 世界美術全集 XII (Chūgoku). Tokyo: Kadokawa Shoten, 1962.

Kane, Virginia. "The chronological significance of the inscribed ancestor dedication in the periodization of Shang dynasty bronze vessels." *Artibus Asiae* XXXV.4 (1973), 335–70.

———. "The independent bronze industries of the south of China contemporary with the Shang and Western Chou Dynasties." *Archives of Asian Art* XXVIII (1974/5), 77–107.

———. "A re-examination of Anyang archaeology", *Ars Orientalis* X (1975), 93–110.

Kang Yin 康殷. *Wenzi yuanliu qian shuo* 文字源流淺說. Beijing: Rongbaozhai, 1979.

Karlgren, Bernhard. "The Book of documents." *Bulletin of the Museum of Far Eastern Antiquities* XXII (1950), 1–81.

———. "Glosses on the Book of documents." *Bulletin of the Museum of Far Eastern Antiquities* XX (1948), 39–315; XXI (1949), 63–206.

———. "Grammata serica recensa." *Bulletin of the Museum of Far Eastern Antiquities* XXIX (1957).

———. "Legends and cults in ancient China." *Bulletin of the Museum of Far Eastern Antiquities* XVIII (1946), 199–365.

———. "New studies on Chinese bronzes." *Bulletin of the Museum of Far Eastern Antiquities* IX (1937), 1–117.

———. "Some characteristics of the Yin art." *Bulletin of the Museum of Far Eastern Antiquities* XXXIV (1962), 1–28.

———. "Yin and Chou in Chinese Bronzes." *Bulletin of the Museum of Far Eastern Antiquities* VIII (1936), 99–156.

Keightley, David N. "Akatsuka Kiyoshi and the culture of early China: a study in historical method." *Harvard Journal of Asiatic Studies* XLII (1982), 267–320.

———. "Ping-ti Ho and the origins of Chinese civilization." *Harvard Journal of Asiatic Studies* XXXVII (1977), 381–411.

———. "Religion and the rise of urbanism." *Journal of the American Oriental Society* XCIII.4 (1973), 527–38.

———. "The religious commitment: Shang theology and the genesis of Chinese political culture." *History of Religions* XVII (1978), 211–35.

———. "Reports from the Shang: a corroboration and some speculation." *Early China* IX–X (1983–5), 20–37.

———. *Sources of Shang history: the oracle bone inscriptions of bronze age China.* Berkeley: University of California Press, 1978.

———, ed. *The origins of Chinese civilization.* Berkeley: University of California Press, 1983.

Kirk, G. S. *Myth: its meaning and functions in and ancient and other cultures.* Berkeley: University of California Press, 1970.

Langer, Susanne K. *Feeling and form.* New York: Charles Scribner & Sons, 1953.

Levi-Strauss, Claude. *Mythologiques* I: *Le cru et le cuit* (Paris: Plon, 1964) [*The raw and cooked* (London: Jonathan Cape, 1970)]; II: *Du Miel aux cendres* (Paris, 1967) [*From honey to ashes* (London, 1973)]; III: *L'Origine des manieres de table* (Paris, 1968) [*The origin of table manners* (London, 1978)]; IV: *L'homme nu* (Paris, 1971) [*The naked man* (London, 1978)].

———. *The savage mind.* Chicago: University of Chicago Press, 1966.

———. *Structural Anthropology.* New York: Basic Books, 1963.

———. *Totemism today.* Translated by Rodney Needham. London: Merlin Press, 1964.

———. *The way of the masks.* London: Jonathan Cape, 1983.

Li Chi (Li Ji 李濟). *Anyang.* Seattle: University of Washington Press, 1977.

Li Deyong 李德永. "Wuxing tanyuan" 五行探源. *Zhongguo zhexue*《中國哲學》 IV (1980), 70–90.

Li Xiandeng 李先登. "Guanyu jiaguwen zui chu faxian qingkuang zhi bianzheng" 關於甲骨文最初發現情況之辨證. *Tianjin Shida Xuebao*《天津師大學報》 1984.5, 51–2.

Li Xiaoding 李孝定. *Jiagu wenzi jishi*《甲骨文字集釋》. Nangang, Taiwan: Zhongyang yanjiuyuan lishi yuyan yanjiusuo, 1965.

Li Xueqin 李學勤. "Di Yi shidai de feiwang buci" 帝乙時代的非王卜辭. *Kaogu Xuebao* 考古學報 1958.1, 43–74.

———. "Guanyu Shizu buci de yixie wenti" 關於自組卜辭的一些問題. *Guwenzi yanjiu*《古文字研究》III (1980), 32–42.

———. "Ping Chen Mengjia Yinxu buci zongshu" 評陳夢家殷墟卜辭綜述. *Kaogu Xuebao*《考古學報》1957.3, 119–30.

———. "Tan Anyang Xiaotun yiwai chutu de you zi jiagu" 談安陽小屯以外的有字甲骨. *Wenwu* 1956.11, 16–17.

———. "Xiaotun Nandi jiagu yu jiagu fenqi" 小屯南地甲骨與甲骨分期. *Wenwu* 1981.6, 27–33.

———. *The wonder of Chinese bronzes*. Beijing: Foreign Languages Press, 1980.

———, ed. *Zhongguo meishu quanji*《中國美術全集》, Vol. 4: *Qingtongqi Shang* 青銅器. 上. Beijing: Wenwu Press, 1985.

Li Zongtong 李宗桐, ed. *Chunqiu Zuozhuan jinzhu jinyi*《春秋左傳今注今譯》. Taibei: Commercial Press, 1970.

Liang Siyong 梁思永, and Gao Quxun 高去尋. *Houjiazhuang* 侯家莊. 7 vols: (*Xibeigang damu* 西北岡大墓 1001 號, 1002 號, 1003 號, 1217 號, 1004 號, 1550號, 1550 號). Taibei: Institute of History and Philology, 1962–76.

Lin Yun 林澐. "Xiaotun nandi fajue yu Yinxu jiagu duandai" 小屯南地發掘與殷墟甲骨斷代. *Guwenzi yanjiu* IX (1984), 111–54.

Loehr, Max. "The bronze styles of the Anyang period." *Archives of the Chinese Art Society of America* VII (1953), 42–53.

———. *Ritual vessels of bronze age China*. New York: Asia House, 1968.

Loewe, Michael. *Ways to paradise: the Chinese quest for immortality*. London: George Allen and Unwin, 1979.

Luo Zhenyu 羅振玉. *Sandai jijin wencun* 三代吉金文存. Pojuezhai, 1936.

Ma Chengyuan. *Ancient Chinese bronzes*. Edited by Hsio-yen Shih. Oxford: Oxford University Press, 1986.

Ma Weiqing 馬薇頃. *Weiqing jiaguwen yuan* 薇頃甲骨文原, Huweizhen, 1971.

Major, John S. "Myth, cosmology and the origins of Chinese science", *Journal of Chinese Philosophy* V (1978), 1–20.

———. "Notes on the nomenclature of winds and directions in the early Han." *T'oung Pao* LXV (1979), 66–80.

Malinowski, Bronislaw. *Myth in primitive psychology*. London: Psyche, 1926.

Maspero, Henri. "L'astronomie chinoise avant les Han." *T'oung Pao* XXVI (1929), 267–356.

———. "Legendes mythologiques dans le Chou king", *Journal Asiatique* CCIV (1924), 11–100.

Miyazaki Ichisada 宮崎市定. "Chūgoku jōdai no toshi kokka to sono bochi— Shōyū wa doko ni attaka" 中國上代の都市國家とその墓地—商邑は何處にあったか. *Tōyōshi Kenkyū*《東洋史研究》XXVIII (1970), 265–82.

———. "Hoi 補遺, *Tōyōshi Kenkyū*《東洋史研究》XXIX (1970), 147–52.

Mizukami Shizuo 水上靜夫. "Jakuboku kō" 若木考. *Tōhōgaku* 東方學 XXI (1961), 1–12.

———. "Soju shinkō ron" 桑樹信仰論, *Nippon Chūgoku gakkaihō* 日本中國學會報 XIII (1961), 1–18.

Mori Yasutaro 森安太郎. *Zhongguo gudai shenhua yanjiu* 中國古代神話研究. Translated by Wang Xiaolian 王孝廉. Taibei: Di Ping Xian Chubanshe, 1974.

Mundkur, Balaji. "The bicephalous 'Animal Style' in Northern Eurasian religious art and its Western hemisphere analogues." *Current Anthropology* vol. XXIV, no. 4 (Aug.–Oct. 1984), 451–82.

———. *The cult of the serpent: an interdisciplinary survey of its manifestations and origins*. Albany: State University of New York, 1983.

Munke, Wolfgang. *Die klassische chinesische Mythologie*. Stuttgart: Ernst Klett Verlag, 1976.

Munsterberg, Hugo. *Symbolism in ancient Chinese art*. New York: Hacker, 1986.

Needham, Joseph. *Science and civilisation in China*. Vol. III. Cambridge: Cambridge University Press, 1959.

Needham, Rodney, ed. *Right and left: essays on dual symbolic classification*. Chicago: University of Chicago Press, 1973.

Nivison, David S. "1040 as the date of the Chou conquest", *Early China* VIII (1982–3), 76–8.

———. "The dates of the Western Chou." *Harvard Journal of Asiatic Studies* XLIII (1983), 481–580.

———. "A new study of *Xiaotun Yinxu Wenzi Jiabian 2416*", paper presented to the International Conference on Shang culture, Anyang, P.R.C., September 1987.

———. "The pronominal use of the verb *yu* in early archaic Chinese." *Early China* III (1977), 1–18.

———. "The question question." *Early China* Supplement I (1986), 30–1.

Pankeneier, David. "Astronomical dates in Shang and Western Chou." *Early China* VII (1981–2), 2–37.

———. "Mozi and the dates of Xia, Shang and Zhou: a research note." *Early China* IX–X (1983–5), 179–81.

Paper, Jordan. "The meaning of the 't'ao-t'ieh." *History of religions* XVIII (1978), 18–41.

Qi Wenxin 齊文心. "Guanyu Shangdai chengwang de fengguo junzhang de tantao" '關於商代稱王的封國君長的談討'. *Lishi yanjiu* 歷史研究 (1985.2), 63–78.

Qiu Xigui 裘錫圭. "Lun 'Lizu buci' de shidai" 論「歷組卜辭」的時代. *Guwenzi yanjiu* VI (1981), 262–320.

———."Shuo buci de fen wuwang yu zuo tulong" 說卜辭的焚巫尪與作土龍, *Jiaguwen yu Yin-Shangshi* 甲骨文與殷商史 I. Shanghai: Guji Chubanshe, 1983, 21–35. Translated by Vernon K. Fowler in *Early China* IX–X (1983–5), 290–306.

Rao Zongyi 饒宗頤. *Yindai zhenbu renwu tongkao* 殷代貞卜人物通考. Hong Kong: Hong Kong University Press, 1959.

Rawson, Jessica. *Chinese bronzes: art and ritual.* London: British Museum, 1987.

———. "Dragons in Shang and Zhou bronzes." paper delivered to the Early China Seminar III (1984), abstract in *Early China* IX–X (1983–5), 371–3.

Rickett, W. Allyn. "An early Chinese calendar." *T'oung Pao* LXIII (1977), 195–255.

———. *Guanzi: political, economic and philosophical essays from China.* Vol. 1. Princeton: Princeton University Press, 1985.

Rong Geng 容庚. *Shang Zhou yiqi tongkao* 商周彝器通考. Beijing: Harvard-Yenching Institute, 1941.

Rosemont, Henry Jr., ed. *Explorations in early Chinese cosmology.* Chico, California: Scholars Press, 1984.

Roy, D. T., and Tsien, T. H., ed. *Ancient China: studies in early civilization.* Hong Kong: Chinese University Press, 1978.

Rudolph, R. C. *Han tomb art of West China.* Berkeley: University of California Press, 1951.

Schafer, Edward H. "Ritual exposure in ancient China." *Harvard Journal of Asiatic Studies* XIV (1951), 130–84.

Sebeck, Thomas A., ed. *Myth: a symposium*. Bloomington: Indiana University Press, 1974.

Segal, Robert A. "In defense of mythology: the history of modern theories of myth." *Annals of Scholarship* I (1980), 3–49.

Shaanxi chutu Shang-Zhou qingtong qi 陝西出土商周青銅器. Beijing: Wenwu Press, 1979.

Shaanxisheng Bowuguan 陝西省博物館, and Shaanxisheng Wenguanhui 陝西省文管會. *Shanbei Dong Han huaxiang shike xuanji* 陝北東漢畫象石刻選集. Beijing: Shaanxisheng Bowuguan, 1959.

"Shandong Yidu Sufutun yihao nuli xunzang mu" 山東益都蘇阜屯一號奴隸殉葬墓. *Wenwu* 1972.8, 17–30.

Shandongsheng Bowuguan 山東省博物館. "Shandong Anqiu Han huaxiang shi mu fajue jianbao" 山東安丘漢畫象石墓發掘簡報 *Wenwu* 1964.4, 30–38.

Shang Chengzuo 商承祚. *Yinqi yicun* 殷契佚存. Nanjing: Jinling Daxue Zhongguo Wenhua Yanjiusuo congkan jia zhong, 1933.

Shanghai Bowuguan Qingtongqi Yanjiuzu 上海博物館青銅器研究組, Shang-Zhou qingtong qi wenshi 商周青銅器紋飾, Beijing: Wenwu Press, 1984.

Shaughnessy, Edward (夏含夷). "Recent approaches to oracle-bone periodization: a review." *Early China* VIII (1981–2), 1–13.

———. "Shi Yu fang" 釋𥁕方. *Guwenzi yanjiu* 古文字研究 IX (1984), 97–110.

Shi Zhangru 石璋如. "Henan Anyang Hougang de Yin mu" 河南安陽後岡的殷幕, *Bulletin of the Institute of History and Philology* XIII (1947), 21–48.

———. "Xiaotun C-qu de muzang qun" 小屯C-區的墓葬群. *Bulletin of the Institute of History and Philology* XXIII (1951), 447–87.

———. *Xiaotun* 小屯, I (Yizhi de faxian yu fajue 遺址的發現與發掘), Part 2: *Jianzhu yicun* 建築遺存. Taibei: Institute of History and Philology, Academia Sinica, 1959.

Shima Kunio 島邦男. *Inkyo bokuji kenkyū* 殷墟卜辭研究. Hirosaki: Chūgokugaku kenkyūkai, 1958.

———. *Inkyo bokuji sōrui* 殷墟卜辭綜類. Tokyo: Kyuko Shoin, 1971.

Shirakawa Shizuka 白川靜. *Chūgoku no shinwa* 中國の神話. Tokyo: 1975.

Shuowen jiezi gulin 說文解字詁林. Shanghai: Yixue Shuju, 1928.

Sichuansheng Wenwu Guanli Weiyuanhui 四川省文物管理委員會, and Sichuansheng Bowuguan 四川省博物館. "Guanghan Sanxingdui yizhi 廣漢三星堆遺址. *Kaogu Xuebao* 《考古學報》1987.2, 227–54.

Sichuansheng Wenwu Guanli Weiyuanhui 四川省文物管理委員會; Sichuansheng Kaogu Yanjiusuo 四川省考古研究所; and Guanghanshi Wenhuaju Wenguansuo 廣漢市文化局文管所. "Guanghan Sanxingdui yizhi erhao jisi keng fajue jianbao"廣漢三星堆遺址二號祭祀坑發掘簡報. *Wenwu* 1989.5, 1–20.

Soper, Alexander. "Early, middle and late Shang: a note", *Artibus Asiae* XXVIII (1966), 5–38.

Staatliche Museen Preussischer Kulturbesitz, Museum für Ostasiatische Kunst. *Ausgewahlte Werke Ostasiatischer Kunst*. Berlin-Dahlem: Staatliche Museen Preussischer Kulturbesitz, 1970.

Sun Sen 孫森. *Xia Shang shi gao*《夏商史稿》. Beijing: Wenwu Press, 1987.

Sun Yirang 孫詒讓, ed. *Mozi jiangu*《墨子間詁》. Shanghai: Commercial Press, 1936.

Suzuki Torao 鈴木虎雄. "Sōju ni kansuru densetsu" '桑樹に關する傳説'. *Shinagaku*《支那學》 I.9 (1921), 1–15.

Thorp, Robert L. "The date of tomb 5 at Yinxu, Anyang." *Artibus Asiae* XLIII (1982), 239–46.

Tōdō Akiyasu 滕堂明保. *Kanji gogen jiten* 漢字語源辭典. Tokyo: Gakutosha, 1967.

Vandermeersch, Leon. *Wangdao ou la voie royale: Recherches sur l'esprit des institutions de la Chine archaique*. Paris: Ecole Francaise d'Extreme Orient, 1977 (Vol. I); 1980 (Vol. II).

Wang Fuzhi 王夫之. *Chuci tongshi* 楚辭通釋. Beijing: Zhonghua Shuju, 1959.

Wang Guowei 王國維. *Guantang jilin* 觀堂集林. Wu Cheng, Zhejiang: Mi Yun Lou of the Jiang family, 1923.

Wang Yunwu 王雲五. *Xia kao xin lu* 夏考信錄. Shanghai: Commercial Press, 1937.

Waterbury, Florence. *Early Chinese symbols and literature: vestiges and speculations*. New York: E. Weyhe, 1942.

Watson, William. *The genius of China: an exhibition of archaeological finds of the People's Republic of China*. London: Times Newspaper Ltd., 1973.

———. *Style in the arts of China*. Harmondsworth: Penguin 1974.

Wen Yiduo 聞一多. *Gudian xinyi* 古典新義 in *Wen Yiduo quanji* 聞一多全集. Shanghai: Kaiming Shudian, 1948.

Wu, Nelson. *Chinese and Indian architecture*. New York: Prentice-Hall, 1973.

Wu Qichang 吳其昌. "Buci zhong suojian xian gong xian wang san xu kao" 卜辭中所見先公先王三續考. *Yanjing xuebao* 燕京學報 XIV (1933), 1–58.

Wu Shan 吳山. *Zhongguo xinshiqi shidai taoqi zhuangshi yishu* 中國新石器時代陶器裝飾藝術. Beijing: Wenwu Press, 1982.

Xu Fuguan 徐復觀 Zhongguo renxinglun shi 中國人性論史. Taibei: 1969.

Xu Xusheng 徐旭生. "1959 nian yu xi diaocha 'Xia Xu' de chubu baogao" 1959年預西調查"夏墟"的初步報告 . *Kaogu* 1959.11, 592–600.

Xu Zhongshu 徐中舒, ed. *Xia wenhua lunwen xuanji* 夏文化論文選集. Henan: Zhongzhou Guji Press, 1985.

Xu Zongyuan 徐宗元, ed. *Diwang shiji jicun* 帝王世紀輯存. Beijing: Zhonghua Shuju, 1964.

Yang Jianfang: see Yeung Kin-fong.

Yang Junshi 楊君實. "Kang Geng yu Xia hui" 康庚與夏諱. *Dalu zazhi* 大陸雜志 I.3 (1960), 6–11.

Yang Kuan 楊寬. *Gushi xin tan* 古史新談. Beijing: Zhonghua Shuju, 1965.

Yang Xizhang 楊錫璋. "Anyang Yinxu Xibeigang da mu de fenqi ji youguan wenti" 安陽殷墟西北岡大墓的分期及有關問題. *Zhongyuan Wenwu* 中原文物 1981.3, 47–52.

Yang Xizhang 楊錫璋, and Yang Baocheng 楊寶成. "Cong Shangdai jisi keng kan Shangdai nuli shehui de rensheng" 從商代祭祀坑看商代奴隸社會的人牲. *Kaogu* 1977.1, 13–19.

Yeung Kin-fong (Yang Jianfang 楊建芳). *Jade carving in Chinese archaeology* (*Zhongguo chutu gu yu* 中國出土古玉). Hong Kong: Chinese University Press, 1987.

Yin Shun Fashi 印順法師. *Zhongguo gudai minzu shenhua yu wenhua zhi yanjiu* 中國古代民族神話與文化之研究. Taibei: Huagang Chubanshe, 1975.

Yiwen leiju 藝文類聚. Shanghai: Zhonghua Shuju, 1965.

Yu Xingwu 于省吾. "Lue lun tuteng yu zongjiao qiyuan he Xia Shang tuteng" 略論圖騰與宗教起源和夏商圖騰. *Lishi yanjiu* 歷史研究 X (1959), 60–69.

Yuan Ke 袁珂. *Gu shenhua xuanshi* 古神話選釋. Beijing: Renmin wenxue Press, 1979.

———. *Zhongguo gudai shenhua* 中國古代神話. Shanghai: Commercial Press, 1957.

———. ed. *Shanhaijing jiaozhu (Haineijing)* 山海經校注. Shanghai: Guji Chubanshe, 1980.

Zhang Bingquan 張秉權. "Jisi buci zhong de xisheng" 祭祀卜辭中的犧牲. *Bulletin of the Institute of History and Philology* XXXVIII (1968), 181–237.

Zhang Guangzhi: see Chang, K. C.

Zhang Xincheng 張心澄. *Weishu tongkao* 偽書通考. Shanghai: Commercial Press, 1954.

Zhang Zhenglang 張政烺. "Shi shi Zhou chu qingtonqi mingwen zhong de yigua" 試釋周初青銅器銘文中的易卦. *Kaogu xuebao* 考古學報 1980.4, 403–15.

Zhongguo gu qingtong qi xuan 中國古青銅器選. Beijing: Wenwu Press, 1976.

Zhongguo Lishi bowuguan 中國歷史博物館 (*Zhongguo bowuguan*, V), Beijing: Wenwu Press, 1982.

Zhongguo Shehui Kexueyuan Kaogu Yanjiusuo 中國社會科學院考古研究所. *Xiaotun nandi jiagu* 小屯南地甲骨. Beijing: Zhonghua Shuju, 1980.

————. *Xin Zhongguo de kaogu faxian he yanjiu* 新中國的考古發現和研究. Beijing: Wenwu Press, 1984.

————. *Yin-Zhou jinwen jicheng* 殷周金文集成. Beijing: 1985.

————. *Yinxu Fu Hao mu* 殷墟婦好墓. Beijing: Wenwu Press, 1980.

Zhou Fagao 周法高. *Jinwen gulin* 金文詁林. Hong Kong: Chinese University Press, 1975.

————. *Jinwen gulin bu* 金文詁林補. Taibei: Institute of History and Philology, Academia Sinica, 1984.

Zou Heng 鄒衡. *Shang Zhou kaogu* 商周考古. Beijing: Wenwu Press, 1979.

————. *Xia Shang Zhou kaoguxue lunwenji* 夏商周考古學論文集. Beijing: Wenwu Press, 1980.

INDEX